KT-439-034

HISTORY OF ENGLISH

Routledge English Language Introductions cover core areas of language study and are one-stop resources for students.

Assuming no prior knowledge, books in the series offer an accessible overview of the subject, with activities, study questions, sample analyses, commentaries and key readings – all in the same volume. The innovative and flexible 'two-dimensional' structure is built around four sections – introduction, development, exploration and extension – which offer self-contained stages for study. Each topic can be read across these sections, enabling the reader to build gradually on the knowledge gained.

History of English:

❏ provides a comprehensive introduction to the history of English
❏ covers the origins of English, the change from Old to Middle English and the influence of other languages on English
❏ provides key readings from well known authors such as Jean Aitchison, Joseph P. Crowley, Douglas Kibbee, Dick Leith, Albert C. Baugh, Thomas Cable, David Graddol, Geoffrey Leech, H. L. Mencken, Bruce Mitchell and Nick Smith
❏ is accompanied by a supporting website.

Structured to reflect the chronological development of the English language, *History of English* describes and explains the major changes in the language over a span of more than fifteen hundred years, and covers aspects from structural change to attitudes towards usage. The book also considers international varieties of English and how contemporary events are continuing to influence the development of English as a global language.

Incorporating examples from a wide variety of texts, *History of English* provides an interactive and structured textbook that will be essential reading for all students of English language and linguistics.

Dan McIntyre is a lecturer in English Language at the University of Huddersfield, UK.

ROUTLEDGE ENGLISH LANGUAGE INTRODUCTIONS

SERIES EDITOR: PETER STOCKWELL

Peter Stockwell is Professor of Literary Linguistics in the School of English Studies at the University of Nottingham, UK, where his interests include sociolinguistics, stylistics and cognitive poetics. His recent publications include *Cognitive Poetics: An Introduction* (Routledge, 2002), *The Poetics of Science Fiction, Investigating English Language* (with Howard Jackson), and *Contextualized Stylistics* (edited with Tony Bex and Michael Burke).

SERIES CONSULTANT: RONALD CARTER

Ronald Carter is Professor of Modern English Language in the School of English Studies at the University of Nottingham, UK. He is the co-series editor of the forthcoming *Routledge Applied Linguistics* series, series editor of *Interface*, and was co-founder of the Routledge *Intertext* series.

OTHER TITLES IN THE SERIES:

Grammar and Vocabulary
Howard Jackson

Psycholinguistics
John Field

World Englishes
Jennifer Jenkins

Practical Phonetics and Phonology 2nd edition
Beverley Collins and Inger Mees

Stylistics
Paul Simpson

Language in Theory
Mark Robson and Peter Stockwell

Child Language
Jean Stilwell Peccei

Sociolinguistics 2nd edition
Peter Stockwell

Pragmatics and Discourse 2nd edition
Joan Cutting

HISTORY OF ENGLISH

A B C D

A resource book for students

DAN McINTYRE

Routledge
Taylor & Francis Group

LONDON AND NEW YORK

First published 2009
by Routledge
2 Park Square, Milton Park, Abingdon, Oxon OX14 4RN

Simultaneously published in the USA and Canada
by Routledge
270 Madison Ave, New York, NY10016

Routledge is an imprint of the Taylor & Francis Group, an informa business

© 2009 Dan McIntyre

Typeset in 10/12.5 pt Minion by
The Running Head Limited, Cambridge, www.therunninghead.com
Printed and bound in Great Britain by
TJ International Ltd, Padstow, Cornwall

All rights reserved. No part of this book may be reprinted or reproduced or utilised in any form
or by any electronic, mechanical, or other means, now known or hereafter invented, including
photocopying and recording, or in any information storage or retrieval system, without
permission in writing from the publishers.

British Library Cataloguing in Publication Data
A catalogue record for this book is available from the British Library

Library of Congress Cataloging-in-Publication Data
McIntyre, Dan, 1975–
History of English: a resource book for students/Dan McIntyre.
    p.   cm.—(Routledge English language introductions)
  Includes bibliographical references.
  1. English language—History.   I. Title.
  PE1075.M59 2008
  420'.9—dc22   2008002316

ISBN10: 0–415–44429–2 (pbk)
ISBN10: 0–415–44430–6 (hbk)

ISBN13: 978–0–415–44429–3 (pbk)
ISBN13: 978–0–415–44430–9 (hbk)

HOW TO USE THIS BOOK

This book spans over fifteen hundred years of linguistic history in little more than 200 pages and is therefore necessarily selective in what it covers. My aim has been to provide a basic introduction to the main themes and events of both the external and internal history of English, with the intention that, armed with this outline knowledge, students will be able to go off and explore for themselves the various stages of the language's development in more detail. Inevitably there are elements of the history of English that I have presented in a simplified form. For example, the development of Standard English in the Early Modern period involved a greater number of steps than I have space to cover. The dialects of Middle English would need an entire book to themselves. Nevertheless, to my mind it is more important for the beginning student to gain an overall picture of the key issues than to focus straight away on the complexities of English's development over time.

In keeping with the Routledge English Language Introductions format, this book is organised into four sections. Section A presents an external history of English, taking into account the main social, political and economic factors that influenced the development of the language from its earliest inception right up to the present day. Section B focuses more on the actual linguistic form of the language at each of its stages, as well as on some of the specific changes that took place and the attitudes towards English that have prevailed at various times. Section C provides exercises and activities to allow you to try out the knowledge and understanding you will have gained from reading sections A and B. Some of these exercises are followed by commentaries while others allow you scope to investigate the issue alone. Finally, section D presents a series of readings in the history of English, chosen to allow you to further the basic knowledge of the history of English that you will gain from sections A, B and C.

CONTENTS

List of figures   xi
Acknowledgements   xiii

SECTION A: INTRODUCTION   1

An external history of English   2

A1   Origins of English   3
A1.1   The Romans in Britain   3
A1.2   The arrival of the Anglo-Saxons   4
A1.3   English: what's in a name?   4
A1.4   Christianity reaches England   6
A1.5   Viking raids   7

A2   The history of English or the history of Englishes?   8
A2.1   Old English dialects   8
A2.2   The rise of West Saxon   9
A2.3   Dialect boundaries   10

A3   Language contact in the Middle Ages   11
A3.1   1066 and all that   12
A3.2   From Old English to Middle English   12
A3.3   The decline of French and the rise of English   14
A3.4   Middle English dialects   15

A4   From Middle English to Early Modern English   16
A4.1   External influences on pronunciation   16
A4.2   The translation of the Bible into English   18

A5   The process of standardisation   20
A5.1   Dialects and emerging standards   20
A5.2   Caxton and the impact of the printing press   22
A5.3   Dictionaries and grammars   23
A5.4   The boundaries of Early Modern English   24

A6   Colonialism, Imperialism and the spread of English   25
A6.1   English in the New World   25
A6.2   The expansion of the British Empire   26

A7   Moves towards Present Day English   28
A7.1   The Industrial Revolution   28
A7.2   The *Oxford English Dictionary*   29

A7.3   A spoken standard   20
A7.4   The linguistic consequences of war   30
A7.5   Technology and communication   31

A8   **Global English and beyond**   31
A8.1   English: a global language   31
A8.2   Globalisation and changes in English   33
A8.3   Assessing the linguistic impact of historical events   34

SECTION B: DEVELOPMENT   35
A developing language   36

B1   **Understanding Old English**   36
B1.1   Spelling and sound in Old English   36
B1.2   The vocabulary of Old English   39
B1.3   Old English: a synthetic language   40
B1.4   Case, gender and number   41
B1.5   Old English verbs   43

B2   **Varieties of Old English**   44
B2.1   Old English and Scots   45
B2.2   Old English dialectal differences   45

B3   **The emergence of Middle English**   47
B3.1   The context of change   48
B3.2   Spelling and sound in Middle English   48
B3.3   Changes in the system of inflections   51
B3.4   Middle English vocabulary   53

B4   **Sound shifts**   53
B4.1   Speech sounds   54
B4.2   Changes in the long vowels   57
B4.3   The Uniformitarian Principle in relation to the Great Vowel Shift   58
B4.4   Consequences of the Great Vowel Shift   59

B5   **Writing in Early Modern English**   60
B5.1   Orthography in Early Modern English   61
B5.2   Some grammatical characteristics   62
B5.3   Expanding the lexicon   66

B6   **The development of American English**   66
B6.1   Causes of linguistic development in the American colonies   67
B6.2   A developing standard   68
B6.3   'Archaisms' in American English   68
B6.4   The beginnings of African American English   69

B7   **International English**   70
B7.1   Australian English   70

B7.2	Indian English	72
B7.3	Pidgins and creoles on the West African coast	74
B8	**The globalisation of English**	76
B8.1	Attitudes towards global English	76
B8.2	World Standard English	77
B8.3	Fragmentation or fusion?	78

SECTION C: EXPLORATION   79

Exploring the history of English   80

C1	**The roots of English**	81
C1.1	Language family trees	81
C1.2	Pronouncing Old English	84
C1.3	Case	84
C2	**Regions and dialects**	86
C2.1	Dialectal differences in an Old English text	86
C2.2	Place names	87
C3	**From Old English to Middle English**	91
C3.1	Loanwords	91
C3.2	*The Canterbury Tales*	93
C3.3	A Middle English *Pater noster*	95
C4	**Codification and attitudes towards English**	95
C4.1	*A Table Alphabeticall*	96
C4.2	*English Orthographie*	97
C4.3	Problems with prescriptivism	100
C5	**Further elements of grammar in Early Modern English**	102
C5.1	More on pronouns	103
C5.2	Gradable adjectives	104
C5.3	What did *do* do?	106
C6	**English in the New World**	108
C6.1	Loanwords in American English	108
C6.2	The politics of spelling	110
C6.3	Early African American English	112
C7	**Present Day Englishes**	113
C7.1	Unknown words from Australian English?	114
C7.2	Enlarging the lexicon	115
C7.3	Tok Pisin	120
C8	**The future of English**	122
C8.1	The cost of global English	122
C8.2	Scare stories: declining standards	122
C8.3	Future developments in English	124

SECTION D: EXTENSION   127

Readings in the history of English   128

D1   Vocabulary in Old English   128
D1.1   Other differences between Old English and Modern English
        (Bruce Mitchell)   128
D1.2   Issues to consider   133

D2   Old English dialects   134
D2.1   The study of Old English dialects (Joseph P. Crowley)   134
D2.2   Issues to consider   138

D3   The influence of French   139
D3.1   Who spoke French in England? (Douglas Kibbee)   139
D3.2   Issues to consider   143

D4   Changes in pronunciation   144
D4.1   The Great Vowel Shift (Dick Leith)   144
D4.2   The Mad Hatter's tea-party (Jean Aitchison)   147
D4.3   Issues to consider   154

D5   'Fixing' the language   154
D5.1   The appeal to authority, 1650–1800 (Albert C. Baugh and Thomas Cable)   154
D5.2   Issues to consider   160

D6   The development of American English   160
D6.1   The beginnings of American (H. L. Mencken)   160
D6.2   Issues to consider   166

D7   A corpus approach to linguistic development   166
D7.1   Recent grammatical change in written English, 1961–1992: some
        preliminary findings of a comparison of American with British English
        (Geoffrey Leech and Nick Smith)   166
D7.2   Issues to consider   177

D8   The future of English?   178
D8.1   English as a transitional phenomenon (David Graddol)   178
D8.2   Issues to consider   182

Glossary of linguistic terms   183
Further reading   189
        General histories of English   189
        Old English   189
        Middle English   190
        Early Modern English   190
        Eighteenth-century English to the present day   190
        World Englishes   191
References   193
Index   201

FIGURES

Map 1	The Anglo-Saxon heptarchy	6
Map 2	Middle English dialect areas	15
B4.1.1	Pure vowels in English	56
B4.1.2	The diphthong [aʊ]	57
B4.2.1	The Great Vowel Shift in English	58
C.1	Hierarchy of language	81
C1.1.1	A language family tree for the Indo-European languages	82
C4.2.1	Title page of Owen Price's *English Orthographie*	98
C4.2.2	Extract from *English Orthographie*	98
C4.2.3	Extract from *English Orthographie*	99
C4.3.1	Article from *The Observer*, 28 October 2007	102
D4.2.1	The Great Vowel Shift	148
D4.2.2	Examples of the Great Vowel Shift	148
D4.2.3	Drag and push chains	149
D4.2.4	High German or Second Consonant Shift	150
D4.2.5	Examples of High German or Second Consonant Shift	150
D4.2.6	Drag chain in Yiddish dialect of northern Poland	151
D4.2.7	The Great Vowel Shift of Late Middle Chinese	151
D4.2.8	Examples of the Great Vowel Shift of Late Middle Chinese	151
D4.2.9	Chronology of the Great Vowel Shift of Late Middle Chinese	152
D4.2.10	Combined push and drag chain	152
D4.2.11	English diphthongs: conventional (older) pronunciation	153
D4.2.12	Estuary English vowels	153
D7.1.1	The Brown, Frown, LOB and FLOB corpora	167
D7.1.2	Declining profile of the core modals in AmE and BrE	168
D7.1.3	Overall frequencies of semi-modals	170
D8.1.1	Estimates of first-language speakers of English from 1950 to 2050 as calculated by the engco model, together with speculations regarding L2 and EFL communities	179

ACKNOWLEDGEMENTS

Innumerable friends, colleagues and students have given me enormously helpful comments and advice which have made this book better than it would otherwise have been. I am especially grateful to Richard Marsden, for his excellent advice on Old and Middle English; to Beatrix Busse, for equally good advice about Early Modern English; to Rocío Montoro, for reading and commenting on most of the book in draft and for being an incredibly supportive friend; to Lesley Jeffries, for advice on phonetics and for much-needed reassurance about the nature of textbook-writing; and to the series editor, Peter Stockwell, for his enthusiasm for the project and encouragement in the final stages of writing. Dawn Archer, Carol Bellard-Thomson, Derek Bousfield, Jonathan Culpeper, Robert Foot, David Gill, Ella Jeffries, Jessica Malay, Lauren McIntyre and Sara Pons-Sanz all read and/or discussed parts of the book with me and I am grateful to them all for their input. Such was the extent of their help that the only parts of the book I can lay sole claim to are any errors that remain. I must also thank the team at Routledge for their unstinting practical support.

Most of this book was illicitly written during a sabbatical term when I should have been working on other things, and I am grateful to my colleagues at the University of Huddersfield for covering my absence during this period. The book is dedicated to my wife Eszter, who deserves my eternal thanks for putting up with my sustained mental absence from normal life as I was finishing it, as well as for giving me the benefit of her own knowledge of the history of English.

DM

CREDITS

D1 – Bruce Mitchell (1995) *An Invitation to Old English and Anglo-Saxon England* (pp. 25–30), Blackwell Publishing. Reproduced by permission of the publisher.

D2 – Joseph P. Crowley (1986) 'The study of Old English dialects', *English Studies* 67 (pp. 97–104), Taylor & Francis Ltd, http://informaworld.com, reprinted by permission of the publisher.

D3 – From Douglas Kibbee (1991) *For to Speke Frenche Trewely. The French Language in England 1000–1600: Its Status, Description and Instruction* (pp. 8–11, pp. 186–8). With kind permission by John Benjamins Publishing Company, Amsterdam/Philadelphia. www.benjamins.com, and the 'Foundation of Language'.

D4.1 – Dick Leith (1983) *A Social History of English* (pp. 145–9), Routledge, reproduced by kind permission of the author.

D4.2 – Jean Aitchison, *Language Change: Progress or Decay?* 3rd edition. Cambridge University Press (pp. 183–93, inc. figs 11.1, .2, .3, .4, .5, .6, .7, .8), 2001. Copyright © 1991, 2001, reprinted with permission.

D5 – Albert C. Baugh and Thomas Cable, *A History of the English Language*, 5th edition, © 2002, pp. 264–9, 271. Reprinted by permission of Pearson Education, Inc., Upper Saddle River, NJ. Copyright © 2002. Reproduced by permission of Taylor & Francis Books UK.

D6 – From *The American Language*, 4th edition by H. L. Mencken. Copyright 1936 by Alfred A. Knopf, Inc. and renewed 1964 by August Mencken and Mercantile-Safe Deposit and Trust Co. Used by permission of Alfred A. Knopf, a division of Random House, Inc.

D7 – Geoffrey Leech and Nick Smith (2006) 'Recent grammatical change in written English 1961–1992: some preliminary findings of a comparison of American with British English' in A. Renouf and A. Kehoe (eds) *The Changing Face of Corpus Linguistics*, Amsterdam: Rodopi, pp. 185–204 (including figures).

D8 – David Graddol (1997) *The Future of English?* London: British Council (pp. 60–1). Reproduced with permission.

Section A
INTRODUCTION

AN EXTERNAL HISTORY OF ENGLISH

Sometimes when we talk about language we discuss it almost as if it is an actual substance – something that you can put under a microscope and examine, or dissect in a laboratory. For instance, Jeffries (2006: 7) suggests that 'the only real way to understand how language works is to get your hands dirty and pull it to pieces'. For some areas of language study, thinking about language in this way can be useful. When we study grammar, for example, we often use the metaphor of cutting a sentence up into its constituent parts. Indeed, Crystal (1994: 6) talks about grammar as 'the business of taking a language to pieces, to see how it works'. However, sometimes it is better to take a more realistic view of what language is like. Language is not a tangible substance. The outward expression of language might be speech or written text but language itself cannot be separated from the people who use it. For its speakers, language has many different functions. It provides a means of performing certain actions (e.g. naming a ship or making a bet), it can be used to promote particular ideologies, and it is the means by which people communicate their ideas and identities to others. One of the particularly interesting things about language is that it is constantly changing and developing. But so too, of course, are the people who use it. It follows, then, that if we want to know how a language develops over time, inevitably, we need to know something about the society in which its speakers live and how historical events have affected them and their development. This is what we will concentrate on in section A of this book. Before we do this, however, it is useful to understand the distinction between the **internal history** of a language and its **external history**.

A language's internal history is a record of its linguistic development over time – for example, how its vocabulary, grammar and phonology have changed. Its external history is a record of its speakers and how they and their societies have developed. It follows that language change can be caused by both intralinguistic and extralinguistic factors (Samuels 1972).

In the case of the former, a change in one element of a language can cause the development of other related elements. For example, a change in the way that one vowel sound is produced can affect the sound of the surrounding vowels. (You can read about this aspect of the development of English in B4 and D4).

Extralinguistic change, on the other hand, comes about when external, non-linguistic events begin to affect the development of a language. For example, in computing the invention of a palm-sized device to move a cursor on a computer screen necessitated the coining of a name to describe it – i.e. mouse. In this case, the word *mouse* widens in meaning to refer to both the rodent and the computer device. Hence, an external, non-linguistic event has had an effect on the development of the language. Section A of this book focuses particularly on the external history of English.

ORIGINS OF ENGLISH

The earliest form of English is **Old English (OE)**. Old English was derived from the Germanic languages of the Anglo-Saxons who settled in Britain, and most linguists agree that Old English emerged in the fifth century, around 449 AD. The language in this form was used for over 600 years, but during those 600 years it was constantly changing. By 1100, it looked and sounded very different to the language it had been in its earliest stages.

A1.1 The Romans in Britain

Where did English come from? The origins of English are usually dated to the arrival of the Anglo-Saxons in Britain in the mid-fifth century. To understand what led to their arrival, we need to know a little bit about events in Britain before then.

At the beginning of the fifth century AD, Britain was an occupied country. Its occupiers, the Romans, had arrived in Britain in 43 AD, under Emperor Claudius. The native inhabitants of Britain at this time were the Britons – or the Celts, as they are often referred to. In addition to the Britons there were also, in the north of the country, the Picts. The Picts had arrived in Britain from Scythia and had settled in what is now Scotland. They had come to Scotland via Ireland, where the native inhabitants, rather confusingly for us, were called Scots. The Scots had refused to let the Picts settle in Ireland and so the Picts had been forced to move on, finally ending up in Britain. The Scots, though, despite their apparent uncongenial treatment of the Picts, felt no compunction about also trying out Britain, and numerous groups of them subsequently settled in Pictish areas. Following the Roman invasion, then, the people in Britain feeling the effects of the occupation were the **Britons**, the **Picts** and the **Scots**, all living in disparate tribal groups and all speaking variant dialect forms of Celtic languages. The Romans brought with them Latin and, it is to be assumed, vernacular dialects of this language. (Your **vernacular** dialect/language is the one that you speak most naturally, i.e. your 'mother tongue'. The term is also sometimes used to refer to low-status varieties of a language.) This was not the first time the Latin language had been used in Britain. There had been a previous attempted Roman invasion in 55 BC, led by Julius Caesar. This was not hugely successful and it took a further year and another invasion for Caesar to actually establish a settlement in Britain. Even so, Caesar achieved only moderate success and an occupation in any real sense did not occur until Emperor Claudius's invasion almost a hundred years later. Despite its success, Claudius's conquest of Britain did not go unchallenged. In 61 AD, for instance, Boudica (sometimes referred to as Boadicea), a widow of a native leader of the Britons, led a revolt against the occupying forces which resulted in the massacre of over 70,000 Romans.

Nevertheless, throughout their time in the country the occupying Roman forces established a firm ruling presence in most parts of Britain. The influence of the Romans was considerable. Major roads were built, towns and cities had bath houses, theatres and places of worship. Roman houses had water supplies and heating. Britain was beginning to look like the other provinces of the Roman Empire. A further indicator of this was the use of Latin, which was established as the language of officialdom.

It is likely that Latin had a prestige value and was spoken not just by those for whom it was a first language but also by the upper-class native inhabitants of cities and towns. Latin, however, never supplanted the Celtic dialects of the native Britons and it began to decline in use with the arrival of the Anglo-Saxons.

A1.2 The arrival of the Anglo-Saxons

At the beginning of the fifth century the Roman Empire was under threat and the Roman garrisons in Britain were withdrawn to Rome. By 410 AD the last Roman legion had left. The native Britons now found themselves facing something of a problem. During the Roman occupation there had been occasional attacks from the Picts and the Scots in the border regions, but the presence of the occupying armies had always been enough to suppress them. Now, though, the Britons found themselves open to increasingly frequent attacks from the Picts and the Scots and in the unfortunate position of not being able to adequately defend themselves. The Britons appealed to Rome for help, but Rome had problems of its own and was able to do little to help. As the situation worsened, Vortigern, one of the leaders of the Britons, made an appeal to the Germanic tribes of north-west Germany and Denmark for help in repelling the attacks. There was something of an irony in appealing to the Saxon nations, as the Saxons had made numerous attacks on Britain throughout the Roman occupation, causing difficulties for the occupying Roman armies (whose garrisons are likely to have included at least some soldiers of Germanic descent). Nevertheless, the Saxons agreed to come to the aid of the Britons and the first boatloads of Saxon warriors, along with two further groups, the Angles and the Jutes, began arriving in 449 AD. The **Saxons** came from north-west Germany, the **Angles** from the Danish mainland and islands, and the **Jutes** from northern Denmark. Collectively, these groups are known as the Anglo-Saxons.

Some older histories of English will tell you that what happened from 449 onwards was an invasion of Britain. This is not strictly true. For a start, the Anglo-Saxon newcomers were invited. Secondly, while it is true that once they had arrived they quickly subjugated the Britons, to talk of the Anglo-Saxons as invading Britain is to suggest a degree of organisation to the venture that was not there. The Anglo-Saxons were not a unified, invading army. They came in relatively small groups and continued to arrive throughout the sixth century. They succeeded in dispelling the Pictish and Scottish attackers and, once they had done this, decided to settle in Britain.

A1.3 English: what's in a name?

Much of what we know of the events of this period comes from the work of the Venerable Bede, a monk who lived and worked at the Jarrow Monastery in the northeast of Britain. In 731 Bede completed his now famous *Ecclesiastical History of the English People*, which is a rich source of information about the OE period. It is Bede who tells us that the Germanic 'invaders' were Angles, Saxons and Jutes. However, when interpreting Bede's work we have to be careful for several reasons. McCully and Hilles (2005: 51) point out that Bede was writing about the coming of the Anglo-Saxons almost 300 years after the event, at a time when there would have been no contemporary records of these events. Bede wrote his history based almost entirely on stories that had been passed from generation to generation orally. Crystal (2005: 16) questions some of Bede's terminology and suggests that his description of the Angles, Saxons and Jutes as being 'nationalities' is not entirely accurate. Crystal explains that Bede's reference to three distinct communities is a simplification. Names for communities of people at the time did not necessarily equate to our modern concept of nations. Some groups would consist of people related by blood. Others might be considered a community because they grouped themselves together under a particular leader. And sometimes a community name might refer to a group (or groups) of people who had come together specifically for the purposes of attacking another group or defending themselves against attacks from others. The history of English is not as neat as it is often packaged!

So if the Anglo-Saxon population was made up of numerous different communities, how then did they come to be known collectively as the *English*? Why not the *Saxons*, for example? We might imagine that this is because the Angles were the more dominant of the groups who settled in the country. After all, *England* means 'land of the Angles'. However, it is not the case that there were simply more of the Angles than any other group. First of all, we have to remember that the idea of three separate communities (Angles, Saxons and Jutes) is an oversimplification. Bede himself sometimes uses the Latin terms *Angli* and *Saxones* interchangeably. *Angli*, then, could refer to groups other than the Angles. The OE equivalent of *Angli* was *Engle*, so the name *Engla lande* – clearly an early form of *England* – is derived from an OE word which could, like *Angli*, be used to refer to any inhabitant of the country. Furthermore, the historian Peter Hunter Blair (1962: 12–13) suggests that the term *Angli Saxones* was used by some Latin writers to refer not to the Angles and the Saxons together, but to differentiate the *English* Saxons from what Bede called the 'Old Saxons' living on the continent. From the eleventh century onwards, then, Britain began to be referred to as *England*, though spellings of this word varied considerably until the fourteenth century.

Gradually, the Anglo-Saxons settled in England. It's not entirely clear how the Britons got on with the new inhabitants. We can assume that in some areas the Britons and the Anglo-Saxons might have lived together peaceably. But in the West Saxon area (along the south coast) there was considerable fighting as the settlers struggled to establish themselves. It is likely that some of the Britons from this area were forced out into nearby Cornwall, or perhaps into Wales (*Wales* actually derives from the OE word *wealas*, meaning *foreigner*, which was hardly a very charitable way for the Anglo-Saxons to describe the native inhabitants of the country!) As the Anglo-Saxons asserted themselves, the civilisation that the Romans had created was gradually destroyed. One of the reasons for this, as Baugh and Cable (2002) point out, is that the Anglo-Saxons lived a different kind of life to the Romans, with the emphasis on hunting and agriculture. But by the seventh century, a number of significant settlements had become established. These were Northumbria, Mercia, East Anglia, Essex, Kent, Sussex and Wessex. Collectively, these seven kingdoms are sometimes referred to as the **Anglo-Saxon heptarchy** (see Map 1).

The boundaries between these kingdoms were by no means stable and over the next 200 or so years, the balance of power fluctuated between them. Political power has always had an influence on the prestige of particular dialects (see Stockwell 2007: 16–17) and things were no different in Anglo-Saxon times. The effect of this on the developing English language was to raise to a position of prestige the dialect of

Map 1 The Anglo-Saxon heptarchy (from Pyles and Algeo 1993: 98)

whichever kingdom happened to be exerting influence at the time. We'll look at dialects in more detail in A2.

A1.4 Christianity reaches England

What we now call Old English emerged as the Germanic dialects of the Anglo-Saxon settlers converged over time. But Celtic and Latin also had an influence on Old English (though of the two, Celtic was significantly less influential). However, the influence of Latin did not come from the period of Roman occupation, even though Christianity had been introduced to parts of Britain during this period. There was no direct contact between Latin and Old English until Christianity was re-introduced to Britain in 597 AD by Augustine, a missionary sent by Pope Gregory I. Augustine's first success was baptising Ethelbert, the King of Kent, just months after arriving in England. No doubt he was helped by the fact that Ethelbert's Frankish wife, Bertha, was herself a Christian (the Franks were a Germanic tribe from around the Rhine, who eventually crossed into – and gave their name to – the country that is now France). Just four years later, Augustine became the first Archbishop of Canterbury. All things considered, the spread of Christianity was quick, and within a hundred years England was a Christian country. (It should be noted, though, that many people continued to practise Christianity and paganism at the same time, not initially accepting the notion of Christianity as an exclusive religion.)

As Christianity spread, Latin was once again introduced to the country and became established as the language of the church and the language of learning. The effect on English was to infuse it with numerous Latin words, and so the vocabulary of English increased further.

A1.5 Viking raids

Although the Anglo-Saxons had succeeded in subjugating the native Britons, they themselves were not immune to attack. Between 787 and 850, Britain was the victim of a series of raids by Scandinavian aggressors. Later on, the raids increased in scale and in terms of the objectives of the Scandinavian invaders, and in time these groups settled in England too and exerted their own influence on the development of English.

The Scandinavian invaders of this period are commonly known as **the Vikings**, though the Anglo-Saxons called them **the Danes**. Initially, they carried out isolated attacks on towns and monasteries (the first being Lindisfarne in Northumbria in 793) for the simple purpose of looting. One of these raids, in 794, was on the monastery at Jarrow – the home of Bede.

The south of the country also suffered Viking raids but the greatest attack came in 865, when a large and well-organised Danish army, led by the memorably named Ivar the Boneless and his brother Halfdan, conquered East Anglia. (Ivar the Boneless and Halfdan were the sons of Ragnar Lothbrok, whose own name is no less memorable; James (2001: 221) translates it as 'Hairy-breeks' – or 'Hairy-trousers'!) Having, conquered the greater part of the East of England, in 870 the Vikings attacked Wessex, where Ethelred was king. Initially, Ethelred repelled the attacks but just weeks later he was himself defeated. Ethelred died in 871 and was succeeded as king by his brother Alfred ('Alfred the Great'), who essentially paid off the Danish attackers. Five years later, though, the Danes were back. This time, however, Alfred was far better prepared and won a clear victory over Guthrum, the Danish King of East Anglia, who had led the assault. The Danes were pushed back from Wessex and Guthrum agreed to accept Christianity and was subsequently baptised. A treaty was drawn up in 886 whereby the Danes agreed to settle in a territory to the east of an imaginary line running diagonally from the Thames to Chester, which was to become known as the Danelaw. This territory was so-called because within it Danish law applied, as opposed to the West Saxon, Mercian and other laws and customs that applied in the west. The Danelaw extended from the east of England into the north. On the other side of the Danelaw, Alfred became the first King of the Anglo-Saxons.

Despite Alfred's victory over Guthrum, this was not the end of the Viking attacks. The famous Old English poem *The Battle of Maldon* tells the story of how, in 991, Byrhtnoth, an East Saxon leader, was defeated by a Viking army led by Olaf Tryggvason, who was later to become King of Norway. In 994, Tryggvason was joined by the King of Denmark, Svein Forkbeard, and together they continued the attacks against the Anglo-Saxons. Finally, in 1014, Svein drove the second King Ethelred (the great-great grandson of Alfred; often referred to as 'the unready', meaning unwise) into exile in Normandy and was crowned King of England. He died the same year and was succeeded by his son, Cnut. And so, the Danes had finally gained power in England, and English was to be influenced by Scandinavian too.

The Scandinavian languages, which included Old Norse, had a significant effect on the development of Old English. Close contact between the Scandinavians and the Anglo-Saxons led to the borrowing of Old Norse words. In C2.2, for example, you can read about the influence of Scandinavian on place-names. Many now common lexical items came originally from Old Norse, including such words as *take*, *die*, *wrong*, *call* and *law* (see C3.1 for more examples). Additionally, the <–s> inflection on third-person present simple singular forms of the verb is a result of Scandinavian influence.

A2 THE HISTORY OF ENGLISH OR THE HISTORY OF ENGLISHES?

There are many different varieties of English in Britain (and, indeed, across the world). These various forms of English are dialects. A dialect is a variety of a language which is distinct from other varieties of that language by virtue of particular lexical and grammatical selections that are not common to other dialects. For example, students of mine who are not from West Yorkshire often find it somewhat confusing (not to mention amusing) when they arrive in Huddersfield and find that there are words used here that seem unique to the region and, conversely, that words they might use at home are not recognised here. In Huddersfield, for instance, a *teacake* is a bread roll – an item that speakers from other regions might call a *cob*, a *breadcake*, a *huffkin* or a *batch*, to list but a few options. Dialectal differences also extend to grammar. I am originally from Yorkshire and when I went to university in Lancashire, my sister accused me (note the strong feelings often associated with particular dialects!) of 'betraying' my Yorkshire roots because I unknowingly started to use elements of Lancashire dialect when I spoke. For example, I would form questions differently – 'Do you not like carrots?' as opposed to 'Don't you like carrots?' (see Stockwell 2007: A2, B2, C2 and D2 for more on dialectal variation). Dialectal differences along these lines were also common in Anglo-Saxon times, though geography does not necessarily account for all the differences that existed, as we shall see. Just as there are different dialects today, so too were there different dialects of Old English.

A2.1 Old English dialects

The four main dialects of Old English which scholars have been able to determine are Kentish, West Saxon, Mercian and Northumbrian (the similarities between Mercian and Northumbrian mean that these two are sometimes grouped together and referred to as Anglian). Kentish was the dialect of the Jutes who had settled around Kent, West Saxon was spoken south of the River Thames, Mercian in an area extending from the Thames to the River Humber (but not including Wales), and Northumbrian, as the name suggests, by people living north of the Humber. It is, of course, likely that there were more than these four dialects in use at the time. Our knowledge of Old English and its dialects is gleaned from a relatively small amount of data. Only around three million words of Old English text have survived (Crystal 2005: 34), so it is perhaps not surprising that scholars have only been able to determine four dialects with any confidence, especially when we consider that Anglo-Saxon culture was largely oral (though we might also say that is it impressive that scholars have managed to glean so much from such a sparsity of material). A further problem that scholars have, of course, is that they are trying to reconstruct Old English dialects from written manuscripts. Of course, written language can give us some insight into dialectal characteristics but, naturally, it can only give us a limited insight into what the spoken form of that dialect might have been. Some dialectal differences that existed may never have been recorded in writing. It is also worth remembering that at this time there would still have been no conception among Anglo-Saxon speakers of 'an English language' shared by all the inhabitants of a country. This is important because the definition of what constitutes a language is as much a political matter as a linguistic one. For example, if you are from the south of England you may find it extremely difficult to understand someone who speaks a strong Newcastle dialect; nevertheless you would still consider them to be speaking English. However, imagine if the northeast of England were politically independent of the rest of the UK – and hostile at that. In such a circumstance, a London-based government might perhaps think very differently and consider Newcastle English to be a completely separate language. Politics, then, plays a large part in the definition of a particular variety as a language, and at this stage in the development of English the Anglo-Saxons were in no sense a politically unified people.

A2.2 The rise of West Saxon

Of the four dialects listed above, West Saxon was the most prestigious. Because of this, and the fact that West Saxon is the predominant dialect found in surviving manuscripts, most introductions to Old English (e.g. Mitchell and Robinson 2007, Hough and Corbett 2007) tend to concentrate on this dialect. But why was West Saxon viewed as prestigious? The answer to this is the same reason that particular accents and dialects are seen as prestigious in Present Day English (PDE): power. It has always been the case that the language variety used by the group that has a considerable degree of political and economic power will be viewed as more prestigious than those varieties used by less powerful groups. This was the case in Anglo-Saxon times, though, as we have seen, the balance of power between the Anglo-Saxon kingdoms was in no way stable. During the late seventh and early eighth centuries, for example, Northumbria dominated both culturally and politically. This situation came about when in 633 Oswald, a Christian, became ruler of Northumbria. Although Christianity was by no means widespread in Britain before the arrival of Augustine, it had not entirely died out after the departure of the Romans and had survived in Ireland. An Irish monk called Columba had founded a monastery on the Scottish island of Iona in an effort to spread the faith to the Picts and Oswald had been introduced to Christianity while on Iona in 616. As ruler of Northumbria, Oswald set about further spreading Christianity through the founding of churches and monasteries, such as those at Lindisfarne and Jarrow (the home, you'll remember, of the Venerable Bede). The monasteries were places of learning. Latin flourished once more as monks engaged in scholarship to disseminate their faith. Strong leadership and the success of the monasteries established Northumbria's political and cultural influence, which in turn would have increased the status of Northumbrian as an OE dialect. However, the Viking raids of the late eighth century effectively put paid to Northumbria's political dominance. You'll recall that when the Vikings invaded they looted towns and monasteries. Among these were the monasteries at Jarrow, Lindisfarne and Iona, and the raids halted the advance of scholarship in these places.

Political and cultural power had not belonged exclusively to Northumbria though. Mercia too had some influence in the eighth century and texts survive that were written not just in Latin but also in Anglo-Saxon. Among these are Old English glosses of Latin texts. But Mercia was also to suffer at the hands of the Vikings, as described in A1.5. This left Wessex, under the rule of Alfred, as the remaining Anglo-Saxon stronghold, the power and influence of Mercia and Northumbria having declined substantially.

Alfred, as we have seen, managed to defeat the Danes (as the Saxons called the Vikings), who were pushed back into the Danelaw. However, since one of the consequences of the Viking raids was a decline in scholarship, owing to the attacks on the monasteries that were the great centres of learning at the time, in the years following these raids, the ability even among the clergy to read Latin had declined. Alfred, being politically very shrewd, recognised the importance of this ability; Latin, for instance, was the language used in Royal Charters to circulate instructions from the King – and, of course, if people were having trouble reading it, as Stenton (1955: 43) points out, then Alfred's legislation would not be widely recognised. Alfred therefore made the decision to revitalise learning and scholarship. He taught himself Latin but recognised as well the importance of having Saxon translations of Latin texts. He himself translated numerous works and it is thanks to his efforts at reform and the Anglo-Saxon manuscripts produced under his guidance that we know so much about Old English today.

Inevitably, the translations made by Alfred and his associates were in West Saxon. The importance of Wessex as a political and cultural centre meant that the West Saxon dialect attained a prestige that set it apart from other varieties. Furthermore, since copies of translations made in Wessex were often sent elsewhere in the country for further copies to be made, West Saxon became established as a kind of literary standard.

A2.3 Dialect boundaries

Of course, we have to be careful when speculating about the geographical boundaries of particular dialects. It was obviously not the case that there was a clear dividing line between areas where, say, West Saxon was spoken and areas where Mercian dominated. Indeed, there was likely to be a strong degree of overlap of dialects at the geographical borders between the Anglo-Saxon kingdoms. It is also the case that just because a text may exhibit characteristics of, say, the Mercian dialect does not automatically mean that it reflects that dialect in full. It was common for the monks who produced such texts to travel around from monastery to monastery, and as they interacted with people from other areas of the country it is inevitable that they would have picked up certain elements of other dialects. It is likely then that texts may contain elements of a number of dialects – for example, the copyist's own as well as elements he may have absorbed both from hearing the speech of people from other areas and from reading their variant spellings of particular words. The scribes who produced Anglo-Saxon translations of Latin texts under Alfred may not all have come from Wessex. Although they may have been influenced by the West Saxon dialect, it is also likely that a few of their own dialectal features found their way into the manuscripts they produced.

Furthermore, it has also been suggested that the dialectal differences apparent in some OE manuscripts may be due in part to particular monasteries having their own styles of writing. Nevertheless, we can be confident that these styles must at least in part have been influenced by the dialect common to the region in which they were originally produced.

What should be clear by now is that when we talk about the history of English, we are really talking about the history of *varieties* of English. We may often concentrate on **Standard English** (and we'll look at the development of this form in A5) but we should be aware that there were and still are many different varieties of English in existence.

LANGUAGE CONTACT IN THE MIDDLE AGES   A3

Following the death of Alfred the Great, the West Saxons, under Alfred's heir, Edward, and later his grandson, Athelstan, managed to keep the Danes in check and retain the strength of Wessex. They even managed to take back areas of the Danelaw and in 937 Athelstan secured his most decisive victory over the Danes at the battle of Brunan-burh. Following this, Athelstan had himself proclaimed King of the Anglo-Saxons and Danes (James 2001: 246) and it is now that we start to see the beginnings of a unified England.

However, this success was not to last (see A1.5). The Viking attacks of the late tenth century saw the Danes reclaim power, ultimately leading to Svein Forkbeard claiming the throne of England in 1014. This then passed to his son Cnut who ruled until 1035. Following Cnut's death, his son, Harthacnut, ruled from 1040, when he took over from his half-brother Harold Harefoot, until 1042. As Harthacnut had no son, the throne then passed to Edward, later to become known as Edward the Con-fessor. Edward was Harthacnut's half-brother. They had the same mother – Emma of Normandy – who had given birth to Edward while married to Ethelred the Unready (the great-great grandson of Alfred the Great). The result of Edward's accession to the throne was a restoration of the Saxon line (remember that Ethelred, Edward's father, was from Wessex) after many years of Danish kings.

Now, returning to the issue of language (all these kings get in the way!), what is significant about Edward the Confessor becoming king is that he had been brought up in Normandy as a result of his father's exile there. Consequently, when Edward took up the throne of England, he filled his court with French advisors. Indeed, the his-torian Norman Davies describes him as 'a Trojan horse' for the rising power of Nor-mandy (Davies 2000: 232). Because of Edward's reliance on his French advisors, the French and English languages would have come into contact to a considerable degree. The influence of French turns out to be hugely important in explaining how English developed next.

A3.1 1066 and all that

Because Edward the Confessor's Royal Court included numerous French speakers, it is likely that even at this stage French was beginning to have an influence on English. Words from one language may have been adopted into the other as French and English speakers attempted to communicate with one another. But the impact of French on English was to increase even further following Edward's death in 1066.

Edward died in January of that year and as he had died childless it was not exactly clear who his heir to the throne should be. Nevertheless, immediately after Edward's death, Harold Godwinson had himself proclaimed king. Harold's father, Godwin, had been one of Edward's most powerful earls. Indeed, Godwin had had significant influence over the running of the country, and upon his death, his son Harold had taken over that position as Earl of Wessex. Harold claimed that Edward had promised him on his deathbed that he would be his successor to the throne. As Harold was effectively ruling England anyway, it was not a huge step for him to proclaim himself king once Edward had died.

Harold, though, was not the only claimant to the throne. William of Normandy, a second cousin of Edward's, also wished to succeed Edward. The fact that he was a second cousin of the former king did not in itself make him a rightful heir. However, like Harold, William claimed that Edward had promised him the throne during a visit that William made to England in 1052. The situation was complicated further by the fact that Harold had been shipwrecked off Normandy in 1064, during which time William had come to his aid in return for Harold promising to support him in his claim to the throne. At least, this is what William claimed. Harold maintained that he had been tricked into making this promise, and as it had been made under duress, probably felt no responsibility to honour it. This, then, was the situation that led to the infamous Battle of Hastings in 1066, and ultimately to the rise of French as a language of prestige in Britain.

The dispute over the throne of England left no option for William but to try and take the crown by force. In September 1066 he landed at Hastings with a formidable army. Harold's forces were badly depleted following their actions in the north of England to repel an invasion by the King of Norway, who was also keen to take the English throne (clearly England was hot property!). Nevertheless, when they arrived at Hastings they were able to take up a position on a hill above the Norman army, which gave them a significant advantage. It was only by pretending to retreat that William was able to lure the English down the hill, and once that had happened the battle was all but over. In the midst of the fighting Harold was killed (allegedly as a result of an arrow piercing his eye). And on Christmas Day, 1066, William of Normandy – William the Conqueror – was crowned King of England in Westminster Abbey. The French language had well and truly arrived in England.

A3.2 From Old English to Middle English

The Norman invasion of England had far reaching consequences for the development of the English language. Of course, the language did not change overnight but gradually French began to have an influence that was to change English substantially and lead it into its next stage of development – Middle English. You can explore what Middle English was like in sections B3 and C3.

We have already seen how, because of Edward the Confessor's Norman origins, the language of the Royal Court would have become dominated by French. This would have continued to an even greater extent under William the Conqueror, especially since so many of his advisors at Court would have also come from Normandy. Furthermore, the language of administration favoured by William would have been Latin, since this was what would have been used at home. So, French became the vernacular language of the Royal Court and Latin the language of administration (and, of course, religion). One of the knock-on effects of this would have been to downgrade the status of English so that it lost a lot of the prestige it had gained under the Saxon monarchy.

The influence of French would also have been felt further afield. One of the immediate consequences of William becoming king was his replacement of many English noblemen with his own Norman nobles (partly because William would have favoured his own men but also because so many of the English nobility had been killed at Hastings). According to the Domesday Book, which William had commissioned to discover exactly what his new kingdom consisted of in terms of land and who owned it, by 1086 most landholders in England were Norman. In terms of linguistic consequences, this meant that French was coming into contact with English and also that French would have gradually attained the prestige that English had formerly enjoyed, since French was now the language of the ruling class. But just how was French affecting English?

In the immediate aftermath of Hastings, it should be said that the effect of French on the majority of the native English population was probably very minimal. Townspeople would have heard it spoken much more than people in the country and the extent to which they experienced it would have depended on the amount of contact they had with the type of people for whom French was the vernacular language. For instance, traders in and around London were much more likely to come into contact with French speakers than farmers in the countryside. And when they did communicate with French speakers, this would more than likely have involved a good deal of effort to understand each other. Over time, some of these efforts would begin to affect English itself. For example, Old English was a language that made use of inflections (see B1.3, B1.4 and B1.5) which tended to be unstressed in spoken language. The fact that some French speakers may therefore not have heard the inflections when listening to Anglo-Saxon speakers meant that their own efforts at speaking and writing in English would not necessarily have included these grammatical elements. Over time, this was a contributory factor to the decline of an inflectional system in English, though it should be noted that the breakdown of the system of inflections had already begun in the Old English period among speakers of different dialects of Old English (see B3.3 for more detail).

The other way in which French affected English was by English borrowing words from French. This was the source of a lot of new vocabulary in English. In short, French began to affect English at many linguistic levels, including vocabulary, spelling, grammar and pronunciation. The extent to which French began to mix with English would have been increased by, for example, inter-marriage between French and English nobility. The children of such unions would have grown up bilingual and would have been likely to engage in code-switching (the sociolinguistic term for the mixing of two languages), which would have further increased the hybrid nature of English.

Trade, too, would have led people to mix languages, to borrow vocabulary and generally to be influenced by each other's ways of speaking and writing.

All of this development changed English to such an extent that linguists refer to the English of this period as **Middle English (ME)**. Middle English is usually said to refer to English from around 1100 to 1500. The reason Middle English is not dated from the arrival of William the Conqueror in 1066 is, of course, because change is never immediate and it would have taken several years for French to start having an influence on English. Linguists often make a distinction between Early Middle English (1100 to 1300) and Later Middle English (1300 to 1500). There are some clear linguistic differences between these periods and some of these can be ascribed to the wider social, political and cultural changes that were taking place at the time (see B3 for more details).

A3.3 The decline of French and the rise of English

Although in the years following the Norman Conquest French replaced English as the most prestigious language, this is not to say that English disappeared. Its status simply became downgraded. It went from being a language of officialdom, with a developing written standard, to once more being primarily a spoken language. Even so, it remained the language spoken by the majority of people in the country. However, its status was to rise again, following a number of events that led to a gradual decline in the use of French.

Among the first of these was King John's loss of Normandy in 1204. John was a descendant of William the Conqueror, and losing Normandy to the French meant that the English lost an important territorial connection with France. One of the long-term consequences of this was to generate a stronger sense of English identity among the nobility of England. This identity was bolstered by the actions of Henry III later on in the thirteenth century. Some of the English nobility began to accuse Henry of favouring those of his subjects who were of French descent. Henry responded by issuing a royal proclamation in English as well as French. In effect, this was a kind of propaganda, designed to emphasise Henry's commitment to his English nobility. As you can see, English is not just a means of communicating a message – here it was being used strategically to foster identity.

The use of English for this purpose increased during the fourteenth century. Between 1337 and 1453, the so-called **Hundred Years War** was waged between England and France. During this period, Henry V (who ruled from 1413 to 1422) began to use English to write despatches home from his campaigns. Again, this is an example of English being using for the purposes of propaganda. To write in French would have been to write in the language of the enemy. Using English emphasised the division between the English and the French and worked to create a greater sense of national identity.

All of these events led to the very considered use of English for particular political purposes. But another event that occurred during the fourteenth century led to an increase in the use of English that was not so obviously determined by politics. This was **the bubonic plague** – or, **the Black Death**. The bubonic plague had already swept across Europe and arrived in England in 1348. Its effect was devastating. Historians estimate that it killed around a third of the population of the country at the time. So how did this affect the development of English? One of the consequences of

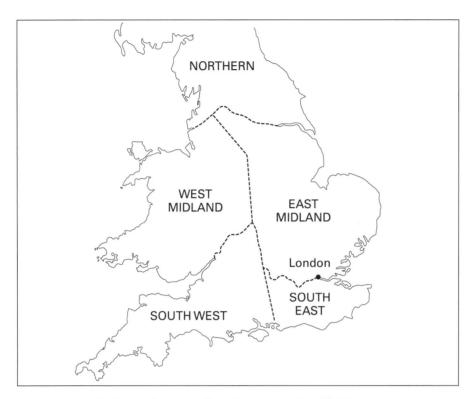

Map 2 Middle English dialect areas (from Burrow and Turville-Petre 1996: 7)

the drastic reduction in population was to reduce the country's workforce. Inevitably, this shortage of labour pushed up workers' wages as demand outstripped supply. This meant that the working classes were able to climb the ladder of social hierarchy and attain a level of prosperity that would have been impossible before the Black Death. And, as we have seen, the greater the influence a particular group has within society, the more likely it is that the language spoken by that group will be seen as prestigious. English was on the rise once again. However, it was an English that had been greatly affected by its contact with French and it remained the case that in some domains of life (e.g. religion), English was still not the dominant language used.

A3.4 Middle English dialects

In the Middle English period there was no established standard form of English such as there is today, either written or spoken. Middle English writers wrote as they spoke (Burrow and Turville-Petre 1996: 6). The upshot of this is that looking at Middle English writing can give us a clue as to the different dialects that were used at the time. Burrow and Turville-Petre (1996) distinguish five different dialects of Middle English: Northern, West Midland, East Midland, South East and South West. The divisions between these dialects can be seen in Map 2.

The dotted lines between geographical areas are isoglosses. An isogloss is a boundary denoting the point at which a difference can be noticed in the use of particular linguistic items (e.g. particular spellings, pronunciations, etc.). Isoglosses are not absolute divisions, of course, as is explained in A2.3. At these boundaries we are likely to find more than one particular linguistic form being used (perhaps two different pronunciations of the same word, for example). A useful analogy is to imagine what would happen if you were to try and colour in the different sections of Map 2 using watercolour paints. If you didn't wait for the paint to dry before starting on another section, you would find that the different colours would bleed into each other at the points where they touched. In effect, this is what happens linguistically at the points where isoglosses intersect.

FROM MIDDLE ENGLISH TO EARLY MODERN ENGLISH

It should be clear by now how, in the history of English, external events have impacted upon the language and been causal in its development and change. Sometimes we can point to one event as being particularly significant (e.g. the Norman Conquest led to English coming into greater contact with French) but even in such apparently clear-cut scenarios, the reality is that a host of different occurrences – some linguistic, some non-linguistic – contrive to generate change in the language. This can be seen particularly in the development of Middle English into **Early Modern English (EModE)**.

The events that caused English to develop into a language that is much more similar to Present Day English are many and varied. Because of this, there is some disagreement among scholars about when EModE might be said to begin and end. Again, we have to remember that boundary dates between linguistic periods are in no way markers of overnight change, but simply serve to indicate the points at which the language noticeably begins to alter. As a rough guide, EModE might be said to begin around 1500, while the changes that were to affect its development into present day English were beginning to be felt around 1700. The reasons for this choice of dates will become clear once you have read about the various events that occurred in this period, which you will find in the rest of this section and in A5.

A4.1 External influences on pronunciation

One of the key developments of English that occurred between the Middle English and Early Modern period involved significant changes to the way in which certain vowel sounds were pronounced, a development which has come to be known as the Great Vowel Shift. This occurred mainly between 1400 and 1650 (though change was ongoing until the eighteenth century) and involved a gradual modification in the pronunciation of the long vowels in English. 'Long' in this sense refers to the duration of the pronunciation. For example, the word *sit* contains the short vowel [ɪ], while the word *seat* contains its 'long' counterpart [iː]. (Try extending your pronunciation of *sit* – it should sound more like you are pronouncing *seat*.) In very simplified terms, what happened during the Great Vowel Shift was that the way in which people pronounced long vowel sounds altered and the long vowels in English were 'raised'. That is, the position of the tongue during the production of long vowel sounds changed over time so that gradually it moved closer to the roof of the mouth. The Great Vowel Shift thus had a considerable impact on the pronunciation of words and also on spelling, as we will see in A5.1, though it is not the case that every area of the country was affected in the same way.

You can read more about the linguistic complexities of The Great Vowel Shift in B4 and in the readings in D4, but since we are for the moment focusing on the external events that affected the development of English, it is worth considering the role that social factors might have played in causing it. Not surprisingly, this is a complex issue. The causes of the Great Vowel Shift have never been definitively established and there has been a considerable amount of disagreement between scholars. Nevertheless, one view, put forward by the sociolinguist William Labov, is that we can hypothesise about the causes of the Great Vowel Shift based on what we know about the causes of linguistic change in contemporary English. In the mid-1960s Labov carried out a groundbreaking sociolinguistic study of the varieties of English used in New York City (Labov 1966) and concluded that in terms of social groups the main driver of change in language was the middle classes. The British sociolinguist Peter Trudgill came to similar conclusions in his famous study of language use in relation to social class in Norwich (Trudgill 1974). In an article written in 1978, Labov suggest that the same might also have been true in the Early Modern period. The Great Vowel Shift may have been motivated by the merchant classes being influenced by varieties of English that they viewed as being particularly prestigious, and which they then either consciously or subconsciously emulated. To understand the theory behind such a hypothesis it is worth quoting at length Labov's outline of the social process of sound change in language:

> A linguistic change begins as a local pattern characteristic of a particular social group, often the result of immigration from another region. It becomes generalized throughout the group, and becomes associated with the social values attributed to that group. It spreads to those neighbouring populations which take the first group as a reference group in one way or another. The opposition of the two linguistic forms continues and often comes to symbolize an opposition of social values. These values may rise to the level of social consciousness and become *stereotypes*, subject to irregular social correction, or they may remain below that level as unconscious *markers*. Finally, one or the other of the two forms wins out. There follows a long period when the disappearing form is heard as archaic, a symbol of a vanished prestige or stigma, and is used as a source of humor until it is extinguished entirely. If the older pronunciation is preserved in place names or fixed forms, it is then heard as a meaningless irregularity.
>
> (Labov 1978: 280)

Labov's hypothesis is useful in that it provides an external reason for the sound changes that took place in this period. You can read more about the intralinguistic aspects of the Great Vowel Shift and the processes of internal change by which it occurred in B4.

A4.2 The translation of the Bible into English

One of the events that was to have an impact on the development of English in the Early Modern period was the publication of the Bible in English. In actual fact, there had been a number of translations produced before the definitive King James Bible of 1611, the first of which had been completed in the late Middle Ages. It is worth following the development of the Bible in English in order to assess its impact on English.

We have seen that during the Middle English period there were effectively three languages in use in England: French, English and Latin. French was the language of the Royal Court, English the language of the ordinary person in the street, and Latin the language of administration and religion. There was a clear hierarchy associated with the use of these languages. Only the educated would have been able to read and understand Latin and, at the time, being educated largely meant being a member of the clergy. Church services were held entirely in Latin and consequently few people would have had much beyond a surface level comprehension of what was going on. It is easy to see how, for most people, the images and statues that adorned churches and cathedrals were of far more value in conveying biblical stories than the Bible itself. But the situation changed when John Wycliffe, an Oxford professor, produced an unauthorised translation of the Bible into English between 1380 and 1382. The translation of the Bible into English was to affect the English language in a number of ways over the Early Modern period and to comprehend the changes it is necessary first of all to understand the impact of Wycliffe's translation in the late Middle Ages.

Wycliffe's Bible was distributed around the country by the Lollards, an organisation of itinerant priests. One side-effect of this was an increase in literacy among common people. Literacy was not widespread at the time but people learned to read in order to be able to read Wycliffe's Bible for themselves. Nevertheless, not everyone was pleased by this development, particularly not the Church. In 1382, at Blackfriars in London, Wycliffe was put on trial by a Special Synod. He was found guilty of heresy, a parliamentary ban was imposed on his English translation of the Bible, and the arrest and prosecution of all Lollards was ordered. But this was not to be the end of the Bible in English. By the late 1300s, political events were shaping up that would affect the status of English and once more lead to its being used in the translation of the scriptures.

We have seen how, during the Hundred Years War with France, Henry V began to use English almost as a method of propaganda, for the purpose of establishing a common national identity that was at odds with that of the French. One of the ways in which he did this was to start using English to write his despatches home from his campaigns in France. Previously, these had all been written in French. Increasingly, English began to be used in government, and the fact that it was necessary for civil service documents to be understood as far apart as London and Carlisle was in part what gave rise to the emergence of a standard form of English that superseded rural dialects. This is sometimes known as **Chancery English** (see A5.1) because it was the form of English preferred by the Chancery – i.e. the Royal bureaucracy. The development of Standard English meant that the possibility existed to spread the word of God in English to even more people. The next major breakthrough in doing this came with the setting-up of a printing press at Westminster by William Caxton in 1476. (We will explore the role of the printing press in the development of a standard form of English in detail in A5.) Mechanising the process of book production meant that more texts could be produced than ever before, and Caxton's printing press also helped to standardise English spelling even further. However, English translations of the Bible were still banned by parliament. Many in the upper classes worried about the difficulty of controlling the spread of ideas that the printing press had augmented. It was not until 1525 that someone else proved brave enough to attempt another translation of the Bible. This was William Tyndale.

Tyndale went one step further than Wycliffe by translating the Bible from the original Hebrew and Greek. Tyndale, too, was passionate about his translation. John Foxe, in *Actes and Monuments*, reports a heated argument between Tyndale and 'a learned man', during which Tyndale is reported to have said 'I defie the Pope and all his lawes' and 'if God spare my lyfe ere many yeares, I wyl cause a boye that dryueth þe plough, shall knowe more of the scripture then thou doest' (Foxe 1563: 514). The advent of the printing press meant that multiple copies of Tyndale's translation could be produced for relatively little outlay. Thousands of pocket-sized copies were printed in Cologne and smuggled into England. So fearful was the Church of the potential effects of Tyndale's translation that Henry VIII put the whole country on alert and many of the Bibles were intercepted. The Bishop of London went so far as to buy an entire shipment simply to destroy them. But Tyndale was not to be outdone. Using the profits from the sale of his Bible, he went on to produce an even better translation, this time of the Old Testament as well as the New Testament.

The influence of Tyndale's Bible was tremendous. It triggered the growth of literacy, with people learning to read specifically so that they could study the Bible in English. As Knowles (1997: 96) explains, 'Bible reading would be a strong motivation for learning to read in the first place, since it enabled readers to form opinions independently of the traditional authorities of church and state'. Tyndale's Bible gave us many words and phrases that we still use today.

Nevertheless, despite the reformation pre-empted by Henry VIII having split from the Roman Catholic Church to initiate the Church of England, Tyndale's translation of the Bible was still seen as heretical. In 1536 he was charged with heresy, strangled and then burned at the stake. Tyndale's last words were a prayer – that God might 'open the King of England's eyes'. It might have surprised Tyndale to learn that just three years later the King had indeed changed his mind. By this time, Henry had married his third wife, Jane Seymour, a follower of the new Protestant religion. She was instrumental in persuading Henry that a Bible in English was just what the new religion needed. Consequently, in 1539 Henry ordered the production of the first official English Bible, and every church in England was instructed to buy one. It was this 'Great Bible' (so-called because of its size) that was to be the basis of the King James Bible, or the 'Authorised Version', published in 1611. The writers of this text looked to Tyndale's and Wycliffe's translations in an effort to create the definitive English Bible, and in doing so they were responsible for many of the idiomatic phrases still in use today. Crystal (1995: 64) lists some of these as *to spy out the land* (Numbers 13), *the apple of his eye* (Deuteronomy 32), *the skin of my teeth* (Job 19), *go from strength to strength* (Psalms 84), *the straight and narrow* (Matthew 7), *the sign of the times* (Matthew 16), *in the twinkling of an eye* (1 Corinthians 15), *filthy lucre* (1 Timothy 3), *rule with a rod of iron* (Revelations 2), and *out of the mouth of babes* (Psalms 8). The real impact of the King James Bible was to make English the language of religion in England. The days of English as a poor relation to Latin and French in terms of prestige were now gone.

The spread of ideas and the impact of the Bible both on literacy and on the development of English generally were greatly affected by the development of a standard form of English. In turn, the production of multiple copies of books reinforced this standard and helped in making it more widely recognised.

A5 THE PROCESS OF STANDARDISATION

The Early Modern period is generally seen as a period in which English underwent a process of standardisation. Of course, it is not the case that with the emergence of a standard form of the language dialect variation was lost. When we talk about Standard English, we are effectively concentrating on a written form of the language.

A5.1 Dialects and emerging standards

Although in the Old English period it was West Saxon that had come closest to being a standard form of the language (at least for written literary texts), this was replaced in the Middle English period by the dialect of the East Midlands, because the centre of political power had moved to London. Indeed, Present Day English derives ultimately from the East Midlands dialect (Nevalainen and Tieken-Boon van Ostade 2006: 271). However, the development of this dialect into a written standard form was not a straightforward process. Samuels (1963) identifies four different types of written Standard English in the fourteenth and fifteenth centuries that were all used at one point or another before finally being subsumed by Chancery English. These were:

Type 1: Central Midlands Standard

This is the form of English that is found in those texts produced by the Wycliffite movement, for example in the Lollard Bible referred to in A4.2. According to Samuels, 'until 1430, it is the type that has most claim to the title "literary standard"' (Samuels 1963: 85). It eventually died out towards the end of the fifteenth century.

Type 2: Early London English

This was in use up until the late 1300s and included characteristics of East Anglian dialects, suggesting that it was developed at least in part by writers originally from that area of England.

Type 3: London English

This form was in use from around 1380 to around 1425 and includes elements of a Central Midlands dialect. Some versions of *The Canterbury Tales* by the Middle English writer Geoffrey Chaucer are in this dialect, suggesting that this may have been the dialect preferred by him (though we should not discount the role of printers in deciding on the dialect in which a text was published and it is important to bear in mind that the first copies of *The Canterbury Tales* were scribal copies as opposed to printed texts).

Type 4: Chancery Standard

This standard form was used in government documents from around 1430. (The Chancery was a royal court. 'Chancery Standard', therefore, is often used as a short-hand term for the variety preferred by the royal bureaucracy, though the category is perhaps not as discrete as its label would suggest, as we shall see.) It includes characteristics of Midlands and Northern dialects, suggesting that it was not solely a regional dialect from the London area, but that its development was also affected by writers from elsewhere incorporating their own dialect forms into this particular standard.

To illustrate the differences between London English (type 3) and the Chancery Standard (type 4), look at the differences in spelling of the following words (based on Samuels 1963: 89):

Type 3: London English	Type 4: Chancery Standard
nat	not
bot	but
swich(e)	such(e)
thise	thes(e)
thurgh	thorough

You will notice that the Chancery Standard spellings are much closer to (and in some cases, the same as) Present Day English spellings.

However, while it is sometimes claimed that Chancery Standard was deliberately cultivated by the Chancery (see Fisher 1996 for details of this argument), it is important to bear in mind that features associated with Chancery Standard did not necessarily originate from the Chancery itself. Recent research by Michael Benskin suggests that Samuels's Type 4, although very common, was not the sole form of government English in use and that so-called Chancery Standard was not the fixed variety linguists have sometimes claimed it to be. As Benskin points out:

> Had Henry V's Signet clerks [Chancery scribes] really been concerned with institutional spelling norms, then the word England would surely have been a prime candidate for fixity, whereas their letters show at least seven variants: Eng(e)lond, England(e), Engeland, Ingelond, Ingeland.
>
> (Benskin 2004: 21)

One Chancery writer quoted by Benskin (2004: 32) uses forms that are of a north midland variety. These include the spellings *sich* and *syche* (PDE *such*; compare these with Samuels's *suche*), *ich* (PDE *each*), *ony* (PDE *any*) and *mych* (PDE *much*). Another Chancery scribe uses the variants *soche* (PDE *such*), *hafe* (PDE *have*) and *gyf, gyve* and *yif* (PDE *give*), suggestive of a north-west midlands variety. Consequently, says Benskin (2004: 32), 'such cases do little to support the belief that Chancery, as a matter of policy, trained its clerks to write English of a certain type'. As he points out, 'The development of a written standard, even in the offices of government, was more complex and less determined than it has sometimes been made to appear, and government English is not the whole story' (2004: 36). Much more research is needed to determine the exact means by which Standard English emerged, but it seems likely that other institutions than Chancery would have played their part. Crystal (2005: 232), for example, makes the point that 'material emanating from the civil service, law offices, ecclesiastical bodies and business centres always operates with a rather special cachet'. He goes on to point out that since such material would generally have originated from London, it would be London norms of usage that were gradually spread around the country. The point is that not all of these norms would necessarily have originated from Chancery.

A5.2 Caxton and the impact of the printing press

A key date in the development of a standard form of English is 1476, when William Caxton, an English merchant, set up a printing press at Westminster. Caxton did not invent the press but had been successful as a printer in Bruges. What is significant about his work in England is that he chose to publish books in English. This did much to establish the legitimacy of English as a language of learning (as opposed to Latin) as well as contribute to the development of a standard form, as we shall see. However, standardising the language was not a primary concern of Caxton's. Rather it was a by-product of a number of decisions that Caxton and his fellow printers (men like Richard Pynson and the memorably named Wynkyn de Worde) had to make as they typeset manuscripts to copy. The process of standardisation was lengthy and cannot be attributed to Caxton alone. Indeed, some scholars (e.g. Scragg 1974: 64) have pointed out that, initially, printing actually caused problems for the establishment of consistency in written English. For example, the variety of different ways in which a word could be spelled was often useful for printers, who would add or subtract a letter in order to ensure that a line of type was justified on both margins. Nevertheless, over time consistency became more commonplace.

A primary issue facing Caxton was which variety of English to use in his work. Dialectal variation was commonplace in speech and also in writing (as it is today, of course). But the mass-production of books and pamphlets necessarily involved the replication of one particular dialect. Caxton had set up his printing press at Westminster and so, unsurprisingly, veered towards London English as the variety of choice, specifically incorporating elements of what Samuels denotes as Type 4, Chancery English, which was becoming established as a standard among the educated classes. Chancery English was a form of the East Midlands dialect and it is from this form of East Midlands dialect that Standard Present Day English derives. Note that the earlier 'standard', West Saxon, had long been supplanted by this stage. Dialects can become prestigious for many different reasons. The rise of the so-called Chancery English has much to do with the power and wealth of the merchant classes trading in London at the time, whose dialect it was. This and the fact that the royal court was based in London meant that the dialect was associated with powerful people – and, as we have already seen, power equals prestige.

The impact of the printing press was huge. Mechanising the process of book production meant that more texts could be produced more quickly and for less cost than ever before. This made the rapid spread of ideas possible and the printing press played a huge role in the success of Tyndale's 1525 translation of the Bible into English. The rapid spread of books and pamphlets also meant the spread of a particular variety of English – the London Standard that was so often used in book production. It should be noted, however, that this 'standard' was not entirely a regional dialect. It would have included elements of other dialects as London-based writers originally from elsewhere in the country struggled to adapt to the emerging standard (in A2.3 we saw something similar happening with the Old English scribes writing in West Saxon). It was also the case that some choices made by printers may have been little more than a 'house standard', in much the same way that modern publishers adhere to conventions that are entirely arbitrary – for example, advising authors to use <-*ize*> rather than <-*ise*> when spelling words such as *organize*.

A5.3 Dictionaries and grammars

Although throughout the Early Modern period a standard form of English gradually emerged, there were those who felt that a greater hand could be taken in the process of standardisation, and particularly in what was referred to as the 'fixing' of the language. In 1712 Jonathan Swift (the author of the satirical works *A Modest Proposal* and *Gulliver's Travels*) proposed that it would be valuable to 'fix' English, in *A Proposal for Correcting, Improving and Ascertaining the English Tongue*. There is an interesting presupposition here, namely that it is in fact possible to 'fix' a language in the sense of regularising and standardising it. You can read more about the efforts of Swift and his compatriots to fix English in D5 but it should be apparent by now that English, like any other language with native speakers, is constantly changing and evolving in response to external and internal stimuli.

Nevertheless, the calls from some quarters for the fixing of the language did at least reflect a growing need for some kind of description and explanation of the English language. English had not always enjoyed the same level of prestige as French or Latin, and because it had been primarily a spoken language during the Old and Middle English periods, no grammar books or guides to its usage had been produced – there had been no need. Now, though, the increase in the number of books in circulation caused by the use of the printing press led to a greater call for dictionaries and grammars of English. People wanted instruction on how to read English so that they could take advantage of the increasing number of texts available. Furthermore, since the Reformation, education was no longer controlled solely by the Church and English had begun to be used in academic circles (previously Latin had been the primary language of education). Consequently, there was a demand for schoolbooks that outlined the workings of English.

The first dictionaries of English were bilingual dictionaries, produced to allow the translation into English of Latin and French texts. Caxton himself produced an English–French dictionary in 1480. The first monolingual dictionary of English appeared in 1604 and was written by Richard Cawdrey. It was called *A Table Alphabeticall* and contained the definitions of around 2500 words, though, unlike today's dictionaries, Cawdrey's focused entirely on what he called 'hard' words – i.e. he ignored words that he thought his readers were likely to have no problems in understanding. The words that Cawdrey focused on were those that had been borrowed into English from other languages, for example, Greek, Latin and French. It was not until later on that dictionary writers began to extend their remit. In 1691 Stephen Skinner produced *A New English Dictionary* in which so-called 'common' words were defined along with their **etymologies** (i.e. the histories of the individual words; for example, the languages they were derived from, etc.). John Kersey's identically titled dictionary was published in 1702 and contained the definitions of approximately 28,000 'common' words. With the understanding of language and linguistics that we have today, we can see that there are numerous problems with the works of the early dictionary writers; they were, for instance, extremely subjective accounts of the **lexicon** (the 'word-stock' of a language). Nevertheless, it is important not to be too critical of their efforts. Nowadays we take dictionaries for granted so it is easy to underestimate the enormity of the task that the early scholars set themselves. To produce a dictionary of a language without recourse to computer technology or the wealth of supplementary material that we have at our disposal today is admirable. Rather than be overtly critical of these early texts, we need to understand where their flaws come from. You can explore some of these issues in C4.

Easily the most impressive and most authoritative dictionary produced in the Early Modern period was that published by Samuel Johnson in 1755. Although Johnson realised fairly early on in the project that he had bitten off significantly more than he could chew, it was still an impressive achievement. The dictionary was compiled over a period of nine years and contained definitions of almost 43,000 words. What made Johnson's dictionary especially noteworthy was the fact he used quotations from other texts to illustrate the meaning in context of the words he defined. Johnson also recognised that the changing nature of language meant that it was impossible to produce a dictionary that would be authoritative for all time. In his preface he says: '[. . .] no dictionary of a living tongue ever can be perfect since while it is hastening to publication, some words are budding, and some falling away[.]' (Johnson 1983 [1755]).

As well as dictionaries, the Early Modern period also saw the production of grammar books. Where a dictionary defines the vocabulary of a language, a grammar explains its syntax; i.e. the 'rules' that govern the formation of meaningful sentences in that language. As with the dictionary writers, the writers of grammars were often simply wrong in some of their assertions. You can explore some of their misconceptions in C4. Nevertheless, the efforts of these scholars did much to promote consistency of usage in English (even if this was sometimes based on false premises) and to establish a standard form for written English.

A5.4 The boundaries of Early Modern English

It is perhaps harder to 'see' the boundaries of Early Modern English than it is to discern the points at which Old and Middle English can be said to begin and end. This is perhaps because Early Modern English does not seem so alien to speakers of Present Day English so it is harder to see the major differences between EModE and PDE. It is also perhaps because we feel that we know a bit more about the EModE period than earlier periods in history, and so it is harder to identify just one or two events that have affected the development of English. Clearly the Great Vowel Shift was of importance, as was the development of the printing press. The production of dictionaries and grammars also played a part, as did the economic and political climate that caused Chancery English to become established as standard. The point, of course, is that there is hardly ever just one event that causes a change in language. More often than not it is a combination of events, and this is true for all periods of linguistic history. Most historians of English suggest the boundaries of EModE to be 1500 to 1800. By 1500 the printing press would have begun to have some influence and the Great Vowel Shift would have begun to take effect. By 1800, Johnson's dictionary had become famous and the language was beginning to look and sound much more like the English we write and speak today. But, of course, such temporal boundaries are not hard and fast and change in language is happening all the time. And while these boundary dates reflect major developments in the standard variety of English, they don't necessarily correspond to developments in the regional dialects of English.

COLONIALISM, IMPERIALISM AND THE SPREAD OF ENGLISH   **A6**

We have already seen how during earlier periods Britain was effectively a trilingual nation, with English, French and Latin having varying degrees of status and being used in particular areas of life. This was in addition to the numerous Celtic and Gaelic languages (e.g. Cornish and Welsh) that would also have been spoken in various parts of the country. So, the idea that languages belong to countries (i.e. English is the language of England, French the language of France, etc.) is a popular misconception. Indeed, English now extends far beyond England and is generally considered to be a global language. It was in the Early Modern period that the spread of English overseas began. This was as a result of **colonisation**, whereby British communities were established beyond the British Isles. These colonies were under the political control of Britain, and constituted part of the **British Empire**.

A6.1 English in the New World

The English had made a number of attempts to found colonies in America in the late 1500s and early 1600s, with settlements in Newfoundland and in what was later to become North Carolina (Jones 1995: 5). These early attempts failed and it was not until 1607 that a lasting colony was established in Jamestown, Virginia, on the east coast of America. In 1620 a further colony was established in what is now Plymouth, Massachusetts. The Puritan settlers who later became known as the Pilgrim Fathers arrived on the ship *The Mayflower*, fleeing religious persecution in England. These early settlers inevitably brought their own varieties of English to the New World. The Jamestown settlers originated from areas of Gloucestershire and Somerset, while the pilgrims of *The Mayflower* came from areas of the Midlands such as Lincolnshire and Nottinghamshire, as well as London and the surrounding areas of Essex and Kent.

By 1732, thirteen British colonies had been established along the east coast of America. The British were not the only ones in the country though. The French had a significant presence in Canada, while the Spanish had settled in Florida. The Dutch had a colony along the eastern seaboard known as New Amsterdam which, when the English wrested control of it in 1664, was renamed New York in reference to the then

Duke of York. In addition to settlers from Spain, France, the Netherlands and England, there were also immigrants from Ireland, Scotland and Germany. From 1619, there was also a rapidly increasing number of black African slaves brought to the colonies, initially to work on tobacco plantations. The presence of people from a multitude of backgrounds meant that the colonies were places of great linguistic diversity and it is easy to imagine new varieties of English emerging from the cultural mix.

In 1763, following a series of bloody conflicts, England seized control of Canada and the land east of the Mississippi River, as well as Florida, which Spain relinquished in exchange for Cuba and the Philippines. Britain had become the largest colonial power in the world. Because of the expansion of their American empire, the British quickly found it necessary to reform their colonial system in order to streamline the process of providing effective government and defence (Jones 1995: 37). The measures that were taken in pursuit of this goal (including increases in taxation and customs duties) were factors that contributed to the outbreak of the **American Revolution**, or the **War of Independence (1775–83)**. The war ended in 1783 and the Treaty of Paris recognised the independence of the United States. The first US President, George Washington, took office in 1789, following the ratification of the US constitution.

We have seen how powerful language can be in creating identities, both for individuals and for countries. In the USA, the integration of people from a wide range of backgrounds inevitably led to new forms of English. But moves were also made to actively develop a variety of English that was distinct from the standard form that was emerging in England, and that would demonstrate the uniquely American character of English in the US which would inevitably form some part of the identity of the new country.

What Samuel Johnson had done for the English language in England, **Noah Webster** did for English in America. Webster was born in 1758 and educated at Yale College, graduating in 1778. Following several smaller (though highly influential) works on English, in 1828 Webster published *An American Dictionary of the English Language* which contained around 70,000 entries. Webster's dictionary had a major influence on American spelling and pronunciation but perhaps more importantly it played a significant role in establishing a linguistic identity for American English. You can explore some of Webster's ideas in more detail in C6.

A6.2 The expansion of the British Empire

Although Britain had lost its American colonies in the American War of Independence, this had done nothing to reduce the status of English as America's unofficial national language. The spread of English was to continue with the expansion of the British Empire into such places as Canada, the Indian subcontinent, Africa and Australasia.

The British position in India had come about as a result of the formation of the **British East India Company** in 1600, for the purposes of trade. The British initially established settlements in the Indian cities of Calcutta (now called Kolkata), Bombay (now Mumbai), and Madras (now Chennai) and ultimately India came under British control. British rule in India (the so-called **Raj**, derived from the Hindi word for 'rule') began in 1765 and lasted until 1947, during which time English was established as the language of administration and education. The universities set up in Calcutta, Bombay and Madras would have played a significant role in this, and part of the motivation for the introduction of English into the education system was to produce bilingual speakers who would be able to act as interpreters for the British (Kachru 1984: 355). However, Kachru (1984) explains that English was not necessarily imposed against the will of the local population. In the early years of the British presence in India, some of the local people had specifically asked that English be taught so that they would have 'access to the scientific knowledge of the West' (Kachru 1984: 354). As English became established in India it would also have come into contact with the variety of other languages (e.g. Hindi) and dialects used in the country, leading to spoken forms of English that may have differed substantially from the standard written form of English.

As the British Empire expanded, English also became the official language of administration and government in such places as Malaysia, Singapore and Hong Kong. British colonies were also established in South Africa, East Africa and West Africa. Alongside the standard varieties of English that were in use for official purposes, there also emerged language varieties which sociolinguists call **pidgins**. A pidgin is a language that arises when two or more different speech communities use their respective languages as the basis for a very basic language with a limited set of functions. For example, English-based pidgins were common along the west coast of Africa for the purposes of trade.

As a result of colonisation, English also found its way to Australia and New Zealand. In the case of Australia, the English language arrived when the British established a penal colony at Sydney in 1788. At the time it was felt to be a simple solution to the problem of overcrowding in English prisons. The settlement of New Zealand by the British occurred later, in 1840. In contrast with Australia, New Zealand was settled as a free colony and attracted immigrants from southern England and from Scotland, many of whom were given assisted passage to help with the cost of the trip. As with the original settlers in the North American colonies, it is easy to imagine how the immigrants' dialects would have mixed and how, consequently, new pronunciations and new vocabulary would have emerged over time. There would also have been a certain amount of contact with the indigenous populations of the countries: Aboriginal Australians in Australia and the Maori in New Zealand. However, because of the differences in lifestyle between the settlers and the indigenous people, not to mention the often racist attitudes that prevailed among the immigrant populations, contact between cultures was limited (Eagleson 1984: 431). Consequently, as Eagleson explains, only a small number of words from the indigenous languages of Australia and New Zealand were borrowed into English.

By the beginning of the nineteenth century, then, English had spread across the globe as a consequence of the expansion of the largest empire ever. In the first half of the twentieth century, though, the British Empire began to decline. Nevertheless, by this time English was well estalished as a language used far beyond the boundaries of the British Isles. Furthermore, the spread of English would continue throughout the twentieth century and into the twenty-first. However, the mechanism that would turn English into a truly global language was not colonisation but a combination of technology, economics and politics.

MOVES TOWARDS PRESENT DAY ENGLISH

By the beginning of the eighteenth century English had developed to the stage where a present-day speaker of English would have little or no trouble understanding it. Although there are some vocabulary differences and some grammatical forms that are not common today (especially when we consider regional dialects), for the most part it is only stylistic differences that distinguish eighteenth-century English from Present Day English. This is not to say that English stopped changing at this point. As we have seen, language is always in a state of flux. Throughout the nineteenth and twentieth centuries there were major social events that were instrumental in affecting the development of English – and not just the standard variety. What follows is a selection of some of the most significant events to have affected the course of English in Britain during the nineteenth and twentieth centuries (you may well think of more) as well as a summary of some of the developments that took place. In the next unit we will consider in more detail the status of English beyond the British Isles.

A7.1 The Industrial Revolution

We have seen that in the Old and Middle English periods regional dialect differences in Britain were much more apparent than they are today. Part of the reason for this is that contact between regional communities was not as common as it is today. The relative isolation of rural communities meant that it was the norm for dialects to develop along different lines. The fact that speakers of these dialects mixed predominantly with other speakers of the same dialect meant that varieties were not exposed to outside influences in anything like the way that they are today. In the nineteenth and twentieth centuries this situation was to change significantly and consequently affect the development of dialects. In Britain, the **Industrial Revolution** was instrumental in causing the movement of people around the country which led to dialects coming into much greater contact with one another than ever before, with resultant linguistic changes and developments. This had substantial effects on English in the nineteenth and twentieth centuries. Later, this contact between different varieties of English (both in Britain and beyond) would be caused by developments in communication technologies.

The Industrial Revolution began in the late 1700s when inventions such as Richard Arkwright's water frame transformed the textile industry in Britain. Almost in tandem with this, the **Enclosure Acts** of the 1700s, which prevented the grazing of animals on common land, had the effect of forcing many families from rural farming backgrounds into the cities in search of work. Almost inevitably, they found themselves working in the factories and mills that had sprung up as a result of the Industrial Revolution. This migration to the cities which continued into the nineteenth and twentieth centuries meant that people would encounter different accents and dialects, which would over time begin to have an effect on their own – perhaps generating new pronunciations and contributing vocabulary items and different grammatical structures. This mixing of dialects began to blur the traditional boundaries of rural vernaculars, and urban dialect areas arose as a consequence of the new conurbations.

A7.2 The *Oxford English Dictionary*

The codification of English that had begun in the Early Modern period with the publication of grammars and dictionaries has continued right up to the present day. Perhaps because the *Oxford English Dictionary* (**OED**) is now something of an institution, many of my students are surprised to find that it was not published until fairly recently in historical terms. Work began on the dictionary in 1882 and it was only in 1928 that the final volume was completed. Since then, there has been a second edition (published in 1989) and an electronic version (1992). The OED was first proposed by the British Philological Society who saw the need for a comprehensive and authoritative dictionary of the English language. The first editor, James Murray, was appointed in 1879 and the project was initially intended to take just ten years. As it was, Murray died before the dictionary was finally completed. What made the OED stand out on its first publication was its sheer size (ten volumes comprising over 400,000 words) and comprehensive nature. Each entry contained not just a definition but an **etymology** of the word in question (i.e. an explanation of the word's development over time), a guide to pronunciation, information about **part of speech** (whether the word is a noun, adjective, adverb, etc.), details of when the word was first used and quotations from published sources demonstrating the use of the word in context. The second edition of the dictionary built on this by taking fuller account of the variety of **World Englishes** in existence (e.g. Australian English, Singapore English).

A7.3 A spoken standard

In A5 we looked at the development of written Standard English, but the emergence of a spoken standard did not occur in Britain until much later on. It is also the case that the spoken standard that emerged is not used nearly as widely as the written standard; indeed, there may be a case for reconsidering the extent to which it may be thought of as a standard form in contemporary English usage.

The spoken standard form that eventually materialised is referred to as **Received Pronunciation** ('received' in the sense of 'accepted') or **RP**. RP was a London accent associated particularly with the educated classes. Its emergence as a standard occurred later than the development of a written standard because the mechanisms by which it could be conveyed were not in place until the nineteenth and twentieth centuries. Whereas the development of written Standard English was greatly affected by the printing press and the ability to produce large quantities of uniform texts, the promotion of a standard spoken variety of English needed a different apparatus of transmission. The first part of this was the **Education Act of 1870** which made a certain level of education compulsory for all children. Because of this, children were exposed to Standard English to a much greater extent than ever before, since this would be the variety reinforced by schoolteachers. The mixing of the middle classes and the upper classes in public schools also played a part in establishing RP as a standard. The prestige associated with it led to many people adapting their own accents (either consciously or subconsciously) in order to avoid the stigma that was increasingly associated with regional pronunciations.

The prestige of RP was given a further boost when it was adopted by the **BBC** (the British Broadcasting Corporation, founded in 1921) in its early years as the accent of choice for its continuity announcers. Its appeal was its prestige and its lack of association with any particular geographical area. Its use in broadcasting ensured its recognition by the vast majority of the population, though not necessarily its adoption. Part of the issue was that very few people spoke RP as their natural accent. Effectively it was a social accent as opposed to a regional one, and most people would simply not have come into contact with it beyond experiencing it via radio and television. The likelihood of it becoming the most prevalent accent in terms of number of speakers was, therefore, always low. Furthermore, it suffered from its upper-class connotations. During the latter half of the twentieth century attitudes began to change and nowadays it is quite common to hear regional accents used by radio and television presenters (though notice that most of the time the dialect used is Standard English; it is still rare to hear regional dialects).

RP, then, was never the most dominant accent in terms of the number of people who spoke it. It is usually estimated that only around 3% of Britain's population speak RP as a 'natural' accent. In fact, this percentage may now be even lower. If it seems somewhat unusual that we should consider RP to be a standard form of spoken English when it does not reflect how the majority of native speakers actually speak, then we need only consider the extent to which standard written English reflects how the majority of native speakers write. The answer is that it probably doesn't. This is not necessarily because people are unaware of standard forms, but because we all change our usage depending on the situation in which we find ourselves. It would be unusual if you were to write a job application letter in non-Standard English but it would not be at all unusual if you were to send a text message in a non-standard form. The point is that a standard variety does not necessarily equate to what the majority of people actually do most of the time. It is important to remember that language is about more than communication. The variety of English that we use says a lot about our identity. It is not the fact that RP has very few speakers that will result in its decline, but changing attitudes to what its usage connotes. In fact, it is better to speak of RP *developing* than *declining*. Accents, like dialects, change and develop over time and RP is no different. Many sociolinguists (e.g. Altendorf 2003: 163) believe that RP is taking on more and more of the characteristics of **Estuary English**, an urban dialect increasingly common in the south-east of England.

A7.4 The linguistic consequences of war

The twentieth century saw periods of bloody conflict and these as much as advances in technology and communication affected the development of English. War necessitates invention and one result of this is to contribute new words to the lexicon of a language. The First and Second World Wars did just this for English. Among the many new words (and old words with new meanings) listed by Baugh and Cable (2002) are *blitz, radar, blackout, machine gun, periscope, trench foot, beachhead, landing strip* and *foxhole*. In addition to this development, however, we might also speculate that the large-scale movement of troops would potentially have had some effect on the dialects of individual soldiers as they came into contact with other groups of people who used English differently. This is in much the same way as economic migration during the Industrial Revolution affected rural dialects. Whether such effects were lasting (beyond the borrowing of particular vocabulary items) is more difficult to assess.

A7.5 Technology and communication

The nineteenth and twentieth centuries saw a boom in technological innovation. In the area of communication technologies this was to have a major impact on the development of English. The first **transatlantic telegraph cable** to work successfully was laid in 1868 allowing the rapid spread of news. Because the British controlled a significant part of the telegraph network, English began to be established as a language for international communication. Radio, which had been developed in the early years of the nineteenth century, came into its own in the twentieth and did much to assist the spread of English around the globe, particularly via the BBC's World Service broadcasts. Television, of course, had a similar effect. The **internet**, developed in the 1960s as a resource for the US military, was popularised via the **World Wide Web** in the early 1990s, and has been an immensely important vehicle for the development of English into a global language. It is to this latest development that we turn in A8.

GLOBAL ENGLISH AND BEYOND   A8

English has come a long way since its earliest inception in the Anglo-Saxon period. A unique combination of events has over time led to the development of numerous varieties of English and to the spread of these worldwide. Estimating the numbers of speakers of English worldwide is fraught with difficulties but even a conservative estimate would put the number of speakers of English as a first language at around 400 million (Crystal 2003), with many hundreds of millions more using it as a second language. English is now commonly referred to as a global language, but what does it mean to say this?

A8.1 English: a global language

We could say that English is now a global language simply by virtue of its being spoken by such a large number of people worldwide. However, while this may well be part of the definition, it is not an entirely satisfactory explanation. After all, there are many hundreds of millions of people who speak some variety of Chinese, yet it is English that is so often cited as *the* global language (or, at the least, the language that is most likely to attain such a position in the near future). Clearly, then, the notion of a global language is much more complex than simply being a language with a lot of speakers. In fact, we have already seen in relation to dialects how particular *varieties* of language become popular, and that is as a result of the relative power of their speakers (see A2.2). As David Crystal says: 'Why a language becomes a global language has little to do with the number of people who speak it. It is much more to do with who those speakers are' (Crystal 2003: 57).

Crystal suggests that 'a language achieves a genuinely global status when it develops a special role that is recognized in every country' (2003: 3). For instance, English has been adopted as the official language (i.e. the language of government, law, etc.) of many countries, including, for instance, Ghana, Kiribati, Liberia and Uganda to name but a few. English is also taught as a second and foreign-language worldwide. These are major contributory factors to why it is now seen as a global language. Nevertheless, we still need to account for why English has taken on these special functions that Crystal identifies. In part, we have covered some of the reasons already. The development of the British Empire and advances in communication technology have all played their part, as has the economic rise of the US following the Second World War. But to really understand what is meant when we refer to English as a global language, we need to know how all of these issues fit within the concept of globalisation.

Globalisation is a process that can be defined as 'the widening, deepening and speeding-up of worldwide interconnectedness in all aspects of contemporary social life, from the cultural to the criminal, the financial to the spiritual' (Held et al. 1999: 2). What this means is that communities all over the world are now connected to each other in ways that were not possible in the past. For example, I can communicate via email with colleagues in other countries and receive replies within seconds – something that would have been impossible not so long ago. Television news provides immediate coverage of events going on in countries many thousands of miles away. It is often said that technology has made the world smaller. In fact, technology has connected what would once have been distant and remote communities and this gives us the illusion that we are physically (and sometimes, perhaps, psychologically) closer to such communities than might once have been the case. Furthermore, this 'connectedness' means that what happens in one area of the globe can have direct consequences for others parts of the world. For instance, a sudden bout of cold weather in the US can lead to an increase in demand for crude oil, with the knock-on effect of petrol prices rising in the UK. All of this happens because of the global connections that are now part of our everyday lives.

Now, if we go back to Held et al.'s (1999) basic definition of globalisation, it will be clear that in addition to the cultural and financial aspects of social life (and so on), there is also a linguistic aspect. And in addition to the worldwide connections that have developed in political and economic terms we can also recognise linguistic connections that have come into being as a result of these other developments. For example, the technological dominance of the US has had a major effect in making English arguably the most dominant language currently found on the World Wide Web. (It is difficult to assess in quantitative terms exactly how many of the billions of web pages out there are in English but a search for almost any term via a search engine such as Google reveals just how prevalent English is in comparison to other languages.) The economic dominance of the US financial markets has led to English being seen by many non-native speakers as a necessary language to learn in order to get a good job. In short, English has attained a level of prestige that makes it a highly influential language. But its influence is not a result of any kind of communicative superiority. Despite what lay opinion sometimes suggests, English is no easier or harder to learn than any other language, nor does it offer any greater communicative possibilities. What can be expressed in one language can also be expressed in another, even if not in exactly the same way. So, the reason that English has attained the level of prestige that it currently has is down to social and political reasons rather than linguistic ones. And it is globalisation, and the role that English-speaking communities have played in instigating this process, that has led to English developing the status that it currently has in the world.

A8.2 Globalisation and changes in English

The previous section focussed on how global events – technological, political, economic and social – have all led to English being seen as a global language. English is increasingly being used throughout the world as a **lingua franca**. A lingua franca is a language that is used for communicative purposes by speakers of different languages, often for very specific purposes such as business, commerce, education, etc. For example, Latin was the lingua franca of medieval Europe for such areas of life as religion and education. But in what ways have these latest global developments started to change English? It is, of course, impossible to make generalisations that are true for all varieties of English everywhere, but we can nevertheless make some observations about how some varieties of English have been or are likely to be affected.

Some aspects of globalisation have been responsible for the spread of Standard English. For example, many international organisations, such as the European Union, NATO (North Atlantic Treaty Organization) and the World Health Organization, have adopted English as an official language (sometimes alongside other official languages). International air travel necessitates a common language for air traffic controllers and that language is English. Electronic communication within the global academic community tends to be in English, as is most published research. In areas like these, Standard English is the norm but even so we might imagine that over time new standards will emerge. It is hard to imagine, for instance, the lasting adherence to entirely arbitrary linguistic 'rules' that advise against ending a sentence with a preposition (a practice that Winston Churchill famously said was something 'up with which I will not put') or splitting the infinitive (e.g. saying 'to quickly type' as opposed to 'to type quickly'). Such rules have no basis in linguistic reality, but more importantly they serve no communicative purpose. It is highly likely that in areas such as government and academia we will see the development of a new Standard English. **World Standard English** might avoid the use of idioms (expressions that are common only to some varieties of English) and colloquialisms, and it might utilise particular pronunciations. The important point here is that it is not likely to be an Anglo-centric standard. The notion that English belongs to Britain and America is simply no longer true (if, indeed, it ever was) and we can fully expect to see other communities worldwide exerting an influence on the development of any new standard.

So, the rise of English as a global language may well end up affecting the development of Standard English. Nevertheless, it is highly unlikely to be the case that a World Standard English develops at the expense of regional varieties. In the same way that regional dialects of English are found within Britain, so too is it likely that 'international' dialects will emerge (indeed, there is evidence that this is already happening) as communities forge their own identities and start to use English in slightly different ways in order to achieve this. This might lead to particular grammatical forms emerging, or particular words developing.

In addition to standards and dialects, it is also worth considering the impact that globalisation has had on particular **discourses** of English. You can think of a discourse as the type of language used in a particular domain of life – for example, we can talk about the discourse of law, or the discourse of education. Where once we might have been able to see clear distinctions between particular discourses, now – often as a result of market forces – it is common to see discourses being mixed. So, for example, the discourse of education has (sadly) been infused with elements of a business discourse so that students are often referred to as 'consumers' or 'customers' and they and the people who work in education are referred to as 'stakeholders'. This may not seem like a particularly significant change but when we consider how language shapes our identities, it is easy to see how changing the norms of a particular discourse can lead people to develop new attitudes towards the domain of life that it relates to. If you are no longer a student but a customer, and if education is no longer a process but a product that you buy, does this imply that you are no longer bound to accept uncomplainingly the education that your university provides? The effects of changing discourses are complex and fascinating.

A8.3 Assessing the linguistic impact of historical events

Section A has attempted to provide a very broad outline of some of the non-linguistic events that have had an effect on the development of English from the Anglo-Saxon period to the present day. Needless to say, there are one or two cautionary points that it is worth reiterating. This historical outline, broad as it is, is necessarily selective. It includes those major events that are generally agreed to have been significant in the development of English, but it would not be possible to cover every such event in such a short space. If you go on to do some of the follow-up readings that are suggested elsewhere in the book, you will encounter other such events that you will be able to weave into the rough narrative history of English that section A has attempted to provide. (Indeed, some of these other events are covered in some of the readings in section D.) Another important point to bear in mind when getting to grips with the outline history of English is that not all events affect all *varieties* of English, and even in those cases where an event does impact on the language as a whole, it does not necessarily have the *same* effect on every variety. For example, the Great Vowel Shift did not affect every variety of English in the same way. The Industrial Revolution may well have had an impact on the language use of those people who found themselves migrating from the countryside to the towns, but for those who remained working on the land, the impact on their variety of English would have been much less. Finally, it is important to remember the distinction between written and spoken English. This may sound so obvious as not to be worth stating but it is surprising how often people can confuse the two when considering how particular events have affected the development of English. For instance, while the printing press clearly had a major effect on the emergence of a written standard, its effect on the spoken language was less important. While the world wars may have given rise to lots of new vocabulary that was common in everyday speech, not all of this would necessarily have found its way into written English. Read with a critical eye and when you come across an event that you think is significant in the history of English, before assessing its impact, ask yourself these questions:

❑   Would it have affected spoken English, written English or both?
❑   Would it have affected every variety of English, and if so, would it have affected every variety of English *in the same way*?

Section B

DEVELOPMENT

A DEVELOPING LANGUAGE

The aim of section B of this book is to give you a sense of what English was like at each of its various stages of development, from Old English to Present Day English, and to examine in more detail some of the linguistic and social elements responsible for the development of English. Clearly it is not possible within the scope of this book for us to examine every feature of English's development over time, and so we will concentrate particularly on those characteristics of the language that allow us to distinguish it as, say, Old English or Early Modern English. The units presented here introduce some of the major aspects of the linguistic history of English. Once you have an overall picture in place of what English was like at its various stages of development, doing the suggested further reading will allow you to gain a wider knowledge and deeper understanding of these issues. As we look at the various forms of English we will also begin to examine some of the ways in which English has changed over time, something that you can follow up in section C.

B1 UNDERSTANDING OLD ENGLISH

Old English (OE) is very different from the English that we speak and write today. It is not possible in the limited space available to teach you how to speak, write and understand Old English fully, though if you want to be able to do this well, there are plenty of excellent introductory books that will help you (some of these are listed in the Further Reading section at the back of the book). Fortunately, you do not need to be fluent in Old English to be able to grasp some of the main differences between OE and Present Day English. The aim of sections B1 and B2 is to make clear what some of these differences are and to give you a sense of what OE is like as a language. In doing this, I may sometimes have made things appear simpler than they actually are. For example, there are more nuances to Old English pronunciation than the tables in B1.1 might appear to suggest. For the moment, this doesn't matter. My aim here is to give you a quick introduction to the basics of Old English. When you are comfortable with this, you can explore the language in more detail by consulting more advanced and specialist textbooks.

B1.1 Spelling and sound in Old English

Knowing how to pronounce Old English will sometimes help you to work out what a particular Old English word means. A word may look unrecognisable but may sound very similar to a modern English equivalent. Or, at the very least, it may remind you of a modern English word with which you are familiar. For example, if we pronounce the word *Angelcynn* as it would have been pronounced in the Anglo-Saxon period, we get a clue as to its meaning. You may be tempted to pronounce the first part of the word as the Present Day English *angel* (i.e. winged heavenly creature) but if I tell you that the <*g*> is pronounced roughly as in *go* then you get a pronunciation that sounds like *angle* rather than *angel*. Now recall that in A1.2 we saw that one of the earliest tribes of settlers in Britain was the Angles, from whom the country name *England* developed. Knowing this, it seems plausible that the first part of *angelcynn* refers to the Angles – or the English. The second part of the word – *cynn* – may look rather less familiar. But again, if you know that the <*c*> is pronounced as it would be in the Present Day English word *cake*, and that the <*y*> is a vowel sound pronounced somewhere between <*i*> [ɪ] and <*u*> [ʊ], then the pronunciation of *cynn* may remind you of the perhaps more familiar word *kin*. *Kin* is now a somewhat archaic word but you will perhaps at least know that it refers to people (as in the phrases 'kith and kin' and 'next of kin'). If you do, then it is not difficult to work out that *angelcynn* refers to 'English people'. It is therefore worth investing a bit of time and effort in learning how to pronounce Old English.

In order to pronounce Old English words you need to know what sounds the individual letters of the Old English alphabet represented (see Table B1.1.1 overleaf). You will recognise many of the letters because, following the introduction of Christianity, Anglo-Saxon scribes adopted the Roman alphabet that we still use today. You will also find that the sounds associated with the letters of the OE alphabet have not changed much over the years. However, a few of the letters are different and have sounds that you might not expect and you will need to watch out for these. Below is list of the letters that represented Old English vowel sounds, along with an indication of their pronunciation. In the tables that follow you will find the terms **grapheme**, **graph** and **digraph** rather than *letter*. This is because some sounds need more than one letter in order to be represented visually. The term **grapheme** refers to the symbol or symbols used to represent a particular **phoneme** (a phoneme is the smallest unit of speech – words are made up of combinations of phonemes). There are different sub-types of grapheme. A **graph** is one letter that represents one phoneme – e.g. the graph <m> represents the phoneme [m]. A **digraph** is a two-letter combination that represents one phoneme – e.g. the digraph [sc] represents the phoneme [ʃ] in Old English. For those of you who are familiar with phonemic transcription I have included the relevant IPA symbol. (The IPA is the International Phonetic Alphabet, a system of symbols for transcribing sounds.) If you want to know more about this, try reading section A2 of Peter Stockwell's (2007) *Sociolinguistics* book in this series, or, for a more in-depth introduction, Collins and Mees's (2004) *Practical Phonetics and Phonology*, also part of this series. (NB: The horizontal lines above some of the graphemes in the tables below are called **macrons** and would not have been used by Anglo-Saxon scribes. They are used here as an aid to pronunciation by indicating vowel length.)

Old English vowel sounds

Table B1.1.1 Based on Quirk et al. (1975: 10–11)

OE graph	Pronunciation	IPA symbol
ā	as in the <a> in *rather*	[ɑ:]
æ	as in the <a> in *cat*	[æ]
ǣ	as in the French *bête*	[ɛ:]
e	as in the <e> in *bed*	[ɛ]
ē	a longer form of <e> (say *bed* but extend the vowel sound)	[e:]
i	as in the <i> in *win*	[ɪ]
ī	as in the <ee> in *deed*	[i:]
o	as in the <o> in *hot*	[ɒ]
ō	a longer form of <o> (say *hot* but extend the vowel sound)	[o:]
u	as in the <u> in *full*	[ʊ]
ū	as in the <oo> in *pool*	[u:]
y	try saying the <i> in *sit* but with your lips pursed; this sound is also similar to the <u> in French *tu*	[y]
ȳ	the same as the above but try extending the vowel sound	[y:]

You will notice that many of the vowel sounds are similar to modern English (especially if you are a native speaker of English who has a northern English accent!). The only really tricky ones are the sounds associated with <*y*> and <*ȳ*>, which do not have a real equivalent in Present Day English. Just remember that <*y*> and <*ȳ*> always represent vowel sounds, not consonant sounds. In addition to the vowel sounds listed above, you will also come across **diphthongs**. A diphthong is a combination of two vowel sounds that, when glided together, form a new sound. For example, if you take the vowel sound in *cat* [æ] and run it together with the vowel sound in *put* [ʊ] you will get the vowel sound in *south* [aʊ]. Try saying the vowel sound in *south* slowly and see if you can hear the two individual vowel sounds. The graphemes that represent diphthongs in Old English are shown in Table B1.1.2.

Table B1.1.2 Based on Quirk et al. (1975: 10–11)

OE digraph	Pronunciation	IPA symbol
ea	The symbol [ə], found in the transcriptions on the right, represents a phoneme called *schwa*. It is the vowel sound at the beginning of the word *about* and at the end of the word *sofa*. To pronounce the digraphs in the left-hand column, combine the pronunciation of the IPA symbols on the right.	[æə]
ēa		[ɛ:ə]
eo		[eə]
ēo		[e:ə]

Now let's turn to the consonant sounds.

Old English consonant sounds

As with the vowels, many Old English consonants have the same phonemic value as in Present Day English. Table B1.1.3 shows the ones that differ significantly, and the digraphs that represent these sounds, plus those no longer used in Present Day English.

Table B1.1.3 Based on Quirk et al. (1975: 10–11)

OE grapheme	Pronunciation	IPA symbol
c	usually pronounced as the <k> in *king* but as the <ch> in <church> when between or after vowels	[k] or [tʃ]
f	as the <v> in <van> when between vowels or other voiced sounds, but as the <f> in *four* when at the beginning or end of a word	[v] or [f]
g (sometimes written as ʒ)	usually pronounced as the <g> in *gold* but as the <y> in <yet> when between or after vowels	[g] or [j]
h	as the <h> in *hand* when at the beginning of the word but as the <ch> in *loch* when in a medial or final position	[h] or [x]
s	as the <z> in *snooze* when between vowels or other voiced sounds but as the <s> in *seven* when at the beginning or end of a word	[z] or [s]
þ or ð (these letters were used interchangeably by most scribes)	as the <th> in *clothe* when between vowels or other voiced sounds but as the <th> in *thin* when at the beginning or end of a word	[ð] and [θ]
sc	as in the <sh> in *ship*	[ʃ]
cg	as in the <dg> in *ledge*	[dʒ]

You will see from the tables above that Old English made use of some letters that we no longer have in Present Day English. These are <æ> (ash), <þ> (thorn) and <ð> (eth). Additionally, although <w> was pronounced as it is in Present Day English, it was represented by the character <p> (wynn). The use of these additional letters and the digraphs of OE was motivated by the fact that the Roman alphabet did not have enough letters to represent the variety of sounds in Old English. When you have familiarised yourself with the letters and sounds in the tables above, practise your pronunciation by trying the exercises in C1.3.

B1.2 The vocabulary of Old English

Present Day English (PDE) has borrowed vocabulary from many of the world's languages. Think about words like *chauffeur*, *government*, *gâteau* and *salary* from French; *pasta*, *balcony*, *ghetto* and *umbrella* from Italian; *wok* from Chinese; *rucksack* from German; and *coach* from Hungarian. Sometimes words come directly from one language or sometimes via another. *Coach*, for example, while ultimately from Hungarian, was borrowed into English from French. Once a word has been borrowed it becomes absorbed into the language to such an extent that we no longer see it as 'foreign'. In contrast, Old English contained far fewer borrowed words (though Latin was one source language) and was made up of predominantly Germanic vocabulary. Some Old English words are instantly recognisable and are still used in PDE, even if our modern spellings are sometimes slightly different. Examples include *gold* ('gold'), *saga* ('story' or 'narrative'), *candel* ('candle'), *ripe* ('ripe' or 'mature'), *stenc* ('stench' or 'stink') and *hunig* ('honey'). And some Old English words survive only in regional dialects of Present Day English – e.g. *nesh* ('afraid of the cold') in Northern English (from the OE *hnesc*); *whelp* ('puppy') in the north-east and north-west (from OE *hwelp*) and *oxter* ('armpit') in Present Day Broad Scots (from OE *ōhsta*).

Sometimes, though, what looks like a familiar word means something quite different in OE. The word *drēam*, for instance, does not mean 'dream' but 'joy', 'melody' or 'music'. The word *grin* refers to a region of the groin rather than a smile, *þyncan* means 'to seem' not 'to think' and *sellan* is 'to give' not 'to sell'.

OE made great use of **compounding** to form new words. This is the practice of putting two (or more) words together to form a new word. So, the word *sǣ* ('sea') could be compounded with *grund* ('ground') to form *sǣgrund* ('seaground'; i.e. 'seabed'). *Eorðe* ('soil' or 'earth') could be added to *ærn* (meaning 'dwelling' or 'store') to form *eorðeærn* ('earth-dwelling', or 'grave'). The word *drēam* could be compounded with *cræft* (an 'art', 'skill' or 'science') to form *drēamcræft* ('the art of making music'). Similarly, *stæfcræft*, made up of *stæf* (meaning both 'stick' and 'letter') and *cræft* forms a compound noun that means 'grammar' ('the craft/science of letters'). Notice that, in PDE, we have replaced many of these compounds with words borrowed from other languages. Having a grasp of Old English vocabulary is as important as understanding its grammar. Indeed, Mitchell (1995) suggests that vocabulary is even more important than grammar in understanding Old English texts. You can find out more about OE vocabulary and about Mitchell's view in the reading in D1.1.

B1.3 Old English: a synthetic language

The main difference between Old English and Present Day English is that OE is a **synthetic** (or **inflectional**) language whereas PDE is an **analytic** (or **isolating**) language. An analytic language is one in which the grammatical function of the words and phrases in a sentence (i.e. the 'job' that they do in the sentence) is indicated by the order in which they appear. For example, consider the following simple sentence:

    1 Oswyn shot Sigbert.

In this sentence, it is clear from the word order that Oswyn is the one who did the shooting and Sigbert is the person who was shot. In grammatical terms, Oswyn is the **subject** of the sentence and Sigbert is the **object** (the verb in this example indicates the action). If we reverse the sentence, we get a very different meaning:

    2 Sigbert shot Oswyn.

In this sentence, the change in word order signals a change in meaning. This time, Sigbert is the subject and Oswyn is the object. This is how the grammatical function of words in a sentence is conveyed in an analytic language. However, Old English is a synthetic language that marks grammatical function in a different way: the primary means of conveying the grammatical function of a word is by adding an ending to it. This ending is called an **inflection**. For example, imagine that Present Day English is not an analytic language but is, instead, a synthetic one. And let us imagine that the way the subject of a sentence is marked is by adding an <*x*> to the end of the word, and the way objects are marked is by adding a <*z*> to the end of the word. If this were the case, we would not need to put the words in the sentence in a particular order, as it would be clear from the inflection what job the word was doing in the sentence. For example:

> 3 Shot Oswyn**x** Sigbert**z**.

Here it is quite clear that Oswyn is the person who did the shooting because the word 'Oswyn' has the inflection <*x*>, which we have decided indicates the subject of the sentence. And it is equally clear that Sigbert is the person who was shot because the word Sigbert has the inflection <*z*>, which we know marks the object of the sentence. Because we have these inflections, it is less important what order we put the words in. Providing they have an inflection, it will always be clear which is the subject of the verb and which is the object. For example, sentence 4 means exactly the same as sentence 3:

> 4 Sigbert**z** shot Oswyn**x**.

B1.4 Case, gender and number

In Old English, the grammatical function of nouns was indicated by an inflection on the noun in question. Inflections on nouns are sometimes called **case endings**. You may be familiar with case if you have studied a language such as German or Russian. In Old English, words that are the subject of a sentence are said to be in the **nominative case**. Words that are the direct object of a sentence are said to be in the **accusative case**. You can see how this works in Old English by considering the following (made-up) sentence:

> 5 se wita hilpð þone bodan (The wise man helps the messenger.)

In the above example, the <*-a*> ending marks the subject of the sentence and the <*-an*> ending marks the object of the sentence. Hence, <*-a*> is a **nominative case ending** or **nominative inflection** and <*-an*> is an **accusative case ending** or **accusative inflection**. You will also notice that in the above example there are two different forms of the determiner (*the*). *Se* is the nominative form and *þone* is the accusative form. If a noun is in the nominative case then it must have the nominative form of the determiner in front of it. And if the noun is in the accusative case then it must be preceded by the accusative form of *the*. Because the information about the grammatical role of the nouns in the sentence is encoded in the noun itself and its accompanying determiner, we could alter the word order of our example sentence but retain the same meaning. So, sentences (5) and (6) mean exactly the same thing.

> 5 se wita hilpð þone bodan (The wise man helps the messenger.)
> 6 þone bodan hilpð se wita (The wise man helps the messenger.)

As well as being marked for grammatical function, in Old English words were also marked for gender. (You may be familiar with the concept of grammatical gender if you have studied a foreign language such as French or German.) The genders in Old English were **masculine**, **feminine** and **neuter**. In sentences 1 and 2, both the nouns are masculine and therefore are preceded by masculine forms of the determiner. If we change our example sentences slightly to include a feminine noun, then we also need to change the form of the article that goes before it:

> 7 se cnapa lufode þā hlǣfdigan (The servant loved the mistress.)
> 8 seō hlǣfdige lufode þone cnapan (The mistress loved the servant.)

In sentences (8) and (9) you can see that the form of the word 'hlǣfdige' changes according to whether it is in the subject or object position (the <-e> ending marks the nominative case and the <-an> ending indicates the accusative). And because 'hlǣfdige' is feminine, it has a feminine form of the determiner before it ('seō' if 'hlǣfdige' is the subject and 'þā' if it is the object).

Not all OE nouns, though, have a different case ending for both the nominative and accusative. Consider example (9):

> 9 se cyning hilpð þone æðeling (The king helps the prince.)

If we now make 'the prince' the subject of the sentence and 'the king' the object, we get the following:

> 10 þone cyning hilpð se æðeling.

If you compare (10) with (9) you will notice that 'cyning' and 'æðeling' have the same form in both the nominative and the accusative. In this instance, we have to rely on the determiners to tell us which is the subject and which the object. As you can imagine, as English developed and the case system started to break down, word order became ever more important.

So far we've looked at fairly simple examples. But there are more cases in OE than nominative and accusative and so – surprise, surprise – Old English is more complicated than the examples above might suggest. The other cases are the **genitive case** and the **dative case**.

The **genitive case** indicates possession. In Present Day English we can indicate possession in various ways. We can use either a possessive pronoun (e.g. *his* or *her*) or an apostrophe followed by an <s> on the end of the noun – for example, *Dan's book*. Old English has possessive pronouns like Present Day English does but if we want to make a noun possessive in Old English then we need to add a specific genitive inflection. In the same way that the nominative and accusative cases are indicated with nominative and accusative inflections, the genitive case is indicated by a genitive inflection on the noun. Similarly, if a noun is in the genitive case and it is preceded by a determiner, we need to use the genitive form of that determiner. Consider example 11:

> 11 þæs mannes hund (The man's dog.)

Here the genitive inflection <-*es*> has been added to the noun *mann*, to indicate that this noun is in the genitive case, and the genitive form of the determiner – *þæs* – precedes it. The PDE word *Christmas* derives from the OE form *Cristesmæsse* ('Christ's mass'), in which <-*es*> is a genitive inflection that over the years people have stopped pronouncing (presumably because it is not a stressed syllable).

The **dative case** typically indicates the indirect object in a sentence. Here's an example of a sentence with an indirect object:

12 The crusty old professor	gave	the students	a dull lecture.
subject	*verb*	*indirect object*	*direct object*

In example 13 there are two objects. The direct object is 'a dull lecture' (i.e. the 'thing' that is 'given') and 'the students' is the indirect object. There is a simple test you can do to decide which is the direct and which is the indirect object. You can put a preposition in front of the indirect object but you can't put one in front of the direct object:

13 The crusty old professor gave to the students a dull lecture.
14 *The crusty old professor gave the students to a dull lecture.

In Old English, indirect objects were in the dative case and, as with the nominative, accusative and genitive cases, there was a specific case ending to indicate this.

Finally, there was another element to Old English grammar that could affect the form of a word. This is **number**. This refers to whether a word is singular or plural (a distinction, of course, which remains in PDE). Unsurprisingly, the form of a word could be different depending on whether it was singular or plural. And, of course, the singular or plural inflection used would depend on the case and gender of the word in question, e.g.

15 seō hlǣfdige lufode þone cyning (The mistress loved the king.)
16 seō hlǣfdige lufode þā cyningas (The mistress loved the kings.)

B1.5 Old English verbs

Just as nouns in Old English inflect for case, gender and number, verbs inflect to mark person and tense.

In Present Day English, the only inflection for person is on the third-person singular form of the verb; for example, we say *I walk* but *he walks*. The irregular verb *to be* is an exception, with different forms for the first-person singular (*am*), second-person singular (*are*) and third-person singular (*is*). The origins of these inflections lie in Old English which made use of different forms of the verb to mark person. For example, *ic singe* ('I sing'), *þu singest* ('you sing') and *hēo singeþ* ('she sings'). The third-person *eþ* form is the ancestor of the PDE third-person present tense <*s*> inflection, while the *est* form survived into Early Modern English but then fell out of usage (see B5.2).

To form the past tense form and past participle of most verbs in PDE, we simply add an inflectional ending <-*ed*> (as in *walk/walked*). (The past participle is the form of the verb that is used after the auxiliary verbs *be* and *have*; see Table B1.5.1 for examples.) But notice that to form the past tense of a verb like *sing*, we don't add an inflectional ending. Instead we change the vowel – the past tense of *sing* is *sang*. In grammatical terms, *sing* is a strong verb while *walk* is a weak verb. Here are some more examples of weak and strong verbs in PDE.

Table B1.5.1

Weak verbs			Strong verbs		
Present	*Past*	*Past participle*	*Present*	*Past*	*Past participle*
I *walk* to work.	I *walked* to work.	I have *walked* to work	We *eat* too much.	We *ate* too much.	We have *eaten* too much.
She *laughs* a lot.	She *laughed* a lot.	She had *laughed* a lot.	He *drinks* too much.	He *drank* too much.	He had *drunk* too much.
They *borrow* money constantly.	They *borrowed* money constantly.	They have *borrowed* money constantly.	You *sing* beautifully.	You *sang* a beautiful song.	You have *sung* beautifully.

As you will notice from the table above, weak verbs form their past tense and past participle by the addition of an inflectional ending (notice that in speech this is pronounced either as [t] or [d]). Strong verbs, on the other hand, inflect in a different way. To form the past tense of a strong verb, the vowel of the present tense form is changed. To form the past participle of a strong verb, either the vowel of the present tense form is changed or <*-en*> is added.

You have already encountered some Old English verbs in the example sentences in B1.4. As in Present Day English, verbs in Old English were either weak or strong. However, there were more strong verbs in Old English than in Present Day English. Over time, many of these became weak through a process of regularisation.

B2   VARIETIES OF OLD ENGLISH

In Present Day English we are used to the concept of different varieties of English. Some are regional (e.g. the Black Country dialect of the midlands of England, the Lancashire dialect, etc.) while some are national (e.g. American English, Singapore English, etc.). Perhaps because of the relative sparsity of Anglo-Saxon texts, it is sometimes easy to view Old English as one homogenous language. However, we need to be aware that in the Anglo-Saxon period, too, different varieties of English were used.

B2.1 Old English and Scots

In discussing the notion of Old English being used in Scotland we need to add the qualification that in the Anglo-Saxon period there was little sense of English as a unified language. What we are really talking about is the extent to which a particular variety of Old English extended into Scotland.

We saw in A1.1 that the Scots were originally from Ireland and settled in what is now Scotland around 500 AD. Also present in Scotland at this time were the Picts, and it was not until 843 that Scottish and Pictish dominions were united by Kenneth MacAlpin, the first king of the Scots (Bugaj 2004: 25). As the language of the Picts gradually died out, the predominant language in Scotland became the Celtic language **Gaelic**. However, the Anglo-Saxon kingdom of Northumbria extended into the eastern lowlands of what is now Scotland, and so the OE Northumbrian dialect would also have been common on the English–Scottish border. Bugaj points out that the Viking raids of the ninth century in which Northumbrian settlements were attacked led eventually to the Northumbrian dialect being influenced by the Scandinavian dialects of the aggressors (2004: 27). A Scottish dialect of English emerged in the Middle English period, during the reign of Malcolm III of Scotland (1058–93) who used English as opposed to Gaelic as the language of his royal court, and whose wife, Margaret, was the great-niece of Edward the Confessor. Consequently, Gaelic never achieved the prestigious position it would have needed to survive as the language of Scotland. The importance of considering dialectal variety in the Old English period can be seen when we consider that contemporary Scots, 'a language continuum that ranges from "broad" Scots to "Scottish Standard English"' (Corbett et al. 2003: 1), developed ultimately from Anglian rather than Saxon varieties of Old English, which accounts for why Scots differs from Present Day English (Corbett et al. 2003: 4).

B2.2 Old English dialectal differences

You will have seen from B1.3 and B1.4 that Old English was relatively free in terms of word order. It should not be too surprising to learn, then, that most of the dialectal differences that can be noticed in Old English concern the sound of the particular variety in question (Marckwardt and Rosier 1972). Understanding these dialectal differences fully requires an in-depth knowledge of phonology. Nonetheless, it is possible to grasp some of the differences without too much difficulty if we concentrate on some straightforward examples.

An example of the kind of dialectal difference we encounter in OE is that words which begin with an initial palatal consonant (a consonant produced using the palate – i.e. the roof of your mouth – as an articulator), such as [g] or [k], are followed by diphthongs in West Saxon but by **monophthongs** ('pure vowels') in other dialects. For example, West Saxon *giefan* ('to give') and *ceaster* ('castle') were *gefan* and *cæster* in Kentish, Mercian and Northumbrian (Marckwardt and Rosier 1972: 178). Marckwardt and Rosier (1972) also point out that some sound changes between the dialects affected the inflectional system of Old English. So, the fact that final <-*n*> tended not to be pronounced in Northumbrian (unlike in West Saxon) may well have led to the impression of inflections not being present on particular words (as opposed to their being present, just not enunciated). Considering dialectal differences, then, can help in explaining long-term developments in the language.

One way of investigating dialectal differences is to compare texts which exist in more than one dialect. One such example is *Cædmon's Hymn*. In his *Ecclesiastical History of the English People*, Bede describes how Cædmon, a layman who worked on the estates of the Abbey of Whitby, in what was then Northumbria, was given the gift of poetry by God. The story goes that Cædmon left a feast early because he felt he would be unable to sing and entertain the assembled guests when his turn to do so came. He was subsequently visited in a dream by an angel who commanded him to sing about the creation of the world. Cædmon then found that he was able to sing beautiful poetry in praise of God. After telling the abbess of his new-found ability, Cædmon entered monastic life and became famed for his religious poems. *Cædmon's Hymn* is all that remains of Cædmon's work but what makes it especially interesting for historical linguists is that it exists in both the Northumbrian and West Saxon dialects. Here are the two versions, followed by a translation into PDE (the OE versions are taken from Smith (1933) though I have removed punctuation that would not have been present in the original manuscripts):

Cædmon's Hymn (West Saxon)
Nu þe sculan herian heofonrices þeard
metudes myhte his modʒeþanc
þurc þuldorfæder spa he þundra ʒehþilc
ece drihten ord astealde
he ærest ʒesceop ylda bearnum
heofon to hrofe haliʒ scyppend
middanʒearde mancynnes þeard
ece drihten æfter tida
firum on foldum frea ælmyhtiʒ

Cædmon's Hymn (Northumbrian)
Nu scylun herʒan hefaenricaes uard
metudæs maecti end his modʒidanc
uerc uuldurfadur sue he uundra ʒehuaes
eci dryctin or astelidæ
he aerist scop aelda barnum
heben til hrofe haleʒ scepen
tha middunʒeard moncynnæs uard
eci dryctin æfter tiadæ
firum foldu frea allmectiʒ

Cædmon's Hymn (PDE)
Now must we praise of heaven's kingdom the Keeper
Of the Lord the power and his wisdom
The work of the Glory-Father as he of marvels each
The eternal Lord the beginning established
He first created the earth for the sons [of men]
Heaven as a roof the holy Creator
Then the middle-enclosure of mankind the protector

The eternal Lord thereafter made
For men, earth the Lord almighty

(translation by Trapp et al. 2002: 2)

There are a number of observations we can make about dialect as a result of looking at the two different versions of the text above. At a very basic level, for instance, the different spellings suggest different pronunciations. We can note, for example, the tendency for diphthongs to be used in West Saxon where monophthongs are preferred in Northumbrian. Examples are *peard/uard*, *bearnum/barnum*, *ȝesceop/scop* and *heofonrices/hefaenricaes*. In the West Saxon version we find the grapheme <*p*> (sometimes replaced by <*w*> in modernised versions) where in the Northumbrian text we find <*u*> or <*uu*> (literally, double-u). And it would appear that in Northumbrian, <*c*> is used before <*t*> while in West Saxon it is <*h*>. We can also see in the Northumbrian text the origins of some present day dialectal features. *Bearnum*, for instance, is the ancestor of the Present Day Scots *bairn* (child). The Northumbrian dialect contributed much to the development of Scots, which is just one reason why an awareness of dialectal variation is important if we are to account for the development of English over time. You can examine for yourself some of the other dialectal features of Northumbrian and West Saxon in C2, where you can also explore what place names can tell us about the Old English dialects.

THE EMERGENCE OF MIDDLE ENGLISH   B3

Units B1 and B2 should have given you some idea of what Old English was like as a language. They do not tell the full story, obviously, and to find out more about Old English you should do the follow-up readings in D1 and D2. Nevertheless, you should at this stage have enough of an awareness of Old English to be able to understand some of the changes that occurred in the Middle English period and afterwards. In this unit we will focus on the emergence of Middle English (ME), looking at what it was like, how it differed from Old English and what caused the changes that occurred between OE and ME.

Linguists often divide up the Middle English period into Early Middle English (EME) (approximately 1100–1300) and Late Middle English (LME) (approximately 1300–1500). There are various reasons why this division is made. One reason is that, in the second half of the Middle English period, substantially more words were borrowed from French. Baugh and Cable (2002: 178) estimate that 40% of the French words borrowed into Middle English came into the language between 1250 and 1400. The enriched vocabulary of LME distinguishes it from EME. Another reason, suggested by Fisiak (1968: 10) is that from the fourteenth century onwards there was more of a move towards the development of 'a single national language', which was made possible owing to a variety of factors, political, social and economic. This latter point reinforces one of the concerns of Section A: namely that the division of English into 'periods' is governed as much by non-linguistic factors as by linguistic ones, and that such divisions are essentially artificial. Language, as we have already discussed, is a process rather than a physical substance.

B3.1 The context of change

If English is your first language, you are perhaps likely to feel more at home with Middle English than with Old English. The vocabulary is more readily recognisable that that of Old English and the grammatical structure seems closer to PDE than OE. Nevertheless, there are still significant differences between ME and PDE and, although to begin with it may seem easier to understand, in many ways ME is harder to get to grips with than OE. This is in part because of the variety of dialects represented in Middle English manuscripts. There was no national standard form of English in the Early Middle English period and scribes wrote in the dialect of wherever in the country they happened to come from. Spellings and grammatical forms varied between dialect areas, and we can assume from this that pronunciation varied widely too. It is, then, impossible to describe a Middle English 'norm', since none existed. Variation and difference were characteristic features of Middle English at its early stage, and while variation is a feature of English at each of its stages of development, the difference is that in the Middle English period there was no standard form available for scribes to use. By comparison, in the Old English period a form of standardisation had taken place which saw the West Saxon dialect become the prominent written form (see A2.2). Indeed, such was its influence that this form was used beyond the regional boundaries of Wessex. Nevertheless, there are some general points that can be made about ME when compared to OE, and these will be the focus of this unit.

In A3 we saw that one of the external events that contributed to the linguistic development of OE into ME was the Norman Conquest of 1066. We must be careful, however, not to attribute linguistic change to this factor alone. The accession of William the Conqueror to the throne led to a rise in the number of French speakers in the country as William appointed his own nobles to prominent administrative positions, and French was eventually to influence English significantly, particularly its vocabulary (see B3.4). But the Norman Conquest did nothing to threaten the survival of English, since English remained the language spoken by the vast majority of the people, most of whom would have had no contact at all with the French ruling elite. English, while influenced by French, was also affected by the Scandinavian languages spoken by the Viking invaders, and a combination of factors was responsible for the development of OE into ME (see B3.3 for example), a process which had started before the Norman Conquest.

What we see in the Middle English era is a period during which a number of languages were used in the country. French was the language of the ruling class, Latin was the language of the Church, and English was the everyday language spoken by the majority of the country's population (English as a written language had also been well established during the Old English period, though comparatively few people would have been able to read and write it).

B3.2 Spelling and sound in Middle English

In the absence of a written standard in the Middle English period, it is common to find considerable variation in the way that words are spelled. But while Middle English spelling may look anarchic, scholars have observed that certain spellings are common to particular regions. As a result of this, we can assume that these different spellings were attempts on the part of Middle English scribes to represent the way that such words would be pronounced. Different spellings therefore give us some insight into how the language was spoken in particular areas of the country (though you should bear in mind that this explanation makes the process of deciphering Middle English spelling seem deceptively easy; writers often used idiosyncratic spellings and sometimes varied the spelling of a particular word within a single sentence).

One major difference between ME and PDE pronunciation is that, while in some PDE words we find silent letters, in their ME equivalents these letters would usually have been pronounced. In PDE, for example, we don't pronounce the <k> or the <w> in *knowledge*. In the ME equivalent, *knowlych* (one of a number of potential spellings, of course), these letters would have been pronounced. An exception is the pronunciation of words borrowed into ME from French, such as *honour* and *heir* whose initial letters are silent. But while this is a case of a French pronunciation being retained following the borrowing of the French word into English, for the most part, French influenced spellings rather than pronunciation. Some examples of how French scribal practices influenced English spelling in the Middle English period are as follows:

❑ The digraph *<th>* replaces *<ð>* to represent [θ], though *<þ>* is still used by some scribes to represent this phoneme, particularly in Early Middle English, e.g. OE *ðrinȝan* ('to press') becomes ME *thringen*.
❑ *<qu>* replaces *<cw>* to represent [kw], e.g. OE *cwen* ('queen') becomes ME *queen*.
❑ The digraph *<ch>* replaces OE *<c>* to represent the phoneme [tʃ], e.g. OE *cīld* ('child') becomes ME *chīld*.
❑ The phoneme [ʃ] is now represented by the digraph *<sh>* as opposed to the OE *<sc>*, e.g. OE *sceran* ('to shear') becomes ME *sheren*.

The changes introduced as a result of the influence of French conventions were not mere whims. For example, in the case of *<ch>* and *<sh>*, the <h> part of these digraphs indicated that the pronunciation of the preceding *<c>* or *<s>* was different from that which these letters normally indicated (i.e. /k/ and /s/ or /z/ respectively, as in *cāndel*, *hūs* and *rīsen*). In effect, the <h> was acting as a **diacritic** – an indicator of a different pronunciation. (In some languages diacritics are found above certain letters. In Hungarian, for example, the diacritic <´> above *<a>* indicates that *<a>* is pronounced as in the English word *hat*. The absence of the diacritic indicates a pronunciation of *<a>* that is like the vowel sound in the word *hot*.). In the case of *<ch>* and *<sh>*, then, the <h> indicated that the digraphs represented, respectively, an affricate (as in the initial consonant sound of *church*) and a fricative sound, i.e. the kind of sound produced when air is expelled through a narrow space between the articulators (articulators are those vocal organs such as teeth, tongue and lips that we use in the production of speech sounds. You can find out more about this in B4.1). Try saying *shhhhh* or *zzzzzz* – the sound you produce will be a fricative.

In several instances, however, Middle English scribes misinterpreted the significance of <h>. For example, PDE words such as *where* and *when* which all begin with initial *<wh>* began in Old English with *<hw>*, e.g. *hwǣr* and *hwanne*. But by the Middle English period these words were being spelled with initial *<wh>*: *whēr* and *whanne.* The reason, according to Scragg (1974: 47), is that Middle English scribes assumed that in cases like these the <*h*> was working as a diacritic to indicate a fricative pronunciation of <*w*> – something like the final consonant sound in PDE *loch*. This was not the case though. The <*hw*> digraph did, in fact, sound something like a pronunciation of [h] and [w] in succession. Nevertheless, the graphs <*h*> and <*w*> were reversed in a misperceived attempt at regularisation. This explains why in some dialects of English – Scots, for instance – you will still hear words such as *where* and *when* pronounced with an initial [h] sound.

A problem that arises out of the variation that is to be found in the Middle English dialects is how to conveniently describe Middle English pronunciation in the absence of a standard form. One option is to describe the sounds used by a particular writer whom we know to have written in a particular dialect. Horobin (2007) takes this approach and uses the writings of the famous Middle English poet, Geoffrey Chaucer, to reconstruct the typical pronunciations of the London English dialect. Tables B3.2.1 and B3.2.2 outline the vowel sounds of this dialect – monophthongs and diphthongs.

Table B3.2.1 Adapted from Horobin (2007: 57)

ME phoneme	ME spelling	Pronunciation	PDE phoneme	PDE example
[ɪ]	kyng, is	s*i*t	[ɪ]	king, is
[ɛ]	bed	b*e*t	[ɛ]	bed
[a]	nat	m*a*n	[æ]	cat
[ɔ]	oft	h*o*t	[ɒ]	hot
[ʊ]	but, sonne	p*u*t	[ʊ] [ʌ]	but, sun
[iː]	wyf, wif	b*ee*	[aɪ]	wife
[eː]	mete	f*a*te	[iː]	meet
[ɛː]	mete	f*a*re	[iː]	meat
[aː]	name, taak	f*a*ther	[eɪ]	name
[uː]	toun, town	g*oo*se	[aʊ]	town
[oː]	mo(o)d	v*o*te	[uː]	mood
[ɔː]	bo(o)t	h*oa*rd	[əʊ]	boat

Table B3.2.2 Horobin (2007: 57)

ME	ME spelling	ME examples
[aɪ]	<ai, ay, ei, ey>	day, wey
[ɔɪ]	<oi, oy>	joye
[ʊɪ]	<oi, oy>	destroye
[aʊ]	<au>	taught, law
[ɔʊ]	<ow>	knowe
[ɛʊ]	<ew>	lewed
[ɪʊ]	<ew>	newe, trewe

For the most part, the consonants of Middle English are pronounced as they are in PDE. Some exceptions concern the pronunciation of the following graphemes:

❏ *<c>* retains the pronunciation [k] but no longer has the pronunciation [tʃ]. ([tʃ], as we have seen above, is instead represented by the French digraph *<ch>*.)
❏ *<c>* also now has the pronunciation [s] in French loan words such as *protestacioun*.
❏ *<gh>* and *<ȝ>* are pronounced [x] (similar to the final consonant sound in PDE *loch*) when in the middle of a word.
❏ *<ȝ>* is pronounced [j] when it occurs as the initial letter of a word.

You can practise your pronunciation by reading aloud the texts in C3. But where your knowledge of Middle English sounds (especially vowel sounds) will really come in useful is in understanding the sound changes that occurred in the Early Modern English period. The so-called Great Vowel Shift is explained in B4.

B3.3 Changes in the system of inflections

As we saw in B1.3 and B1.4, the order of words in a sentence was much less important in Old English than it is in Present Day English, because Old English was a synthetic language as opposed to an analytic one. Hence, inflections conveyed grammatical information that in PDE is now indicated by other means, for example through syntactic structure and the use of prepositions. However, towards the end of the Old English period and throughout the Middle English period, this system of inflections began to break down and inflections became ever more scarce. Inflections didn't disappear completely (see B5.2) but by the end of the Middle English period the inflection system was substantially less complex than it had been in Old English.

What caused the loss of inflections in English? There are several potential explanations, outlined below. As you read through these explanations, bear in mind that it is likely that a combination of these factors was responsible (i.e. these are not necessarily competing explanations).

Changes in the sound system of English

Changes in the sound system of Old English were responsible in part for the reduced complexity of the inflectional system. Inflections became unstressed in speech which had the effect of levelling the pronunciation of the vowels in these inflections. This simply means that the vowel sounds in inflections lost their distinctness. For example, consider the following two OE nouns:

> *faru* (journey)
> *fara* (journeys).

Read these words aloud. If you stress both syllables of *faru* and *fara* equally you will hear a clear difference between the vowel sound of the singular inflection (*–u*) and that of the plural inflection (*–a*). However, if you only stress the first syllables of each word, the vowel sounds in the inflections will reduce to schwa and the two words will sound identical. Stressing only the first syllable of the words means that it is impossible to distinguish the type of inflection in the unstressed syllable. And if you can't hear a distinction between the two forms then you are unlikely to produce the inflectional distinctions in your own speech. Inflections, therefore, would have become gradually less important as a means of conveying important grammatical information.

Scandinavian influence

Language contact between the Danes and the Anglo-Saxons is one explanation as to why inflections began to disappear from English. The base form of a word in English was often remarkably similar to the base form of the same word in Scandinavian. The only difference was in the inflections that were appended to these words. Hence, it was the inflections that were a barrier to mutual understanding. Getting rid of the inflections increased the likelihood of the Danes and the Anglo-Saxons being able to communicate effectively. This would have been especially necessary in areas such as the Danelaw (the territory to the east of an imaginary line running diagonally from the River Thames to Chester; see A1.5) where Danish and Saxon communities would have mixed. Consequently this is one factor that may well explain the loss of inflections in English. Later on in the period, when the Danes had gained the throne of England, their position of power was likely to have raised the prestige of the variety of English that they spoke, potentially establishing it – a variety with reduced inflections – as a variety for other speakers to aspire to.

The process of language learning

In a similar process to that described above, it is possible that inflections were omitted in situations where an English speaker was conversing with someone whose first language was not English and who had only limited ability to speak in English (compare this to the situation with the English and the Danes, whose languages were mutually intelligible to at least some degree). For example, some French speakers may well have learned simplified forms of English for the sole purpose of communication. However, the limited number of French speakers who may have done this makes this an unlikely explanation for widespread inflectional change in English.

The breakdown of the system of inflections led ultimately to English becoming an analytic as opposed to a synthetic language. As an example of the difference between ME and OE, consider one of the example sentences from B1.4:

> 1 se cnapa lufode þā hlǣfdigan (The servant loved the mistress.)

In Middle English, this could have been expressed in various ways, for example:

> 2 þe ladde lovede þeo lafdiȝ.
> 3 þe ladde lovede þe lady.

Example 2 uses different forms of the determiner to mark the nominative and accusative, as in OE. But during the Middle English period the different forms of the determiner were gradually replaced with just one form: *þe*. And because the ME nouns *ladde* and *lafdiȝ* have no inflections to indicate case, in example 3, where just one form of the determiner is used, we rely entirely on word order to determine the meaning of the sentence. (You will also notice different spellings in the two sentences, a common feature of Middle English.) By the end of the Middle English period, inflections on nouns had almost entirely disappeared and only one form of the determiner was used (Fisiak 1968).

B3.4 Middle English vocabulary

During the Middle English period, the lexicon of English increased substantially as a result of the borrowing of words from French, and Latin and Norse (of these, French had the most influence). The Viking invasions of the Old English period had also led to significant borrowing, and during the Middle English period many of these borrowed Scandinavian words became more widely used. Borrowing is made possible by language contact. Words can be borrowed directly from one language, or they may come via a second language. English had come into contact with Latin via the work of the early Christian missionaries, whereas contact with French came about both as a result of Edward the Confessor's French-speaking royal court and by the consequences caused by the Battle of Hastings of 1066 (see A3). It is also the case that certain conditions make borrowing more likely. For instance, Smith (2005: 16) suggests that the decline of inflections in the ME period made it easier to integrate words from other languages into English, as their forms did not need to be changed to the same extent. Unsurprisingly, the borrowed words often came from areas of life that the donor languages were specifically associated with. So, for example, Latin contributed many religious words (*pulpit*, *rosary*, *scripture*, *testament*, etc.) though this is not to suggest that this was the only semantic field from which vocabulary was drawn. French borrowings hint at the prestigious position of French speakers in England at the time: *prince*, *princess*, *virtuous*, *hostel*, *debt*, *cathedral*, *chivalry*, *magnificence*, *majesty*. Scandinavian borrowings such as *egg*, *knife*, *freckle*, *root* and *smile* suggest fairly close contact between the Scandinavians and the Anglo-Saxons. You can explore Middle English borrowings further in C3.

SOUND SHIFTS

B4

Because reading Early Modern English is closer to Present Day English in terms of grammar and vocabulary than Old English or Middle English, there is perhaps a tendency to underestimate some of the differences between the two, as well as the significant linguistic changes that occurred during the Early Modern period. Written Early Modern English seems closer to Present Day English because of the process of standardisation that occurred in the Early Modern period, and by the fact that the new standard that emerged was spread via the development of the printing press. But the Early Modern Period also saw major changes in spoken English, specifically pronunciation. In B4 and B5 we will examine these linguistic developments in spoken and written English.

B4.1 Speech sounds

One of the major changes to occur during the transition from Middle to Early Modern English was the so-called Great Vowel Shift, which affected pronunciation in many parts of the country and which led eventually to the pronunciations that we use in Present Day English. Although this was a linguistic phenomenon, it is outlined in A4.1 because of the social events that some linguists (e.g. Labov 1972) have suggested were instrumental in causing it to occur (e.g. the fact that some accents came to be seen as particularly prestigious). In this section I will concentrate on describing what happened linguistically during the Great Vowel Shift.

Understanding the Great Vowel Shift is made easier if you have a grasp of what happens physiologically when we produce speech sounds (and, obviously enough, vowel sounds in particular), so we will start with this. Then we will look at the changes in the pronunciation of the long vowels that occurred in the Early Modern period. Finally, when you feel comfortable with all of this, I would suggest that you move on to the readings in section D4 in order to consolidate your understanding of the Great Vowel Shift as a whole and to explore its complexities in greater depth.

Producing speech sound

To produce **speech sound**, we expel air from our lungs which then passes through the **trachea** (sometimes called the windpipe) and the **larynx** (part of the throat), before leaving the body via the mouth or the nose. The particular sound that comes out depends on how we modify the airflow as it leaves our body. First of all, let's consider how we produce consonant sounds.

Producing consonant sounds

To produce a consonant sound, we use **articulators** (vocal organs such as the tongue, lips, teeth, etc.) to restrict the airflow in some way. If we use our lips as articulators we can create, for example, the sounds [p] and [b]. To do this, we obstruct the airflow by keeping our lips tightly together. The build-up of pressure means that when we move our lips apart there is an explosion of air, creating what phoneticians call a plosive. In the case of [p] and [b], this is a **bilabial plosive**, since it is a plosive that is created as a result of using both lips as articulators (*labia* is the Latin plural of *lip* and *bi* means 'two'; hence *bilabial* means 'two lips'). The difference between [p] and [b] is that [b] is **voiced** and [p] is **unvoiced**. As air from our lungs is expelled it passes over the **vocal folds** (sometimes called the vocal chords). These are two bands of muscle stretched horizontally across the trachea. If the vocal folds are close together when the air hits them they will vibrate, creating a voiced sound. Conversely, if the vocal folds are open, the air will pass through them without causing them to vibrate, resulting in an unvoiced sound. To feel the difference, put your index and middle fingers against your Adam's apple and say the sounds [p] and [b]. When you say [p] you should feel nothing; when you say [b] you should feel the vibration caused by the vocal folds oscillating. All consonant sounds are either voiced or unvoiced and all are dependent on the airflow being restricted in some way. For instance, to produce the unvoiced phoneme [f], we use our teeth and our lower lip as articulators. The air leaves the oral cavity (i.e. the mouth) through the gaps between the teeth and the lower lip. The articulators involved in producing the phoneme [m] are the lips – as with [p] and [b]. The difference is that the air leaves the body via the nasal cavity rather than the mouth. Remember, the common feature of all consonant sounds is that their production relies on our restricting the outflow of air in some way.

Producing vowel sounds

Vowel sounds are produced in a different way. To produce a vowel sound you do not restrict the flow of air from the body. Instead, the shape of the oral cavity and the position of the tongue within it determine the kind of vowel sound that is produced. Moving the tongue to a specific position within the mouth creates a resonating cavity within which a particular vowel sound can be produced. If the tongue is raised up in the mouth it leaves a small resonating cavity. If the tongue is moved towards the bottom of the mouth it leaves a larger resonating cavity. Try saying the sounds [i:] (as in *meat*) and [a:] (as in *bar*). Take notice of where your tongue moves to in your mouth as you say these sounds. When you say [i:] your tongue is high up in your mouth. The resonating cavity in which the [i:] sound is produced is small. Conversely, when you say [a:] the tongue is low down in the mouth and you should feel that there is consequently a much larger space in which the vowel sound is produced.

Phoneticians make use of a trapezium-shaped diagram to represent the resonating cavity in which vowel sounds are produced (see Figure B4.1.1 overleaf). **Close** vowel sounds are produced when the cavity is small (i.e. when the tongue is close to the roof of the mouth, or **raised**). **Open** vowel sounds are produced when the cavity is large (i.e. when the tongue is low down in the mouth). There are other factors that can influence the type of vowel sound produced. One is whether the resonating cavity is towards the **front** or **back** of the tongue. Try saying [i:] and [u:] (as in *boot*). You should feel that for both these sounds the tongue is high in the mouth. However, when you say [i:] it should feel like the sound is coming from the front of the tongue while the [u:] phoneme should feel like it is being produced from the back. This is because [i:] is a front vowel while [u:] is a back vowel. Another factor that can influence the type of vowel sound produced is whether your lips are **rounded** or **unrounded** when you produce the vowel sound in question. Say [i:] and [u:] again. Take notice of the position of your lips as you pronounce these sounds. When you say [u:] your lips will be pursed. [u:] is a rounded vowel while [i:] is an unrounded vowel. Lastly, the length of a particular vowel sound is important in distinguishing it from others. Say [i:] and [ɪ] (as in *pit*). You should feel that these sounds are coming from roughly the same place within your mouth. Both are front vowels, and both are produced with the tongue close to the roof of the mouth (though the height of the tongue varies slightly between the two vowels). Additionally, both are unrounded. One of the main distinguishing features between these two sounds is that [i:] is long while [ɪ] is short.

You will see from Figure B4.1.1 that while some vowel sounds are produced with the tongue high up in the mouth and others with it low down, still other sounds are produced when the tongue is at a mid-point. The horizontal lines in the chart illustrate that different sounds are produced when the tongue is raised to the mid-open and mid-close positions as well. Additionally, while some vowel sounds come from the front of the tongue and others from the back, certain vowel sounds are produced from a resonating cavity in the centre of the mouth. These include schwa (see B1.1), [ɜ:] and [ʌ].

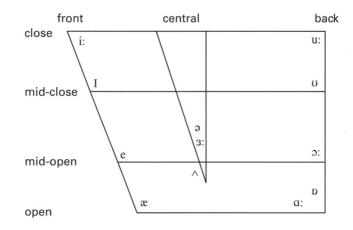

Figure B4.1.1 Pure vowels in English

The vowel sounds represented in Figure B4.1.1 can be found in the following English words:

[iː]	meat, sleep, treat
[ɪ]	bit, tin, lip
[e]	bed, head, said
[æ]	cat, tap, pan
[aː]	rather, far, bar
[ɒ]	hot, rock, mop
[ɔː]	law, caught
[ʊ]	look, cook
[uː]	boot, shoot, loot
[ə]	<u>a</u>bout, sof<u>a</u>
[ɜː]	bird, hurt
[ʌ]	cut, gun

(NB: Speakers of Northern English use [ʊ] in those instances where speakers of Southern English use [ʌ])

The sounds represented in Figure B4.1.1 are all pure vowels or monophthongs. Additionally, English also makes use of vowel sounds called diphthongs, which involve movement between one vowel position and another. For example, for many English speakers the vowel sound in the word *house* is a diphthong: [aʊ]. Producing the diphthong [aʊ] involves the tongue moving between one position and another in the oral cavity. Figure B4.1.2 shows the direction of the tongue's movement during the production of this diphthong.

Of course, not every speaker of English would use the diphthong [aʊ] in the word *house*. Accents vary, and in some parts of the northeast of England and in Scotland, the vowel sound in *house* would be closer to the pure long vowel [uː]. In fact, speakers of English who pronounce the word *house* as [huːs] are demonstrating a pronunciation that would have been common in Middle English. We saw in B3.2 how Middle English pronunciation differed from that of Present Day English. It was the Great Vowel

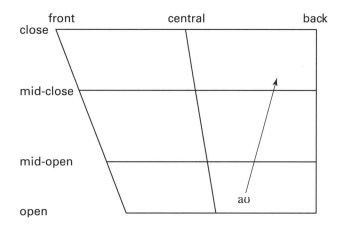

Figure B4.1.2 The diphthong [aʊ]

Shift that was the cause of many of these changes in pronunciation. What happened during the Great Vowel Shift was that the pronunciation of the long vowels was raised. That is, the Great Vowel Shift caused the long vowel sounds to be produced with the tongue higher up in the oral cavity than it would have been during the Middle English period. This resulted in changes to the seven long vowels of Middle English, including the **diphthongisation** (the process of a pure vowel becoming a diphthong) of some of them. We will see why in the next section.

B4.2 Changes in the long vowels

Once you have a basic idea of the movement of the tongue during the production of vowel sounds it becomes easier to grasp what happened during the Great Vowel Shift. The changes that occurred affected the seven long vowels in Middle English: [iː], [eː], [ɛː], [aː], [ɔː], [oː] and [uː]. Notice that not all of these vowels are represented in Figure B4.2.1 (overleaf), since some of these sounds are no longer used in Present Day Standard English (though some occur in regional varieties – e.g. [ɔː] in a Lancashire pronunciation of *bored*).

Let's take a simple example of the kind of change that occurred during the Great Vowel Shift. The Middle English pronunciation of *name* would have been [naːmə] and the Early Modern pronunciation would have been [nɛːm]. The vowel sound in the Early Modern English pronunciation is higher than that of the Middle English pronunciation. That is, when you pronounce the Early Modern English example your tongue is closer to the roof of your mouth than when you pronounce the Middle English example, thereby changing the shape of the resonating cavity inside your mouth that determines the vowel sound that is produced.

What is important here is that a change in the pronunciation of one long vowel has a knock-on effect on the other six. Effectively, what happened is that the [aː] vowel of the Middle English pronunciation was raised, resulting in it being pronounced as [ɛː]. So what, then, happens to the [ɛː] vowel? The answer is that it too was raised so that it took on the quality of the [eː] vowel. Then, as a consequence of this, the [eː] vowel was raised to take on the quality of the [iː] vowel. And what about the [iː]

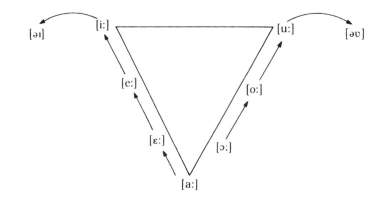

Figure B4.2.1 The Great Vowel Shift in English (Aitchison 2001)

vowel? As the highest front vowel there was nowhere for this to move to, and so the [iː] changed into a diphthong: [əɪ]. This diphthong changed again to become Present Day English [aɪ]. So, the word *ride* would have been pronounced [riːd] in Middle English and [rəɪd] in Early Modern English, before eventually becoming [raɪd] in Present Day English (see the reading by Aitchison 2001 in D4.2 for more examples of changing pronunciations between the Middle English and Early Modern periods).

This deals with the front vowels. The back vowels, too, raised in a similar way. Aitchison (2001) summarises the movement of the long vowels diagrammatically (see Figure B4.2.1). Notice that, like the front vowel [iː], the back vowel [uː] raises to become a diphthong. In the Early Modern period this was [əʊ], which eventually became [aʊ] in Present Day English.

Figure B4.2.1 explains *what* happened during the Great Vowel Shift but it does not explain *why* it happened. In A4 we explored a potential social explanation for why people began to change the way that they spoke. But in addition to this we need a linguistic explanation for why the long vowels moved. Generally, linguists agree that the Great Vowel Shift was caused by a **chain shift**. Imagine the long vowels as links in a chain. As one part of the chain moves, so too do the other parts. There is, though, a further question, and this is whether one vowel sound was *pushing* the others into different positions or whether the converse was true; i.e. that one vowel was *pulling* the others into different positions. This is the difference between a **push chain** and a **drag chain**. You can explore these theories in more detail in D4.2.

B4.3 The Uniformitarian Principle in relation to the Great Vowel Shift

In A4.1 we saw that one potential sociolinguistic explanation of the Great Vowel Shift is Labov's notion that speakers were emulating the sounds they heard in prestigious varieties of English, just as there is evidence of this occurring in PDE. According to Machan (2003: 12), Labov's explanation is an example of the application of the 'Uniformitarian Principle'. Machan explains this as follows:

> Roger Lass [1980: 55] formulates the most general form of the principle in this way: 'Nothing (no event, sequence of events, constellation of properties, general

law) that cannot for some good reason be the case in the present was ever true in the past.'

(Machan 2003: 12)

Essentially what this means is that if something is the case in the present, we can assume that in all likelihood the same was true in the past. For instance, in PDE we have open vowels and close vowels, and so we can assume that earlier forms of English also had open vowels and close vowels (even though these may have differed from PDE slightly). Machan goes on to explain that the Uniformitarian Principle also extends to social aspects of language use:

> In principle, there is no reason that the Uniformitarian Principle cannot be extended from such issues of language structure to those of language use. Indeed, Suzanne Romaine inverts this principle and applies it directly to society and language, whereby the Uniformitarian Principle means that 'the linguistic forces which operate today and are observable around us are not unlike those which have operated in the past. Sociolinguistically speaking, this means that there is no reason for claiming that language did not vary in the same patterned ways in the past as it has been observed to do today' [Romaine 1982: 122–3].
>
> (Machan 2003: 12)

What this suggests is that we can assume the English of the past to have varied in the same ways as different varieties of English do in the present. We know that regional variation was commonplace but on the basis of the Uniformitarian Principle we can assume the social variation was commonplace too. That is, certain varieties and usages would have been seen as particularly prestigious and worthy of emulation. This, then, provides the support for Labov's theory of the sociolinguistic causes of the Great Vowel Shift.

B4.4 Consequences of the Great Vowel Shift

The obvious consequence of the Great Vowel Shift was that the pronunciation of the long vowels changed. But the Great Vowel Shift also begins to explain some of the peculiarities of English spelling. You will recall from A5 that one of the defining aspects of the Early Modern period was that it was an age of standardisation. During this time, the production of grammars and dictionaries of English increased substantially and significant efforts were put into standardising the spelling system. Previously, you will remember, spelling had been largely phonetic – that is, people spelled words in a way that reflected their own pronunciation in their own dialect. The problem, of course, was that all of this standardising was going on at a time when the spoken language was also undergoing significant change, as we have been looking at in this unit. A consequence of this was that the spellings that emerged as a result of the processes of standardisation often reflected the pronunciation of words *before* the Great Vowel Shift was complete. This begins to explain why in PDE there often appears to be no logical connection between the way that a word is spelled and the way it is pronounced. In fact, seemingly arbitrary spellings often reflect an earlier pronunciation. For example, the spelling of the words *mice* and *wine* reflects the fact that in the ME pronunciation the vowel sound in each was a pure vowel, or monophthong. Had the spellings of these words been fixed *after* the Great Vowel Shift had occurred, we might expect them to reflect the fact that both these words are now pronounced with the diphthong [aɪ] – *mais* and *wain*, perhaps?

B5   WRITING IN EARLY MODERN ENGLISH

The Early Modern period saw the emergence of a standard form of written English that was due in no small part to the increasing use of the printing press in England, following Caxton's setting up of a press at Westminster in 1476. The simple fact of there being a press in existence, however, does not in and of itself provide a full explanation for why a standard should emerge. We can gain a better insight into this by considering Haugen's (1966) sociolinguistic explanation of the way in which standard forms develop.

Haugen (1966) considers the issue of how 'dialects' develop into 'languages'. (I have used scare quotes around the terms *dialect* and *language* because the definition of these two terms is informed as much by politics as linguistics – see A2.1; and, of course, Standard English should be seen as just one dialect among many, rather than a superior form). In considering this issue, he is effectively also considering the development of vernaculars into standard varieties. Haugen (1966: 110) suggests there are four stages to the development of a standard. These are:

❑   selection of norm
❑   codification of form
❑   elaboration of function, and
❑   acceptance by the community.

The first of these stages involves the **selection** of a particular variety to become a standard form of the language. In A5.1 we saw how, in the Middle English period, four varieties of English emerged as potential standard forms: Central Midlands Standard, Early London English, London English and Chancery Standard (see Samuels 1963). In Haugen's terms, these were the varieties *selected* as standards (though it is perhaps more accurate to suggest that these emerged as standards). The next stage in the development is **codification**, during which the norms of the selected form are made explicit, usually by the production of printed materials and especially through grammars and dictionaries. Notice that when Caxton began publishing books and pamphlets, the standard he chose to publish in was what is often referred to as Chancery Standard. Essentially, this was the variety that became codified through the publication of books and articles. Later on, this was the variety that scholars wrote about in the grammars and dictionaries of the period. Hence, the norms associated with Chancery Standard were codified during the Early Modern period (see A5.1 for a discussion of the issues surrounding the classification of Chancery English). The fact that the other potential standards of the time were not codified (at least, not to the same extent as Chancery Standard) was responsible for their not becoming established as standard forms in the EModE period. The third stage in Haugen's process is the **elaboration** of the functions of the selected and codified standard. Haugen explains that since the selected and codified standard is 'by definition the common language of a social group more complex and inclusive than those using vernaculars, its functional domains must also be complex' (Haugen 1966: 108). What this means is that the newly emerging standard must be adequate for a variety of purposes. It must have the potential to be used by various classes of people and by different communities. It must be usable for a variety of different functions, including 'high' functions such as official communications and literary writing. If an emerging standard has been selected, codified and elaborated then it stands a strong chance of becoming established as a long-term standard form. Nevertheless, the final stage in Haugen's four-stage process is **acceptance** and requires that the newly developed standard be accepted by the speech community as a whole. That is, it must be seen to be a viable and useful form that offers something to its users, be this power, prestige or the opportunity for social and educational advancement. This four-stage process can clearly be seen to have been in progress during the Early Modern period and was instrumental in the emergence over time of the form of Standard English that is still widely recognised today. Note too that it applies equally to spoken English. However, as Haugen points out, '[t]o choose any one vernacular as a norm means to favor the group of people speaking that variety. It gives them prestige as norm-bearers and a headstart in the race for power and position' (Haugen 1966: 109). We will consider this issue of power and prestige in more detail in B6. Throughout the rest of this section we will examine some of the characteristics of the newly emerging written standard in Early Modern English.

B5.1 Orthography in Early Modern English

At the beginning of the Early Modern period there was little consistency in spelling. The word *mother*, for example, might be spelled variously as *modir*, *modyr*, *moodre*, *modere* and *moder* (all of these forms can be found in the Paston Letters, a famous collection of family letters from the beginning of the Early Modern period). This inconsistency is also found in early printed books of the period. Scragg (1974: 66) puts this down to the fact that William Caxton, who had introduced the printing press in 1476, was likely to have been unfamiliar with developments in orthography during the fifteenth century, as he had spent much of this period away from England. Added to this, he initially employed foreign printers who were similarly unfamiliar with the developing standards of Chancery English. Over the Early Modern period, however, spelling conventions gradually became established and these orthographic norms mean that Early Modern English spelling is not as haphazard as it may at first appear to be. The following are some common features of spelling at the beginning of the Early Modern period:

❑ There are two forms of the letter <*s*> in use. The practice is to use <*s*> when the final letter of a word but <*ʃ*> – sometimes called 'long s' – when the letter is word-initial or appears in a medial position.

❑ <*u*> can represent both the vowel sound [ʊ] and the consonant sound [v]. <*v*> can also represent both the vowel sound [ʊ] and the consonant sound [v].

Nevertheless, the usage is not arbitrary. <*v*> is used in word-initial position, whether the phoneme to be represented is [ʊ] or [v]. Elsewhere, the norm is to use <u>. For example, *have* is typically spelled *haue*, while *up* is spelled *vp*. PDE, of course, treats <*v*> and <*u*> as distinct graphemes, a convention that began around 1630 as a result of continental influence (Barber 1997: 3).

❑ <*i*> tends to be used in places where in PDE we would use <*j*>. According to Barber (1976: 16), the letter combination <*ij*> – as in *diversifijng* – was the only instance in which the letter <*j*> would be used.

An additional point of interest about Early Modern English spelling is the use of <*e*> on the end of particular words. In the Early Modern period, final <*e*> in words like *name*, *moste* and *persone* would not have been pronounced in speech but fulfilled a number of different functions in writing. A summary of these (based on Görlach 1991: 47) is as follows:

❑ The use of final <*e*> was not arbitrary.

❑ Final <*e*> could indicate that the vowel sound in a word was long – e.g. in words like *name* and *nose*. Once established, this convention was applied to other words. So, for example, Middle English *cas* became *case*, *lif* became *life*, *wif* became *wife*, etc.

❑ The use of final <*e*> to indicate vowel length caused a problem in words like *writen* (PDE *written*). The <*e*> suggested that the vowel sound was long, when it was in fact short. The solution was to double the medial consonant, resulting in *written*.

❑ Final <*e*> was also used to differentiate between words that used <*s*> as a plural inflection on the end of the word and those in which <*s*> was simply the final letter. For example, adding a final <*e*> to *divers* indicates that the word is an adjective – *diverse* – not a plural noun. A similar example is *dens* and *dense*.

B5.2 Some grammatical characteristics

Pronouns

Pronouns in Present Day English take different forms depending on a number of factors. The form of the pronoun depends on whether it is the **subject** or **object** of a sentence, or whether it is fulfilling a **possessive** function. (Broadly speaking, these three categories correspond to the nominative, accusative and genitive cases described in B1.4). Other factors that determine the form of a pronoun are person (first-, second- or third-person) and number (whether it is singular or plural). We can summarise the different forms of the pronoun in PDE as in Table B5.2.1.

Table B5.2.1 Pronouns in Present Day English

	First-person	Second-person	Third-person
Subject			
Singular	I	you	he/she/it
Plural	we	you	they
Object			
Singular	me	you	him/her/it
Plural	us	you	them
Possessive			
Singular	mine	yours	his/hers/its
Plural	ours	yours	theirs

Notice that the form of the pronoun changes according to its grammatical function, i.e. the job that it is doing in the sentence. So, while the development of English over time is marked by a tendency towards regularisation and a reliance on word order to convey meaning, it is still the case that in PDE we sometimes change the form of a word in order to denote its grammatical function.

In Early Modern English, there were more forms of the pronouns than there are in PDE (Table B5.2.2).

Table B5.2.2 Pronouns in Early Modern English (after Barber 1997: 152)

	First-person	Second-person	Third-person
Subject			
Singular	I	thou	he/she/it*
Plural	we	ye	they
Object			
Singular	me	thee	him/her/it*
Plural	us	you	them
Possessive			
Singular	mine	thine	his/hers/his
Plural	ours	yours	theirs

* The original form of *it* was *hit,* which was in use until around 1600. The form *it* developed as a result of the initial /h/ being dropped in circumstances where *hit* was unstressed.

You will see from Table B5.2.2 that there are some differences between Early Modern English and Present Day English pronouns. For instance, at the beginning of the Early Modern period it was usual for the masculine singular possessive pronoun *his* to be used in those instances where in PDE we would use *its*. The main difference between pronouns in EModE and PDE, however, is the second-person forms. In Early Modern

English, as in Middle English, the second-person pronoun changed form according to person, number and grammatical function. *Thou*, *thee* and *thine* are singular forms whereas *ye*, *you* and *yours* are plural forms. In Present Day Standard English there is no distinction between singular and plural forms and only the possessive form is different from the others. (Exceptions can be found in certain dialects – e.g. Dublin English and Liverpool English have a plural second-person pronoun, *youse*, and in American English we find a contracted second-person plural, *y'all* – i.e. *you all*.) However, as Leith (1983: 107) points out, the second-person forms also had a particular social meaning in Early Modern English. During the Early Modern period *thou* and *thee* and *ye* and *you* were marked for social status, and when used in this way *ye/you* could be applied as singular pronouns too. A person of higher social standing could address a person lower down the social hierarchy with either *thou* or *thee* and expect *ye* or *you* in response, since using *ye* and *you* showed a deferential awareness of that person's higher social status. Effectively, *ye/you* was a more polite form. Many languages still make a similar distinction and have second-person forms that are marked for politeness, though nowadays the factor that determines their usage is usually a person's age rather than their social class. French, for instance, has the forms *tu* and *vous*. *Tu* may be used between friends as marker of social solidarity, while *vous* is likely to be used by a young person speaking to someone older than themselves (Barber (1997: 153) explains that the *thee/thou–ye/you* distinction most likely developed in English as a result of French influence in the Middle English period). Similarly, Present Day German offers the option of using either *du* or *sie*.

Verbs

Throughout the development of English there has been a tendency towards **regularisation**. During the Middle English period inflections began to fall out of usage, though this was ongoing throughout the Early Modern period and it would be a mistake to assume that Present Day English is inflection-free. PDE verbs, for example, still inflect in the third-person present tense. We say *I walk* but *she walks*, *you drink* but *he drinks* (compare this with the past tense inflection <-*ed*> which is the same for first-, second- and third-person). Unsurprisingly, if we look at Early Modern English verbs we find a greater degree of inflectional complexity than in PDE. Consider, for example, the EModE present tense forms of the weak verb *to walk* (see Table B5.2.3).

Table B5.2.3

	Singular		Plural	
	Present	*Past*	*Present*	*Past*
First-person	I walke	walked	we walke	we walked
Second-person	thou walk(e)st	thou walkedst	ye walke	ye walked
Third-person	he/she/hit walketh	he/she/hit walked	they walke	they walked

As you can see, EModE also included an inflection to mark the second-person singular form of the verb, in both the present and the past tense, which is something that does not survive in PDE.

It is also important to bear in mind that inflections varied according to dialect. For example, the third-person <-eth> form was a southern inflection. In the north of England the third-person present tense inflection was <-es>; e.g. *she walkes*. Notice that this is the form that survives in PDE. Barber (1997: 167) suggests that around 1600, this northern third-person inflection was considered less formal than its southern counterpart. So although the two third-person inflections denoted the same grammatical information, they conveyed different **pragmatic** information, in much the same way that the two EModE forms of the second-person pronoun (*thou* and *ye*) conveyed different social implications.

The example in Table B5.2.3 above is of a weak verb though the same inflectional complexity was present in EModE strong verbs too. Table B5.2.4 is an example.

Table B5.2.4

	Singular		Plural	
	Present	*Past*	*Present*	*Past*
First-person	I giue	I gaue	we giue	we gaue
Second-person	thou giue(s)t	thou gau(e)st	ye giue	ye gaue
Third-person	he/she/hit giueth	he/she/hit gaue	they giue	they gaue

The inflection on the second-person singular form of the verb is something that we no longer have in PDE. Barber (1997: 165) suggests that it fell out of usage when *ye/you* replaced *thou/thee* as the standard second-person singular pronoun in the seventeenth century, since there was no second-person inflection on the form of the verb that agreed with *ye/you*.

The process of regularisation also affected many of the strong verbs in Early Modern English. Many EModE strong verbs regularised over time to become weak verbs. In some cases, however, verbs that are weak in PDE had both a strong *and* a weak form in EModE. Some examples (from Barber 1997: 175) are given in Table B5.2.5.

Table B5.2.5

EModE base form	Strong past tense	Weak past tense
help	holp	helped
melt	molte	melted
swell	swole	swelled
climb	clamb/clomb	climbed

B5.3 Expanding the lexicon

In B1.2 you can read about how new words were formed in Old English via the process of **compounding** (putting existing words together to form new words). In the Middle English period **borrowing** words from Latin and French was the principal means by which the vocabulary of English was expanded (see B3.4 for examples). In the Early Modern period, considerable disagreement arose among certain scholars concerning the most apt way of enlarging the lexicon of English. The disagreement occurred in the second half of the sixteenth century and centred on the appropriateness of expanding the vocabulary of English by borrowing words from Latin and other Classical languages such as Greek. Some writers, such as Sir Thomas Elyot, believed that the expressive capability and status of the English language could be enriched by borrowing vocabulary from such languages. Other commentators felt that these loanwords were unnecessarily complex and that it was better to use 'simple' Germanic vocabulary. This disagreement has come to be known as **The Inkhorn Controversy**. *Inkhorn* is another term for *inkpot*, into which scholars would dip their pens as they wrote. Those writers who scorned the borrowing of Classical vocabulary described such loanwords as **inkhorn terms**, a disparaging phrase that conveys the belief that using such terms was a scholarly affectation. Sir John Cheke, a Cambridge scholar who was famously against the use of inkhorn terms, expressed his objections to the practice of borrowing Classical vocabulary in a letter of 1557:

> I am of the opinion that our own tongue should be written clean and pure, unmixt and unmangled with borrowing of other tongues, wherein if we take not heed by time, ever borrowing and never paying, she shall be fain to keep her house as bankrupt.
>
> (Cheke 1557, quoted in Johnson 1944: 115)

It may seem surprising that the 'inkhorn terms' to which Cheke and others were objecting included such now common words as *audacious*, *celebrate*, *clemency*, *compatible*, *contemplate*, *expectation*, *hereditary*, *insane* and *promotion*. Notice that commentators such as Cheke demonstrated an overtly prescriptive (and proscriptive) view of the development of English.

B6   THE DEVELOPMENT OF AMERICAN ENGLISH

The spread of English overseas from the late 1500s onwards necessitates a change in terminology when we talk about the language. Although *dialectal* variation existed in English from its earliest inception, from the point at which English begins to spread to other countries it becomes necessary to talk also about *international* varieties of the language. **American English** is one such example of an international variety that differs from British English (though it is important not to overstate the differences which, in the twenty-first century, are marginal owing to globalisation and the mixing of cultures that this has led to).

In this section we will consider how English developed in America after the arrival of English speakers in what was then seen as 'the New World' (we will focus specifically on North American English and will look at other international varieties – or **World Englishes** – in B7 and B8). It is important to remember that the first British settlers in America would have spoken varieties of Early Modern English. Initially, then, varieties of English in America would have sounded like varieties of English in Britain. Over time, though, differences emerged as a result of numerous factors: contact with other languages, the influence of other cultures, power struggles, etc. The forging of a national identity distinct from that of Britain was also responsible for developments in the language.

B6.1 Causes of linguistic development in the American colonies

In A6.1 it is noted that the first British settlers in America came from a variety of places in England. London was just one of these. Additionally, settlers originated from such counties as Gloucestershire, Somerset, Lincolnshire, Nottinghamshire, Essex and Kent. What is particularly important here is that the early British settlers were drawn from the lower- and middle-classes of Britain, and consequently the English that was initially spoken in America included many regional dialectal features as opposed to being solely a form of Standard English. Cassidy (1984: 178) makes the salient point that 'people at the top of the social scale do not become colonists'. This is significant when we consider research in sociolinguistics which suggests that change and development in language is generally instigated by the middle-classes.

Cassidy (1984: 179) goes on to suggest what some of the factors might have been that would have caused the development of English in the earliest American colonies. These include:

- ❑ *Numerical majority* – the dialectal forms that were most frequent in the colonies were the ones that were most likely to survive and develop into American English. i.e. The larger the group of settlers from a particular area of Britain, the more likely their regional dialect was to have an influence on what became the norm in the developing American English variety.
- ❑ *Prestige* – the linguistic forms used by community leaders would most likely have been viewed as prestigious and adopted into American English for this reason.
- ❑ *Lack of contact with Britain* – the influence of British English was, over time, reduced as a result of diminishing contact between the settlers and their homeland. Conversely, the experiences of colonial life were more likely to affect the development of American English.

In addition to these factors there is also the significant issue of language contact. In A3 you can read about the importance of language contact for the development of Middle English. Contact between English and other languages played a similarly important part in the development of American English. Languages and dialects that English came into contact with included those of the Native American Indians, as well as **Dutch**, **Spanish**, **French** and **German** (the languages of other immigrant groups in the country at the time).

B6.2 A developing standard

Reed (1967: 16) makes the point that because the early British settlers in America were not from the upper echelons of society (and hence, perhaps, not as well educated), it is likely that spoken language more than written language determined the standard form of American English that developed. The standard that gradually emerged was not as socially charged as, say, written Standard British English and Received Pronunciation, most likely because the social hierarchy of Britain had not been transplanted to the American colonies. In a study of contemporary American English, Toon (1984: 214) claims that '[I]n general, English in the United States is most uniform in the domain of syntax and most variable in pronunciation'. This is an observation also made by contemporary observers of American English in the 1700s (Marckwardt 1980: 70), though it is likely that this was overstated somewhat. Dillard (1985) puts this down to **dialect-levelling**, a process by which the characteristic features of dialects are gradually lost as dialects **converge** (i.e. speakers accommodate their language use to become more like other language users). Dillard explains that this dialect-levelling occurred from the beginning of the 1700s until well into the last quarter of that century (1985: 70) and that, within a generation of settlers, 'access to the levelled dialect was possible' (1985: 62). This rapid development came about in part because of the establishment of schools wherein children would be exposed to standard forms, as well as the peer-pressure that caused colonial children to accommodate their language use to that of their classmates (Dillard 1985: 63). Nevertheless, by the end of the 1700s, dialectal diversity became more commonplace owing to contact with the frontier varieties spoken by immigrants from other countries (Dillard 1985: 71).

B6.3 'Archaisms' in American English

In the early years of the American colonies, in addition to the fact that American English was seen as remarkably uniform in terms of dialect, it was also often observed that it retained a number of 'archaic' forms of British English (the same claim is sometimes made today too). To a certain extent this was true, but it is necessary to exercise caution when investigating this. For example, it is not the case that forms of Early Modern English have been preserved in American English entirely without change (Marckwardt 1980: 71). And while it may sometimes be claimed that a particular word, grammatical structure or pronunciation in American English is an archaic form of British English, it is often the case that the form is still in use in dialects of British English other than SE (remember the necessity of considering varieties of English before making generalisations about linguistic change; see A8.3). Hence, some of the cited archaisms in American English are often simply forms which are no longer in use in Standard British English. 'Archaism' is perhaps not, therefore, the best term to use when describing these differences. As an example, here are some linguistic variables that are commonly cited as being archaic but which still survive in regional British dialects:

❑ Marckwardt (1980: 73) reports that the word *druggist* was used in England until around 1750, when it was replaced by *chemist*. However, *druggist* remained in use in the American colonies. Nevertheless, as Marckwardt points out, while *druggist* fell out of usage in the Standard British English of the time, it was retained in some dialects of Scotland. (In contemporary American English, while *druggist* may be used in the mid-West or on the East Coast, other dialects prefer *pharmacist*. Just to confuse things, you may find that *pharmacist* is now replacing *chemist* in some British English dialects. If you're a speaker of British English, which would you use?)

❑ In RP, *farm* is pronounced [fa:m] while in some accents of American English – that of New York, for example – it is pronounced [fa:rm]. The pronunciation of <*r*> in the latter example is an instance of what linguists call post-vocalic <*r*>; i.e. the pronunciation of /r/ after a vowel sound. Post-vocalic <*r*> can turn up in words like *car, hour, poor, wire, harm*, etc., and is sometimes cited as being an archaism since it used to be prevalent in British English but no longer is, despite being retained in many American accents. However, while it is true that post-vocalic /r/ is no longer used in RP (according to Cassidy (1984: 201), it died out in the early seventeenth century in RP but was retained in the American colonies), it is still common in particular regional varieties of British English – for example, Lancashire. (Interestingly, the prestige value of post-vocalic /r/ differs between British and American English, which reinforces the fact that the social 'value' of particular linguistic variables is determined entirely by non-linguistic factors; see Labov's famous study of New York English (Labov 1966) for more details.)

❑ Baugh and Cable (2002: 360) suggest that *mad* is used in American English to mean 'angry', which was its meaning in Early Modern English. The claim is that PDE *mad* now means 'mentally disturbed'. The problem, of course, is that seeing *mad* in American English as an archaism privileges Standard English in the history of the language and ignores the fact that *mad* to mean 'angry' is commonplace in some British dialects – e.g. Yorkshire English.

The notion of archaism as a trait of American English is, then, somewhat problematic. While it is true that older forms of English are preserved in American English, it is also the case that these forms continue to be used in British English dialects. The only sense, then, in which they are archaic is when compared against Standard British English – and to do this implies that Standard British English is the measure against which all other varieties are to be judged. The current status of English as a global language makes this an untenable position to take.

B6.4 The beginnings of African American English

So far we have been dealing with the developing English of immigrants to America from England. However, there is another variety of contemporary American English whose roots are not yet fully clear to linguists. This is **African American English (AAE)** which has developed from the varieties spoken by the African slaves who were brought to work on plantations in the early seventeenth century. The debate about the origins of AAE has focused on whether it developed from the dialects of the early European settlers in America (as North American English did), or from **creoles**. Creoles develop from pidgins (see A6.2 for the definition of this term) and when a pidgin acquires native speakers – i.e. when the children of pidgin-speakers use that pidgin as their first language – it is said to become a creole. Green (2002: 9) explains how some linguists have suggested that the first African slaves to arrive in America brought with them West

Indian creoles (e.g. Jamaican Creole), which were then adapted and developed into AAE. This hypothesis is formed on the basis that AAE shares numerous patterns with Jamaican Creole (Green 2002: 9). The alternative view is that AAE is a development from the Southern dialects of the plantation owners. Green (2002) explains that recently the **creolist hypothesis** has been questioned and it has been suggested that AAE may have developed in much the same way as North American dialects, and that it is developments in the twentieth century that have led to its becoming significantly different from present day so-called white vernaculars (see Wolfram and Thomas 2002).

B7   **INTERNATIONAL ENGLISH**

The global spread of English from the late 1500s onwards (see A7) has led to the emergence of numerous international varieties of English, or **World Englishes** (see A6 for the example of the early development of American English). In the limited space available it is impossible to provide a comprehensive survey of all of these varieties (though see Jenkins 2003 for a detailed introduction to World Englishes). What I will do instead is to focus on some of the characteristic features of just a few of these international varieties, in order to give a flavour of the variety of forms currently in use. We will consider how these varieties have emerged and what relationship they have with British English. As you read through the sections of this unit, bear in mind the notion that was introduced in A2.1 that the definition of a language is as much a political matter as a linguistic one. As Burchfield (1994: 13) points out, 'it must always be borne in mind that varieties of English, spoken at whatever distance, or however close up, are not discrete entities. [. . .] The similarities greatly exceed the differences'.

B7.1 Australian English

According to Trudgill and Hannah (2002: 16) there is little regional variation in Australian English. That is, dialects of Australian English have a tendency towards uniformity (though this does not discount the social variation that is to be found). Burridge and Mulder (1998: 38) suggest that this is because the settlement of Australia was by and large achieved as a result of Australian settlers sailing from New South Wales to other parts of the country. During this process of settlement whole groups of people might move long distances without coming into contact with other speech communities. This lack of contact had the effect of keeping the settlers' dialects relatively uniform – in effect, the English of the settlers in New South Wales was simply transferred around the country through a gradual process. In terms of accent, there are some obvious characteristic features of Australian English. Trudgill and Hannah (2002: 16–18) suggest the following:

❑   Use of schwa [ə] in unstressed syllable where in RP the phoneme would be [ɪ], e.g. *naked* /neɪkəd/, *David* /deɪvəd/, *honest* / hɒnəst, *village* /vɪlədʒ/, *begin* / bəgɪn/.
❑   Use of non-rhotic /r/ (see B6.3 for details of rhotic /r/ usage – i.e. post-vocalic /r/ – in American English)

❑ Intervocalic /t/ (that is, the pronunciation of /t/ between vowel sounds) becomes closer to /d/ – e.g. *city* /sɪdi:/, *better* /bɛdə/ (this feature, though, is not as common or standard as in North American English).

❑ The /ʊ/ vowel has more lip-rounding than in 'English English' (i.e. the English spoken in England; try saying *put* with and without rounding and listen to the difference in the vowel sound).

❑ Use of /i:/ where in RP /ɪ/ is more common – e.g. *very* /vɛri:/, *many* /mɛni:/, *city* /sɪdi:/ (Trudgill and Hannah note that this feature is similar to southern English non-RP accents).

There are essentially two theories concerning how these distinctive features of the Australian English accent emerged. The first is that they are the result of dialect-levelling among the early settlers and convicts, many of whom came to Australia from the south-east of England and from Ireland and Scotland (note that one piece of evidence here is that the use of /i:/ where in RP /ɪ/ would be the more common phoneme is also a feature of southern English non-RP accents). Burridge and Mulder (1998: 37) explain that the early linguistic situation following the arrival of the first settlers would have been one in which a variety of dialects were spoken. As these converged, certain accentual features would have been lost and others consolidated, giving rise to distinctive features that would over time come to be associated with the new variety of English. The second theory, according to Burridge and Mulder (1998), is that London English (and particularly the **Cockney** dialect – the dialect of East Londoners) is the ultimate basis of the Australian English accent, while features from Irish and Scottish accents took effect later on.

In addition to distinctive phonetic and phonological features, Australian English also makes use of distinctive lexis. The following are extracted from a list put together by Trudgill and Hannah (2002: 20):

Australian English	English English
to barrack for	to support
footpath	pavement
frock	dress
get	fetch
lolly	sweet
parka	anorak
station	stock-farm
station wagon	estate car
stove	cooker
stroller	push-chair

Some of these examples are still relatively uncommon in English English (and other British varieties). *Estate car*, for instance, is still preferred over *station wagon* in British English. Some, on the other hand, *can* be found in British varieties of English. *Footpath*, for instance, which Trudgill and Hannah suggest is only used in English English to refer to a woodland track, is commonly found as a synonym for *pavement* in Northern varieties of English. The problem, of course, is that it is difficult to make generalisations about differences between international varieties of English, since within all of these we also find variation based on a number of non-linguistic factors: geography, social class, the formality of the discourse situation, etc. You can explore these issues some more in C7.

B7.2 Indian English

The legacy of British colonial rule in India (see A6.2) is that English is now an official language in the country and the second language of a significant number of the population. While there is considerable variation in some aspects of Indian English, such as pronunciation (Trudgill and Hannah 2002: 129), there are other features which may be seen as typical of the variety. An example of one of these is the tendency towards regularisation in the formation of plurals of mass nouns. A mass noun is a noun that in Standard English is not countable – i.e. one which cannot be made plural by the simple addition of an <-s> inflection (e.g. *hand* → *hands*) or by changing the vowel in the stem (e.g. *foot* → *feet*). An example of a mass noun is *bread*. In Standard English we cannot say 'I ate two breads'. Instead, we have to add a pluralising expression – 'I ate two slices of bread'. (Sometimes, mass nouns can become countable. A recent example which is particularly appropriate for us is the noun *English* to refer to the language. The explosion of international varieties has led us to talk now about World *Englishes*). In Indian English, however, pluralising mass nouns by the addition of an <-s> inflection is common, giving rise to such examples from Trudgill and Hannah (2002: 130) as:

aircrafts	Many aircrafts have crashed here.
fruits	We ate just fruits for lunch.
litters (rubbish)	Do not throw litters on the street.
furnitures	He bought many furnitures.
woods	He gathered all the woods.

Clearly, what is happening in these instances is that the rules governing the formation of plurals in Standard English have been regularised by the speakers of the Indian English variety. Over time this has come to be a common feature of Indian English and while it may be viewed as non-standard from the perspective of a speaker of British English, we have already seen that British English is no longer an appropriate benchmark (if, indeed, it ever was) against which to judge other varieties. In this case, what is non-standard in British English is standard in Indian English.

Another characteristic difference between Indian English and British English concerns the meaning of some modal verbs. Modal verbs are a type of auxiliary verb – that is, they always occur with a main verb and provide information that the main verb doesn't. In the case of the modals this extra information concerns the speaker's or writer's attitude to the proposition being expressed. For example:

You can go. (The modal auxiliary *can* indicates permission; *go* is the main verb.)
It could be true. (The modal auxiliary *could* indicates possibility; *be* is the main verb.)
You must answer! (The modal verb *must* indicates obligation; *answer* is the main verb.)
He should have tried harder. (The modal verb *should* indicates necessity; *tried* is the main verb; *have* is an additional auxiliary.)

You will notice from the above examples that in Standard Present Day British English the modals do not change their form according to person, number or tense (though this was not always the case) and that they express particular attitudinal perspectives. In Indian English this is also true, but the semantic information (i.e. the meaning) that the modals convey is often different from British English. Trudgill and Hannah (2002: 133) illustrate this with the following examples:

Indian English	English English
This furniture may be removed tomorrow.	This furniture is to be removed tomorrow.
These mistakes may please be corrected.	These mistakes should be corrected.

It would appear that in the Indian English examples the modal verb *may* has been interpreted by the speaker/writer as being a polite form and that this pragmatic function takes precedence over the semantic meaning.

Other grammatical features of Indian English that differ from Standard British English include the following (drawn from Trudgill and Hannah 2002):

Use of present tense as opposed to present perfect with durational phrases

Indian English	I am here since two o'clock.
English English	I have been here since two o'clock.

Lack of subject/verb inversion in direct questions

Indian English	What this is made from?
English English	What is this made from?

Indian English	Who you have come to see?
English English	Who have you come to see?

Unsurprisingly, it is also the case that Indian English has borrowed considerably from other Indian languages. Borrowed words include the following (drawn from Trudgill and Hannah 2002):

bandh	a total strike in an area
crore	ten million
durzi	tailor
hartal	a strike used as a political gesture
sahib	sir, master
swadeshi	indigenous, native, home-grown

Some of these words seem likely to have been borrowed in response to particular situations faced by speakers of Indian English during the colonial era. In addition to borrowings from other Indian languages, Indian English has also created new vocabulary by adapting existing British English words, e.g.:

appreciable	appreciated
backside	behind

biodata	curriculum vitae
hotel	restaurant, café
stir	a demonstration
tiffin	lunch

Some of these newly created words arise from changing the form of an existing word (e.g. *appreciable*), some change the meaning (*hotel*) and some change the degree of formality of the word in question (*stir* is perhaps more colloquial in British Standard English than in Indian English). You can explore the creation of new vocabulary in English in more detail in C7.

B7.3 Pidgins and creoles on the West African coast

Todd (1984: 286) points out that in those African countries where English is used as an official language, it is useful if we think of English as a language continuum. By this she means that English exists in a variety of forms – from pidgins and creoles through to second-language English influenced by the speakers' first languages, and local standards. In this section we will concentrate on pidgins and creoles, since these provide further examples of how English has developed beyond the British Isles.

Pidgin varieties of English developed along the West African coast as a result of contact between the native inhabitants and European sailors and traders. (Indeed, Todd 1974 points out that many pidgins and creoles retain numerous nautical words as a result of their origins as coastal trading languages. She gives the example of *galley* as the term for a kitchen in Krio, a creole language in Sierra Leone.) This illustrates one of the key features of a pidgin, namely that it is a **contact language**. That is, it is no-one's first language but instead emerges to fulfil a limited set of functions for two or more speech communities that otherwise have no language in common. In B6.4 we discussed the notion of African American English emerging out of a pidgin. Pidgins need both a **substrate** language and a **superstrate** language. The substrate (usually the local vernacular) provides the grammatical structure while the superstrate provides the majority of the lexis of the pidgin.

Other key features of pidgins are **simplification**, **mixing** and **reduction**. Simplification involves both regularisation and loss of redundancy. Regularisation means the process of making irregular forms regular – for example, pluralising mass nouns by the addition of an <-s> inflection (see B7.2, above). Loss of redundancy involves the deletion of linguistic elements that repeat information. For instance, a pidgin might not use the third-person present tense inflection on verbs since this is grammatical information that is conveyed by the third-person pronoun. Mixing refers to the tendency of pidgin speakers to incorporate elements of their own language – accent, grammatical structures, lexis, etc. – into the pidgin. Finally, reduction refers to the fact that pidgins have reduced function. That is, the simplification of the contributing languages in the process of **pidginisation** means that the pidgin is only useful for a limited set of functions – basic communication, for example, as opposed to, say, use as a language of administration or law.

This, then, is a pidgin, but in some cases further development takes place. If a situation arises where a pidgin becomes the first language of a speech community (as a result of children learning the pidgin as their mother tongue) it becomes a creole. The process of **creolisation** increases both the complexity and functionality of the language, resulting in increased expressive capability and greater capacity for use in numerous domains of life. What happens next to the creole depends on the particular society in which it has developed. If it has emerged alongside a standard language, it may develop in such a way as to take on more and more features of that standard. If this happens, the creole is said to undergo **decreolisation**. Alternatively, it might remain as a creole. Once a creole has reached a certain stage of development it is also possible for it to generate new pidgins, in which case the whole process begins again.

Cameroon Pidgin well illustrates the concepts discussed above that are typical of pidginisation. For example, the pronoun system of Cameroon Pidgin (Table B7.3.1) demonstrates simplification via regularisation.

Table B7.3.1 Todd (1984: 7)

Subject	Object	Possessive determiner	Subject	Object	Possessive determiner
a	mi	ma	I	me	my
yu	yu	yu	you	you	your
i	i/am	i	he	him	his
i	i/am	i	she	her	her
i	i/am	i	it	it	its
wi	wi	wi	we	us	our
wuna	wuna	wuna	you (plural)	you	your
dɛm	dɛm/am	dɛm	they	them	their

As will be apparent from the above table, a significant amount of simplification has taken place in Cameroon Pidgin. There is no indication of gender, for example, in the third-person pronouns, nor is there a distinction made between subject and object forms. In such varieties, contextual information becomes increasingly important for interpreting speaker-meaning. Nevertheless, the simplification that is typical of pidgins is also governed by linguistic rules – it is not the case that anything goes. For example, Todd (1984: 5) points out that to form a negative statement in Cameroon Pidgin you put *no* in front of the verb. To give extra emphasis *no* can also be put in front of any nouns in the sentence, but without *no* before the verb the sentence is ungrammatical. So, as Todd (1984: 5) demonstrates, *No man no bin kam* ('Nobody came') is an acceptable sentence in Cameroon Pidgin while *No man bin kam* is not.

The mixing that is typical of pidgins can be seen in the vocabulary of Cameroon Pidgin which utilises lexis not only from English but also from the local vernacular that forms the substrate. Todd (1984: 14) gives the following examples:

fɔn	chief
nchinda	chief's messenger
mbombo	namesake
ngɔmbi	spirit, god
birua	enemy

pulpul	grass skirt
akara	beancake
kaukau	sweet potato
fufu	pounded yam
kindam	crayfish

But while borrowing of words from the local vernacular is used as one means of extending the lexicon of a pidgin, communicative necessity means that this cannot be the principal source of vocabulary. **Calquing** is also used, a process in which 'ideas borrowed from the local cultures [are] expressed in English words' (Todd 1984: 15). Some examples from Todd include:

gud hat	sincere (literally, 'good heart')
krai dai	a wake, funeral celebration (literally 'cry die')
biabia mɔt	moustache, beard (literally, 'hair mouth')

Pidgins and creoles, then, demonstrate some of the means by which English has developed and spread globally.

THE GLOBALISATION OF ENGLISH

Unit A8 describes the rapid globalisation of English over recent years. Considering English's current status as a global language it is interesting to speculate on how the language might develop in the future. In this final unit of section B we will consider some of the possibilities.

B8.1 Attitudes towards global English

Perhaps the first issue to consider in a discussion of the globalisation of English is the attitudes that people have towards English as a global lingua franca. Pennycook (2001) summarises some of the debate in this area, pointing out the difference of opinion that exists on the subject. For example, it is not necessarily the case that the spread of English globally is seen as a good thing. If you are a native speaker of English who has never considered the issue, this might surprise you. Surely, the spread of English globally provides numerous advantages? It makes travel easier, it makes international communication more straightforward, it provides more economic opportunities, etc. The answer, of course, is that it does – but not for everyone. If you are a native speaker of British Standard English you will enjoy all of the advantages listed above of English becoming a global language. But what if you are a speaker of an international variety of English that is not recognised as a standard? What if you do not speak English at all? From these latter perspectives the development of English into a global language is perhaps not as appealing. Bear in mind too that diversity is interesting in and of itself. Encountering other languages and cultures is an enriching experience.

A further argument against the global development of English is provided by

Pennycook (2001), who cites Cooke's (1988) and Judd's (1983) assertions that English is a language of imperialism and that its global spread threatens the survival of many of the world's lesser known languages. Their argument is that the prestigious position that English occupies results in people wanting to learn and use English in order to reap the economic advantages that it brings – and this inevitably leads to the downgrading of local vernaculars which, in a worst case scenario, can result in the dying out of languages. Crystal (2000) provides numerous arguments as to why we should be concerned by this. For example, languages are repositories of history. If we lose a language (that is, if it dies out entirely as opposed to simply developing) then we lose the history of the speakers of that language – especially if theirs was an oral culture. Furthermore, language provides a means of expressing individual identity; imagine how your sense of self would be affected if your native variety were to be displaced by a global language which you were then forced to communicate in. Would you still be able to express your identity in the same way? Not least of Crystal's (2000) concerns about the dying out of languages is simply that diversity is an essential part of our humanity. Experiencing difference allows us to understand ourselves better and to empathise with other viewpoints. If the consequences of the global spread of English threaten this, then this is something that should be a cause for concern.

There are, then, complex ethical and moral issues to be taken into account as English spreads globally. Managing the international spread of English requires careful and considerate language planning and policies. If you are reading this book as part of a course, you could debate these issues in class.

B8.2 World Standard English

We saw in A6 that it makes no sense to think of languages as 'belonging' to countries. English does not 'belong' to the English. World Englishes are not corruptions of a British 'norm' but complex and developed varieties in their own right (we saw in B7, for instance, that pidgin forms of English have grammatical 'rules' just as Standard English does). Nevertheless, it is often the case that speakers of British English as a first language perceive international varieties as corruptions, partly out of a misplaced belief that diversification leads to a disregard for standards. As Crystal (2001) points out, though, the development of global English and all the varieties that constitute this *increases* the need for standard forms in order for speakers of World Englishes to communicate with one another. According to Crystal (2001: 58) what is particularly interesting about the future of global English is that speakers are likely to have to master at least two standard forms – what he calls **World Standard Printed English (WSPE)** and **World Standard Spoken English (WSSE)**. In fact, as Crystal explains, World Standard Printed English already exists insofar as Standard English is the common form used worldwide for writing in English. Only occasionally do we find national and/or regional variants in Standard English (for example, slight lexical and grammatical differences between American and British English) – and even in these cases the differences are not a barrier to comprehension. A World Standard Spoken English has not yet emerged but if it does Crystal (2001) surmises that it is likely to avoid such features as regionally based idioms and complex phoneme clusters, and to involve at least some degree of simplification. We already shift varieties according to particular contexts (I am writing this book in Standard English, for instance, though I may revert to my regional dialect when conversing with my family, as an identity marker). Perhaps we will see more of such shifting as global English develops further.

B8.3 Fragmentation or fusion?

What form might we expect English to take in the future? One conundrum concerning the future development of English is whether we can expect it to fragment – that is, to develop into numerous sub-languages that are not mutually intelligible – or whether, alternatively, we might expect it to develop to the extent where there are very few differences between international varieties of English. Crystal (2003) considers these possibilities and admits that with our current levels of knowledge about new varieties of English it is difficult to accurately predict the likelihood of fragmentation happening. He does, however, note that a number of factors might lead us to suppose that this is an unlikely scenario. The weight of material published in standard written English will continue to exert an influence on what is perceived as prestigious in terms of usage. Similarly, the ease with which it is possible to read and hear international varieties of English (via the internet, cinema, etc.) means that developing forms of English will not emerge in isolation from existing varieties. In this respect, mutual unintelligibility is unlikely to develop.

In fact, it is not necessarily the case that we need to consider the notions of fragmentation and fusion as mutually exclusive. In A8.3 I stressed the importance of considering how sociopolitical events do not necessarily affect all varieties of English in the same way. We have seen how English exists in numerous different forms – national varieties, regional varieties, social varieties, etc. It is also the case that individuals use language differently according to particular circumstances – the language you use at work or in the classroom may be very different from the language you use when out with friends. We might therefore expect the globalisation of English to lead to the fusion of certain varieties (a developing World Standard English such as that referred to above, perhaps) while at the same time retaining the diversity associated with particular local varieties of the language that are especially important for conveying identity. Burridge and Mulder (1998: 274) consider this possibility in their discussion of the related concepts of **conformity** and **diversity**. Conformity refers to levelling of difference in linguistic terms. Diversity is the opposite. Burridge and Mulder (1998) suggest that in many cases linguistic diversification is a reaction against conformity, pointing out how linguistic diversity emphasises the connection between language and identity. Developing particular localised varieties of English (even if speakers have command of several alternatives, as is likely) enables the assertion or reassertion of individual identities, which, as we have seen, is as important a function of language as communication.

Section C
EXPLORATION

EXPLORING THE HISTORY OF ENGLISH

In this section you will find language data and exercises to help you investigate some of the major aspects of the history of English for yourself. Some of these exercises are designed to raise your awareness of the language as it was at its various stages of development, some concentrate on social attitudes towards usage, and others allow you to investigate specific aspects of linguistic change. A grasp of all of these elements is important in order to understand why English has developed in the way that it has. Each unit of section C broadly corresponds with the equivalent numbered unit in sections A and B, so if you find yourself getting stuck, re-read the corresponding A and B units and you should find these will help you to make sense of the issues raised here.

As you explore specific elements of change in English over time it is useful to keep in mind two questions:

1   At what structural level does the change occur?
2   What was the motivation for the change?

With regard to the first question, it is often useful to think about language as hierarchically organised. Figure C.1 illustrates this notion by showing how the units of language combine to form progressively larger units.

The elements of the hierarchy are different depending on whether we are dealing with spoken language or written language. For example, in speech morphemes are composed of phonemes, but in written language they are made up of graphemes. Nonetheless, linguistic change can occur at all of the levels in Figure C.1. For example, the Great Vowel Shift (see B4 and D4) involved change at the phonological level – that is, a change in the sound system of English. The development of English into an analytic as opposed to synthetic language involved change at the sentence level – that is, a change in the syntactic structure of the language.

Having identified the level at which the change you are concentrating on has occurred, the next step is to consider question two and ascertain what caused the change to take place. In doing this it is important to remember that the levels in Figure C.1 are interconnected and that change at one level can generate change at another. For instance, the syntactic development of English into an analytic language was caused by the loss of morphological inflections towards the end of the Old English period which was itself caused by the fact that inflectional endings tended to be unstressed in speech. This is an example of **internal change** – a development at one linguistic level causes further developments at others. Sometimes, though, linguistic development occurs as a result of external factors. For example, American English has borrowed numerous words from Native American Indian languages as a result of the contact between the Native Americans and the early settlers in America. Another

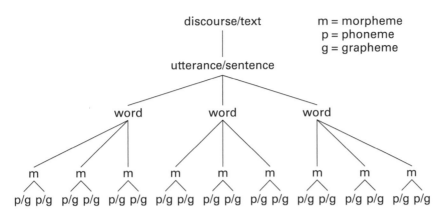

Figure C.1 Hierarchy of language (based on Jeffries 2006: 5)

external influence on the development of English was the introduction of the printing press, which led eventually to a standardised system of spelling.

One important level of change that the structural model in Figure C.1 misses, however, is meaning (this is because meaning is not a structural element of language in the way that, say, morphemes are). The semantic meaning of words can change over time (for example, OE *drēam* originally meant 'joy' or 'music' before it took on its present meaning), as can their pragmatic meanings (consider the development of the EModE second-person singular pronouns). We will consider this issue further in C7.

THE ROOTS OF ENGLISH

`C1`

In this section we will investigate the relationship Old English has with the languages from which it has developed, as well as the nature of Old English as a language in its own right. Bear these origins in mind as you investigate the language in its later stages of development as they will sometimes help you to understand where a particular word, structure or pronunciation has come from.

C1.1 Language family trees

Unit A1 outlines the number of languages that influenced the development of Old English. Celtic, Latin and Scandinavian all had an effect, however big or small, on the expansion of the Germanic dialects of the Anglo-Saxon settlers. One common way of representing the development of languages is to use a family tree to show the various relationships that exist between them. Figure C1.1.1 (overleaf) is a simplified family tree in which the bold line shows the linguistic development of English. If you trace the line back you can see that it is a language of West Germanic descent, which itself derives from a language called Indo-European. If we use the 'family' metaphor, English is the great-great-grandchild of the prehistoric Indo-European.

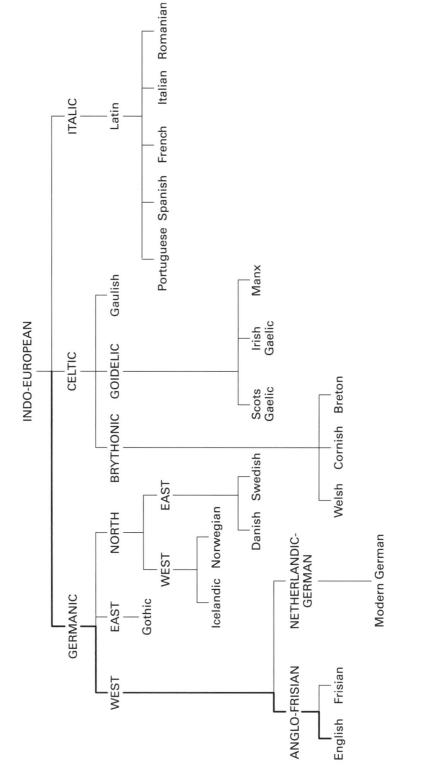

Figure C1.1.1 A language family tree for the Indo-European languages (adapted from Pyles and Algeo 1993: 68–9)

Activity

The family tree metaphor is useful for thinking about languages as it shows how languages group together because of shared characteristics. For example, you will recognise that Spanish, Italian and Portuguese *sound* similar, even if you can't describe in technical terms why. This is because Spanish, Italian and Portuguese all derive from Latin – which is now considered to be a dead language (i.e. no-one speaks it as a first language anymore). However, family trees do not give the complete picture of a language's development. To think through this issue in a bit more detail, try answering the following questions (some suggested answers are given in the Comments below).

i   What important elements of the development of Old English does the family tree *not* show? (Hint: think about the languages that Old English borrowed words from.)

ii   Re-read (or read!) section A1.1. Based on what you know of the earliest inhabitants of Britain (the Britons) and how they lived, how accurate is the family tree in reflecting the language they would have spoken?

iii English is often described as a living language, while Latin is said to be a dead language. Can languages really be dead or alive? How useful is this metaphor?

Comments

i   The family tree misses out quite a lot of important information in the development of Old English. We know, for example, that Old English borrowed a large number of words from Latin, but the family tree suggests that English did not have any contact with Latin at all. Similarly, the family tree shows no contact between English and Celtic, or English and the Scandinavian languages. Later on in the development of English, French had an important effect on the language (see C.3) – but again, the family tree misses this out completely.

ii   The family tree gives the impression that all languages can be traced back to a single, overarching language. But this 'top-down' view gives a false impression of how languages develop. We know, for instance, that the Britons lived in fairly disparate communities, perhaps often far apart from each other. The idea that all these communities would speak in exactly the same way therefore seems a bit far-fetched. It is more likely that they spoke various dialect forms of Celtic. But the language family tree does not show up the contribution that dialects make to a language's development.

iii When we talk about a language being 'dead', we mean that it is no longer spoken as a first language by anyone. This metaphor suggests that languages are living entities. But languages are not born and they do not die. A language only 'dies' when the last of its speakers dies (or, in fact, when the last but one of its speakers dies; after all, if you're the only remaining speaker of a language, who are you going to talk to in that language?). Consequently, using the 'family' metaphor to describe languages might be misleading in that it can lead to incorrect assumptions about how languages are created. It's important to remember that a language is not a tangible thing. The development of a language is to a large extent affected by the development of its speakers, and the society in which they live. A language family tree does not take account of this.

C1.2 Pronouncing Old English

Activity ✪

Using the pronunciation guide in B1.1, try pronouncing the following Old English words. Does your pronunciation help you to work out what each word means?

wǣpen	*forbēodan*	*swīnhyrde*
tōdæg	*dēaþ*	*blæc*
steall	*cirice*	*dægtīd*
smiþ	*wulf*	*scearp*
mancynn	*wulfas*	*ðornig*
hors	*drȳgan*	*ūpweard*
hlaf	*meolc*	

The answers are *weapon, today, stall* (for cattle), *smith* (as in blacksmith), *mankind, horse, loaf* (as in bread), *to forbid, death, church, wolf, wolves, to dry, milk, swineherd, black, day-time, sharp, thorny, upward*. Were you right? Did any (parts) of the words cause you problems? If so, why was this?

C1.3 Case

In B1.3–1.5 we saw how case was more important in Old English than it is in Present Day English, and how nouns and determiners have to 'agree' – i.e. the determiner (if used) needs to be in the same case as the noun it precedes. Table C1.3.1 outlines the different forms of the determiner in Old English. You will also notice the form of the determiner depends not only on its case but also on gender (whether the noun it precedes is masculine, neuter or feminine) and number (whether the noun is singular or plural).

Table C1.3.1 Forms of the determiner in Old English

	Singular		
	Masculine	*Feminine*	*Neuter*
Nominative	se	sēo	þæt
Accusative	þone	þā	þæt
Genitive	þæs	þǣre	þæs
Dative	þǣm	þǣre	þǣm

	Plural		
	Masculine	*Feminine*	*Neuter*
Nominative	þā	þā	þā
Accusative	þā	þā	þā
Genitive	þāra	þāra	þāra
Dative	þǣm	þǣm	þǣm

Activity

Each of the PDE sentences below has one or more determiners missing. If you were going to use the correct Old English determiner, which would you need to fill the gaps? Use the table above to work out which form is needed.

1 _____ king was tired ('king' is masculine).
2 _____ horse was strong ('horse' is neuter).
3 The king loved _____ queen ('queen' is feminine).
4 The king loved _____ swans ('swan' is feminine).
5 _____ king's swans were beautiful ('king' is masculine).
6 _____ queen gave _____ swans food ('queen' is feminine; 'swan' is feminine).

Activity

Now try a similar exercise. This time we'll use a couple of sentences in Old English. These two sentences are extracts from an Old English version of a medieval romance, *Apollonius of Tyre*. You can find the text in Quirk et al. (1975: 15) and the word-for-word translation that I have given below each sentence is based on Quirk et al.'s more natural-sounding translation. For each sentence, I have given you the gender of the words that follow the determiner.

1 _____ ōðer him andwirde ond cwæð: 'Swīga ðū['] ('ōðer' is masculine).
   (The other him answered [i.e. answered him] and said: 'You be silent'.)
2 Ðā ðā Arcestrates _____ cyningc hæfde _____ gewrit oferrǣd [. . .]
   ('cyningc' is masculine; 'gewrit' is neuter).
   (Then when Arcestrates the king had the letter read [i.e. had read the letter].)

The answers are:

1 Se ōðer him andwirde ond cwæð: 'Swīga ðū['].
2 Ðā ðā Arcestrates se cyningc hæfde þæt gewrit oferrǣd [. . .]

C2 REGIONS AND DIALECTS

If we want to investigate different dialects or different international varieties of Present Day English, we can collect data directly from speakers of such varieties simply by recording examples of their speech (it may be costly and time-consuming, but theoretically at least it is fairly straightforward). Investigating different varieties of older forms of English is more difficult, of course, since we don't have access to spoken language or an abundance of evidence of how language was used in different contexts. Nevertheless, it is still possible to gain an insight into regional variation by looking at, for instance, texts which exist in more than one version. This is what we will concentrate on in this unit. We will also look at how place-names provide evidence of different tribal settlements in Britain, which can also provide evidence for the origins of particular dialects.

C2.1 Dialectal differences in an Old English text

Activity ✪

> Here are two versions of an Old English text (from Toon 1992: 432–3). One is in the West Saxon dialect and the other is in the dialect of Northumbria. Read the texts out loud and practise your pronunciation. Does this help you to recognise the text?
>
> ### *Version 1* (West Saxon)
> fæder ure þu þe eart on heofonum
> si þin nama gehalgod
> tobecume þin rīce gewurþe ðin willa
> on eorðan swa swa on heofonum
> ūrne gedæghwamlican hlāf syle us to dæg
> & forgyf us ūre gyltas
> swa swa wē forgyfað ūrum gyltendum
> & ne gelǣd þu us on costnunge
> ac alys us of yfele
>
> ### *Version 2* (Northumbrian)
> fader urer ðu bist in heofnum
> sie ðin noma gehalgad
> to cymeð ðin rīc sie ðin willo
> in eorðo suae is in heofne
> userne [ofer witlic] hlāf sel ūs todæg
> & forgef us usra scylda
> suae uoe wē forgefon usum scyldgum
> & ne inlæd usih in costnunge
> ah gefrig usich fro yfle

⭐ **Activity**

> You may have recognised the text as you read it aloud. It is *the Lord's Prayer*, sometimes called the *Pater noster*, or the *Our Father*. (If you're not familiar with the PDE version, look it up. You will be able to find it quickly on the internet).
>
> Re-read the texts closely and compare the West Saxon and Northumbrian versions. How do they differ? What can you infer from looking at the two versions about how Northumbrian was pronounced? Can you identify any inflections? Do these differ between the West Saxon and Northumbrian versions? What does this suggest about the two dialects?
>
> Now compare both OE versions with a PDE version of the prayer. Which OE words have survived into Present Day English and how have they changed? Have any of the OE words been replaced by words borrowed from other languages? (Use an etymological dictionary to find out the origins of borrowed words.) Do any of the OE forms survive in PDE dialects?

C2.2 Place names

Studying place names can give us an insight into the geographical settlement of particular groups of people, including when such groups settled. Knowing this can help us in tracing the origins of English and can sometimes provide insights into the origins of particular dialects.

Cameron (1996) identifies two different types of place names: **habitative** and **topographical**. A habitative place name is one which denotes inhabited places such as farms, buildings, enclosures, etc. An example is *Lenham*, which is developed from a compound of the personal name *Lēana* and *hām*, the OE word for 'village' (literally, 'Lēana's village'). Note that place names can be formed via **compounding**, in the same way as other words in the lexicon (see B1.2). Indeed, Cameron (1996) notes that many habitative place names are a compound of two elements; the first is often the name of a person or group while the second refers to the type of habitation. Another example is *Heckmondwike*, a compound of the personal name *Hēamund* and OE *wīc* ('house', 'dwelling place' or 'village').

Topographical place names describe some feature of the landscape – either natural or artificial; for example, a tree, a ford, a river, etc. Again, compounding of elements is common and this gives us such names as *Bradford* (broad + ford), *Whitchurch* (white + church; 'white' perhaps in reference to white limestone), *Millbrook* (mill + brook). It is also common to find personal names as the first element in a topographical compound. An example is *Huddersfield*, which derives from a compound of the OE personal name *Hūd(a)* or *Hūdrǣd* and *feld*, meaning 'open land' (or 'field' in PDE).

What makes the study of place names useful in the history of English is that the elements of which they are made up reflect the variety of languages which have been spoken in Britain over the years. Understanding the etymology of place names can help us to see who lived where and give us some indication of how the country was settled. In terms of what place names contribute to our understanding of the

C2

development of English over time, Ekwall (1960: xxix) points out that they 'give hints as to the districts where a British population preserved its language for a comparatively long time'. Tracing the etymology of place names can show how the administration of particular places changed over time. For example, *York* derives ultimately from the Celtic name *Eboracon*, which itself comes from the word *Eburos* – which either means 'yew' or is a personal name (Reaney 1960: 24). *Eboracon* was then Latinised (the practice of re-spelling a word to make it sound and look more like Latin) by Roman settlers to *Eboracum*. Following the departure of the Romans from Britain, York came under the control of the Angles who began to use the name *Eferwic*. Reaney (1960: 24) explains that this was likely to be because in this period <b> had come to be pronounced as [v]. The element *Eber* was therefore likely to have sounded to Anglo-Saxon ears like *eofor* – the OE word for 'boar'. The second element *wīc*, as we have seen above, could refer to a village, resulting in an Anglo-Saxon name meaning something like 'boar-village'. When York later came under the control of the Scandinavian settlers (see A1.5), the Danes once again adopted the existing name but spelt it in a way that reflected their own pronunciation – *Iorvik*. This then went through a series of spelling changes, including *Iork*, *ʒeork* and *ʒork*, before eventually becoming present-day *York* sometime in the thirteenth century. In this example, then, changes in the place name over time reflect wider political changes in society.

To investigate place names you need to be aware of some of the common elements and which languages they come from. Here are some of the most frequent elements and the languages from which they are derived:

Celtic elements

A few Celtic words survive as place name elements. Examples include *brocc* ('badger') in the name *Brockholes* ('badger holes') and *tor* ('hill') in the name *Dunster*. Many river names are of Celtic origin, including *Cray*, *Medway* and *Colne*. *Avon* as the name of a river is from the Celtic word for 'water' which also gives rise to the variant forms *Esk* and *Usk*. Cities with names that were originally Celtic include *Carlisle* (developed from the Celtic personal name *Luguvalos* plus Celtic *Cair* meaning 'city' or 'fortified place'), *York* (from *Eboracon*; see above) and *London* (from *Londinos*). As we have seen in the case of York, Celtic names were often Latinised by Roman settlers. *Londinos*, for instance, became *Londinium*.

Latin elements

Few Latin elements remain in English place names. Ekwall (1960) lists the following:

castra	a city or walled town, a Roman fort or camp (e.g. Lancaster, Lanchester; the similar sounding element in names such as Doncaster and Manchester is OE *ceaster* which is derived from the Latin element)
portus	a port (e.g. Portsmouth, Portland)
strat	street – i.e. a Roman road (e.g. Stratford, Streatham; *strat* was borrowed into OE, becoming *strǣt*)

In addition, Latin elements were added to some place names in later periods. For example, Lyme became Lyme Regis in the thirteenth century (*Regis* meaning 'king'). Weston-super-Mare acquired its Latin element (*super-mare* meaning 'on sea') also in the thirteenth century.

Anglo-Saxon elements

bury/burgh	fortified place (e.g. Loughborough, Canterbury)
bridge/brig	bridge (e.g. (Cambridge, Stocksbridge)
cliff	cliff, rock (e.g. Wharncliffe)
dale	dale, valley (e.g. Borrowdale)
don	hill, down (e.g. Swindon)
ey	island (e.g. Walney)
field	open land (e.g. Sheffield, Wakefield)
ley	clearing, glade (e.g. Honley)
ham	village, manor, estate, settlement (e.g. Rotherham, Rockingham)
hamm	enclosure, bend of a river (e.g. Higham)
ingas	people of (e.g. Hastings, Worthing)
ton	farmstead (e.g. Bolton)

Some place name elements are confusing because of their similarity. For example, *ham* and *hamm* have different meanings but are often spelt *ham* in PDE. It is also common to find place names composed of more than two elements. For example, *Birmingham* derives ultimately from the personal name *Beornmund*, the *–ingas* element meaning 'people of' and *–ham* meaning 'village'; hence, 'the village of Beornmund's people'.

Scandinavian elements (Old Norse and Old Danish)

beck	stream (e.g. Caldbeck, Sandbeck)
by	village, farm (e.g. Quarmby, Whitby)
carr	brushwood, marsh (e.g. Redcar)
rigg	ridge (e.g. Haverigg)
slack	shallow valley (e.g. Witherslack)
thorpe	farm, hamlet (e.g. Grimesthorpe)
thwaite	meadow, clearing (e.g. Slaithwaite)

French elements

A few place name elements can be attributed to French, such as *bel/beau*, meaning 'beautiful'. Examples of such names include *Beaulieu* ('beautiful place'), *Beaumont* ('beautiful hill') and *Beauchief* ('beautiful headland'). Occasionally we find French elements (e.g. the definite article) in place names, such as *Chester-le-Street* or *Chapel-en-le-Frith*. More commonly, French influence on place names is seen in the changed pronunciation of Anglo-Saxon forms. For example, the sound [tʃ] at the beginning of the place name element *ceaster* did not exist in Norman French and so French speakers would commonly pronounce the sound as [s]. The legacy of this can be seen in the pronunciation of such place names as *Gloucester* and *Cirencester*. Finally, some place names include elements which are French personal names. Examples include Melton *Mowbray*, Shepton *Mallet*, Aspley *Guise* and Drayton *Beauchamp* (see Cameron 1996 for more of these).

You may have noticed from the above examples that in addition to place names sometimes being formed from more than two elements, it is also the case that place names are sometimes made up of elements from more than one language. An example is *Redcar* (OE *hrēod* 'reed' + Old Norse *kiarr* 'marsh'). We therefore have to be careful when investigating place names not to jump to conclusions about likely etymologies. Try to find out whether one element came first, or what reason there might be for a mixing of two languages in a place name. Think about what this might tell you about the social contact between different groups of settlers and what consequences this might have had for the development of English.

Activity ✪

The examples in the list of common place name elements above often contain more than one element. In each case I have usually explained just one of these elements. The <-ley> element in *Honley*, for instance, means 'clearing' while the first element is either from OE *hān* ('stone') or *hana* ('woodcock'), or may be a personal name (i.e. 'Hana's clearing'). Using a dictionary of place names, investigate some of the unexplained elements in the examples above. Are they from the same language as the second element? If not, what might this suggest about settlement and integration? What do the elements suggest about the nature of these early settlements?

Activity ✪

The place names *Norfolk* and *Suffolk* refer to 'Northern people' and 'Southern people' respectively and reflect the geographical settlement of the Angles in the northern and southern parts of East Anglia. In a similar manner, *Sussex* means 'south Saxons'. Bearing this in mind, where else in the country are the Saxons likely to have settled? (Think about similar-sounding place names).

Activity ✪

Choose some British place names not listed above (perhaps places nearby if you live in Britain) and investigate their etymologies. An excellent resource for studying place names is the University of Nottingham's online *Key to English Place Names* (http://www.nottingham.ac.uk/english/ins/epntest/keytoepn.html). Alternatively, use a dictionary of place names, such as Mills (1998) to do this. From what historical period do they originate? Which language(s) are they formed from? Can you identify any common elements? Do the names tend to be habitative or topographical, or do they derive from other sources (personal names, for example)? Can you make any connection between the place names you have investigated and wider social events referred to in section A?

In places where one group of settlers were conquered by another, it was often the case that the invaders did not simply replace the existing place name with a different one from their own language. Why do you think this was and what consequences does it have for our interpretation of place names?

FROM OLD ENGLISH TO MIDDLE ENGLISH

C3

The changes that were occurring towards the end of the Old English period eventually gave rise to a form of English that was markedly different from OE. In this section we will consider how the vocabulary of English was expanded as a result of borrowing words from other languages, and we will explore some of the characteristics of Middle English by looking at some extracts from Middle English texts.

C3.1 Loanwords

The rich vocabulary of English is a result of the extent to which it has borrowed from other languages during the course of its history. In the early part of the Old English period borrowing was uncommon though some of the vocabulary of Old English was Latin in origin, having originally been borrowed into Germanic dialects before the arrival of the Anglo-Saxons in England. Following the Viking raids later on in the period, Scandinavian loanwords were introduced into English. During the Middle English period, borrowing as a source of new words increased and Latin and French loanwords entered English.

When investigating the borrowing of words into English we need to be aware that words are not always borrowed directly. That is, a word may have been borrowed into English from French but the word in question may originally have been borrowed into French from Latin. An example of this is the word *charter*, which was borrowed into Middle English from the Old French *chartre*, which itself came from the Latin *charta*. It is also the case that the etymology of a word may be obscured as a result of changes in spelling. For example, *adventure* was originally borrowed into English from French (*aventure*), though the later addition of a *<d>* suggests a Latin origin. A similar case is *debt* which is a French loanword (*dette*), though the later addition of a *<b>* suggests it too originated from Latin. In fact, it didn't and the *<b>* was added as a result of an etymological reinterpretation caused by the influence of Latin. Sometimes, suffixes on Latin loanwords were changed to more common French suffixes, thereby further confusing the origin of the borrowed word. For instance, the French suffix *<-ie>* (which later become *<-y>*) was often used in place of the Latin *<-ia>*, giving rise to *letanie* (*litany*), *familie* and *custodie*. Below are some examples of loanwords borrowed into Middle English.

Scandinavian loanwords

In B3.3 we considered the reasons for the development of Old English into an analytic language and we saw that contact between groups who spoke different languages (or, at least, dialects) from one another was a major influencing factor in this. One such group was the Scandinavians. Unsurprisingly, the arrival of the Scandinavians led to the borrowing of numerous words from Scandinavian dialects into Old English. Although direct borrowing did not occur during the Middle English period, many of the words borrowed into OE dialects found their way into the ME southern dialects. Of those still used in PDE that have a Scandinavian origin, Björkman (1969) lists, among many others, *anger*, *bask*, *booth*, the place name suffix *<-by>* (see C2.2; *<-by>* also survives in the PDE term *bylaw*), *carp* (as in 'to talk' or 'to brag'; still found in some regional British English dialects), *grime*, *husting*, *lug* (as in 'to drag'), *meek*, *rotten*, *rugged*, *same* and *sly*.

French loanwords

Following the Norman Conquest of 1066, loanwords from French were gradually absorbed into English. Section B3 explains how the division between Early and Late Middle English is in part determined by the number of French loanwords in English in these two periods, there being substantially more in Late Middle English. Serjeantson (1935) lists the following words, among many others, as being borrowed into English from French during the Middle English period (I have given you the PDE spellings): *capon*, *court*, *rent*, *ginger*, *justice*, *grace*, *bacon*, *chaplain*, *cardinal*, *mercy*, *purple*, *nunnery*, *acquit*, *debt*, *challenge*, *countess*, *tournament*, *chastity*, *cruel*, *dangerous*, *courtesy*, *feast*, *office*, *baron*, *sergeant*, *sermon*, *parliament*, *angel*, *merchandise*, *dungeon*, *baptism*, *humility* and *treason*.

Latin loanwords

In the Middle English period, Latin borrowings included the following: *implement*, *exorbitant*, *legitimate*, *simile*, *cardamon*, *diocese*, *memorandum*, *requiem*, *abacus*, *conviction*, *persecutor*, *redemptor*, *limbo*, *library*, *credo*, *Pater noster*, *comet* and *equator*.

Activity ✪

> Divide the French loanwords listed above into appropriate semantic categories (for example, you might choose 'food' as one grouping). Based on these categories, can you make any comment on the type of words that were borrowed from French? What does this suggest to you about the nature of contact between French speakers and English speakers? Now try the same activity for the Latin loanwords. Which spheres of life are represented by loanwords from Latin?

Activity ✪

> Among the many words borrowed into English from Scandinavian were the pronouns *they*, *their* and *them*. What do these words and the Scandinavian loanwords listed above suggest to you about the nature of contact between the Scandinavian settlers and the Anglo-Saxon groups already in England at the time of the Viking invasions?

Comments

When we talk about vocabulary we can make a distinction between **open class** words (also called **lexical words**) and **closed class** words (often referred to as **grammatical words**). Open class words include nouns (e.g. *chair, happiness, boxes, silence*), verbs (e.g. *go, ran, followed, is*), adjectives (e.g. *red, heavy, apparent, interesting*) and adverbs (e.g. *slowly, suddenly, fast, carefully*). In the closed class category we find conjunctions (e.g. *and, but, if*), prepositions (e.g. *on, at, in, under*), auxiliary verbs (e.g. *may, must, should, will*), determiners (e.g. *the, a, this, some*) and pronouns (e.g. *he, them, us, you*). Most of the loanwords above are open class words as, indeed, are any new words that are coined in Present Day English.

You will probably have noticed that the loanwords from French relate to spheres of life that would have been dominated by those high up in the social hierarchy. So, for instance, there are words relating to law, administration and finance. Latin – as the language of the church – inevitably contributes a substantial number of religious words. The Scandinavian loanwords, on the other hand, appear to come from spheres of everyday life. Furthermore, the words borrowed from Scandinavian include the pronouns *they*, *them* and *their* – closed class words. For closed class words to be borrowed into English suggests very close contact between Scandinavian settlers and Anglo-Saxons, and the borrowing of these words was likely also to have been motivated by the similarity between the languages of these two groups.

C3.2 *The Canterbury Tales*

As a way into making sense of Middle English, let's have a look at a Middle English text. One of the most famous examples of Middle English is Geoffrey Chaucer's *The Canterbury Tales*, a collection of stories written in the fourteenth century and supposedly told by a group of travellers as they make a pilgrimage to Canterbury. Below is an extract from the beginning of 'The General Prologue', followed by a translation into PDE. Read the Middle English text and try to make sense of it before you read the translation.

Extract from 'The General Prologue'

Whan that Aprill with his shoures soote
The droghte of March hath perced to the roote,
And bathed every veyne in swich licour
Of which vertu engendred is the flour
Whan Zephirus eek with his sweete breeth
Inspired hath in every holt and heeth
Tendre croppes, and the yonge sonne
Hath in the ram his half cours yronne,
And smale foweles maken melodye,
That slepen al the nyght with open ye
(So priketh hem nature in hir corages),
Thanne longen folk to goon on pilgrimages

Extract from 'The General Prologue' (PDE translation)

When April with its sweet showers
Has pierced the drought of March to the root,
And bathed every vein [of the plants] in such liquid
Of which power the flower is engendered [i.e. created]
When Zephirus, also, with his sweet breath
Has inspired [i.e. breathed life into] every grove and heath [i.e. field]
Tender crops, and the young sun
Has run half his course in the ram [i.e. Aries]
And little birds make melody [i.e. sing]
That sleep all the night with open eye
So nature pricks them [i.e. provokes them] in their hearts
Then folk long to go on pilgrimages

Activity ⭐

First, try reading the extract aloud using the guide to pronunciation in B3.2. Once you have done this, read the extract again and consider the following questions:

❏ In what ways does the language differ from Old English?
❏ What do you notice about the pronouns in the extract?
❏ What has happened to the meanings of *licour* and *foweles* over time?

Comments

Did you find it difficult to understand the extract? My guess is that although there may have been particular words that you struggled with (*soote, holt, corages*, perhaps?), in general you will have found it easier to make sense of than the Lord's prayer in C2.1. Middle English seems much closer to PDE than Old English. Nonetheless, there should be elements of the language that you recognise as being clearly developed from OE. For example, some of the verb forms include Old English inflections – *slepen* (from OE *slǣpen*), *mak<u>en</u>* (from OE *macian*) and *goo<u>n</u>* (from OE *gegangen*). You may also have noticed that *whan* is now spelt with initial <wh> as opposed to the initial <hw> of OE *hwanne* (see B3.2). With regard to the pronouns in the extract, *his* is not masculine as you may initially have thought. It was commonly used as an indefinite form in the Early Modern period (see B5.2). In terms of vocabulary, Middle English borrowed extensively from French, as we saw in B3.4. Evidence of this can be seen in the extract: *perced, licour, vertu, engendred, inspired, cours, melodye, corages* and *pilgrimages* are all French loanwords. What you may have noticed about *licour* and *foweles* particularly is that over time they have narrowed in meaning. Whereas *licour* originally meant any form of liquid, it now refers solely to strong alcoholic drinks. And *foweles*, meaning *birds*, now refers specifically to birds that are eaten as food. This narrowing of meaning is considered in more detail in C7, where we concentrate on the formation of new words in English.

C3.3 A Middle English *Pater noster*

In C2.1 you examined two different versions of the Lord's Prayer (or **Pater noster**) in Old English. Here is a version in Middle English taken from *The Pater Noster*, attributed to John Wycliffe, in Arnold (1871: 93–6):

> Oure Fadir þat ert in hevenes, halwid be þi name
> þi rewme come to þee
> þi wille be doon; as it is fulli doon in hevene so be it doon and in erþe
> To ȝive us oure eche days breed to day
> Forȝive us oure dettis, as we forȝive to oure dettouris
> Leed us not into temptacioun
> But, gracious Fader, delyvere us from alle yvel
> Amen

 Activity

Compare the Middle English version of the prayer with the Old English versions in C2.1. What differences in grammar and vocabulary do you notice? What evidence is there that this is a text from fairly early on in the Middle English period?

CODIFICATION AND ATTITUDES TOWARDS ENGLISH

C4

In B4 you can read about some of the important sound changes that occurred in the Early Modern period. As we saw, one of the possible explanations for why such changes occurred is a social explanation; namely that attitudes towards particular varieties of speech may have caused speakers (either consciously or unconsciously) to alter their way of speaking. The important point here is that attitudes to language use can often determine its development. This is also true in the case of written language. Section A5 outlines the importance of the printing press in the development of a standard form of English, and as this standard variety developed so too did a desire to codify the language – that is, to write down the 'rules' that governed its use. A problem that can be seen in many of the early dictionaries, grammars and style guides, however, is that the writers of such texts tended to be **prescriptive** as opposed to **descriptive**. They were intent on explaining what people should and shouldn't do when they used English. In contrast, modern linguists simply describe *how* people use language. They do not judge this usage (though they may sometimes explain *why* certain varieties are often deemed less prestigious than others). The activities below allow you to investigate codification and attitudes towards English in the work of early writers on English usage.

C4.1 *A Table Alphabeticall*

The first monolingual English dictionary was Richard Cawdrey's *A Table Alphabeticall*, published in 1604 (see A5.3 for more details). From the perspective of modern linguistics it is easy to be critical of the problems with such early work on the English language, and so it is important to remember the pioneering steps that such early writers on language were taking. Nonetheless it is worthwhile considering the kinds of misapprehensions such writers had about the nature of language, since an understanding of these helps us to fully appreciate the capacity of language to develop.

Activity ✪

The title page of Cawdrey's *A Table Alphabeticall* (Cawdrey 1604) contains the following statement:

A Table Alphabeticall, contayning and teaching the true writing and vnderſtanding of hard vſuall Engliſh wordeſ, borrowed from the Hebrew, Greeke, Latine, or Frenche, &c.

With the Interpretation thereof by plaine Engliſh wordeſ, gathered for the benefit and help of all vnſkilfull perſonſ.

Bearing in mind the professed aim of *A Table Alphabeticall*, consider the extract from it below. What problems can you see with Cawdrey's definitions? Try comparing the extract with extract 2 from Johnson's dictionary of 1755. What information does Johnson's dictionary convey that Cawdrey's doesn't? What information is not present in either entry that you would expect to find in a PDE dictionary?

Extract 1 – *A Table Alphabeticall* (Richard Cawdrey)
abjure, renounce, deny, forſweare

Extract 2 – *A Dictionary of the English Language* (Samuel Johnson)

To ABJURE. v.a. [abjuro, Lat.]

1. To caſt off upon oath, to ſwear not to do ſomething.

Either to die the death, or to *abjure*
For ever the ſociety of man. *Shakeſp. Midſum. Night's Dream.*

No man, therefore, that hath not *abjured* his reaſon, and sworn allegiance to a preconceived fantaſtical hypotheſis, can undertake the defenc of ſuch a ſuppoſition. *Hale's Origin of Mankind.*

2. To retract, or recant, or abnegate; a poſition upon oath.

Comment

Cawdrey's aim in his dictionary was to define so-called 'hard' words and to be successful in this he needed to be confident that his readers would be able to understand the synonyms (words of similar meanings) he used to define the target word. *Abjure* comes from Middle French and is defined using *renounce* and *deny*, which also come from French, and *forsweare* which is of Old English origin. Whether French-derived words would have been helpful to define another French-derived word depends on how well known they would have been to the reader. At the very least, we can assume that this was a dictionary aimed at an already fairly well-educated speaker. An additional issue is that although Cawdrey's dictionary was aimed at educated readers, there would still have been a problem if Cawdrey's definitions of 'hard' words were hard words themselves – i.e. not known by the reader. What the entries from Cawdrey's dictionary lack is an indication of how the target word is used in context. Johnson's dictionary goes much further towards explaining this by providing quotations containing the target words. Johnson's dictionary also gives the language from which the target word was borrowed, and takes account of the two senses of the target word. It was in all respects a phenomenal achievement for one man. Additional information that you might expect in a PDE dictionary would include a phonetic transcription indicating the pronunciation of the word and, potentially, pragmatic information about the context in which the word is usually used.

C4.2 *English Orthographie*

In C4.1 you considered some of the issues with the first monolingual dictionary of the Early Modern English period. Now let's consider a writing guide of this period. Owen Price's *English Orthographie* was published in 1668 and was aimed at both teachers and students. As with Cawdrey's dictionary, the title page (Figure C4.2.1) gives us an indication of the aims of the book.

⭐ **Activity**

Looking at the title page of *English Orthographie*, it is clear that EModE spelling is on its way to becoming the Standard English that is common today. What specific features of the text on the title page strike you as typical of Early Modern English? Can you note any differences in spellings and orthographic practices between this text and Present Day English? For example, what rules does Price appear to employ concerning when to use word-initial capital letters? When you have thought about this, read through Price's own explanation for his practices in this respect (Figure C4.2.2 overleaf). Which rules are still used in PDE? Can you suggest reasons why some of these rules have fallen out of usage?

Englifh Orthographie

OR

The Art of right fpelling, reading,
pronouncing, and writing all fortf of Englifh Wordf.

WHEREIN

Such, as one can poffibly miftake, are digefted in an Alphabeticall Order,
under their feveral fhort, yet plain Rules.

ALSO

Some Rules for the points, and pronunciation, and the ufing of the great letters.

TOGETHER WITH

The difference between words of like found.
All which are fo fuited to every Capacitie, that he, who
ftudies this Art, according to the Directions in
the Epiftle, may be fpeedily, and
exactly grounded in the
whole Language.

Figure C4.2.1 Title page of Owen Price's *English Orthographie* (Price 1668)

Of the great Letters

Q. How do you know when to write the great Letters?
A. That may be a great Letter, which is the firft in

1. *A proper name of a perfon, or place, as* Charls, England.
2. *The firft letter in a Sentence, as the firft letter in your writing, or the firft after a period.*
3. *The firft letter in a verfe.*
4. *I, by it felf, is a great, I, as I am.*
5. *All thofe words that imply an emphafis, or what is remarkable, must be written with a great letter.*

Figure C4.2.2 Extract from *English Orthographie* (Price 1668: 40)

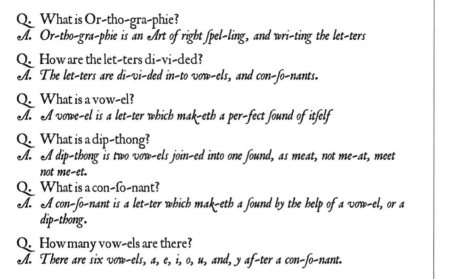

> Q. What is Or-tho-gra-phie?
> A. Or-tho-gra-phie is an Art of right ſpel-ling, and wri-ting the let-ters
>
> Q. How are the let-ters di-vi-ded?
> A. The let-ters are di-vi-ded in-to vow-els, and con-ſo-nants.
>
> Q. What is a vow-el?
> A. A vow-el is a let-ter which mak-eth a per-fect ſound of itſelf
>
> Q. What is a dip-thong?
> A. A dip-thong is two vow-els join-ed into one ſound, as meat, not me-at, meet not me-et.
>
> Q. What is a con-ſo-nant?
> A. A con-ſo-nant is a let-ter which mak-eth a ſound by the help of a vow-el, or a dip-thong.
>
> Q. How many vow-els are there?
> A. There are six vow-els, a, e, i, o, u, and, y af-ter a con-ſo-nant.

Figure C4.2.3 Extract from *English Orthographie* (Price 1668: 4)

✪ Activity

Read through the extract from the book – a series of questions and answers (Figure C4.2.3). What problems can you see with Price's answers to the questions he poses? What assumptions and misconceptions does he make? (NB: In the introduction, Price explains that he has 'syllabicated' words 'for the ease of a beginner' – i.e. he has hyphenated words to indicate the number of syllables in the word when spoken.)

Comment

An interesting point about the extract from Price's book is the presupposition inherent in his definition of orthography as 'the art of right ſpel-ling, and wri-ting the let-ters'. The presupposition, of course, is that there is indeed a 'right' (i.e. 'correct') way of spelling and writing in English and that anything other than this is wrong. As we saw in B5, this is a notion that did not exist in the Middle English period when variation was a defining feature of written language. Similarly, there was considerable freedom of choice for writers during the Early Modern period (see, for example, C5.2 and C5.3). Towards the end of the Early Modern period, however, the pendulum was swinging in the opposite direction and standardisation was being actively promoted. Sometimes, though, the pursuit of a written standard was based more on prescriptive rules than on descriptive ones. In the case of *English Orthographie* it would seem that there is an attempt at descriptive rules, though these are not always useful.

Price's attempt to provide some ground rules concerning English orthography is admirable yet runs into difficulties from the outset. This is because he does not differentiate clearly between letters and sounds. In answer to his question 'What is a vowel'?, Price explains that it is 'a let-ter which mak-eth a per-fect found of itfelf'. The problem is that a vowel is primarily a feature of speech, not writing (see B4.1 for an explanation of how we produce vowel sounds in English). What Price means is that a 'vowel' in written language is a grapheme which may be used to represent a vowel *sound*. Furthermore, his explanation that a vowel 'mak-eth a per-fect sound of itfelf' does not provide enough explanatory detail for us to understand what he means. What is 'a perfect sound'? We can see when we look at his next question ('What is a dip-thong?') that what he means by 'vowel' is 'monophthong', but this is only really clear if you already know what a diphthong is. (Notice that his definition of a diph-thong relies on the reader understanding what a vowel is, thereby resulting in a circular definition!) Price's confusion of letters with sounds continues in his last question and answer, in which he explains that there are six vowels. A more accurate answer would be that there are six letters with which we can represent vowel sounds (there are many more than six vowel sounds in English).

In general, it seems that Price views writing as primary, as opposed to speech. Because of this, he runs into difficulties when trying to explain such concepts as vowels and consonants. Nevertheless, it would appear that Price is at least attempt-ing to provide a description of standard practice (as can be seen in his explanation of when to use capital letters). He is also sympathetic towards students whose teachers may have been using the book in class; in a marginal note next to the extract above, he writes: 'If this correction of the letters will not sink into the blockish, or ignorant Teacher's head, let him go off to spelling'! (Price 1668: 4).

C4.3 Problems with prescriptivism

In linguistics, being **prescriptive** involves telling people how they *should* use language – e.g. telling them that they should always use a capital letter at the start of a new sentence. Being **proscriptive** involves telling them what they *shouldn't* do – e.g. telling them that they should never end a sentence with a preposition. Being **descriptive** involves, obvi-ously enough, describing *how* people use language – e.g. if we notice that people often end sentences in presuppositions when they write, then we don't judge this as wrong; we simply record it as something that people commonly do in written language. It follows from this that a descriptive rule is simply a rule based on having observed what people do when they use language. A descriptive rule regarding Standard English, for example, is that we put an <-*s*> inflection on the third-person singular form of the verb.

Activity ✪

Prescriptivism and proscriptivism became increasingly common in the later part of the Early Modern period (you can read about some of the wilder excesses of this in D5.1), but prescriptive and proscriptive views are also often heard today. Try to come up with answers to the questions below con-cerning the problems with prescriptive and proscriptive attitudes towards language usage. If you are reading this book as part of a class, discuss your answers with other students in your group.

❑ Why does it not make sense to take a prescriptive attitude towards usage? (Hint: think particularly about the focus of section A of this book and the nature of language itself).

❑ Is there any situation in which prescriptivism should be tolerated?

❑ Read the article published in *The Observer* newspaper, concerning the use of English by employees of the BBC (Figure C4.3.1, below). What are the problems with the views expressed by those who believe that 'presenters and correspondents on both television and radio routinely misuse words, make grammatical mistakes and use colloquialisms in place of Standard English'?

Mind your language, critics warn BBC

Mistakes prompt a demand for grammar to be policed

The BBC is being urged to appoint a language chief by critics who claim that its reputation as a bastion of the Queen's English is fading fast.

They claim that presenters and correspondents on both television and radio routinely misuse words, make grammatical mistakes and use colloquialisms in place of Standard English.

Sir Michael Lyons, chair of the BBC Trust, will receive an open letter tomorrow calling for a 'democratic airing' of the proposals, which advocate the creation of a new post to scrutinise 'the syntax, vocabulary and style' of thousands of staff heard on the air.

Although the BBC has a department dedicated to pronunciation, it has no equivalent for vocabulary or grammar.

Among the signatories are Professor Chris Woodhead, the former chief inspector of schools, Lord Charles Guthrie, the former chief of the defence staff, and MP Ann Widdecombe. 'We do so because language deeply affects all branches of society,' says the letter.

Widdecombe argued that the way in which language was used by broadcasters had a huge impact on society. 'I think promoting the proper use of language is important. Whereas the BBC is better than most, even it is starting to get a bit slack,' she said. 'Mass communication has a tremendous effect.'

She and others want managers at the BBC to consider the suggestion by Ian Bruton-Simmonds, a member of the Queen's English Society, that it appoint a head of grammar. Under the proposals, 100 unpaid 'monitors' working from home would note grammatical slips or badly chosen vocabulary. The checkers would then report to a central adviser, who would write to broadcasters outlining what was said and what should have been said.

According to Bruton-Simmonds, also author of *Mend Your English or What We Should Have Been Taught at Primary School*, regular mistakes by BBC correspondents spread fast through society.

He blamed the corporation for ruining a number of words, giving the example of the noun, replica. Correctly defined as a 'copy, duplicate or reproduction of a work of art', Bruton-Simmonds complained that it was now used in place of 'imitation', 'likeness' and 'model'. He first noticed the mistake when a *Blue Peter* presenter, standing by a railway engine, held up a model of it and said: 'It's an exact replica.' Radio 4 presenters such as Jim Naughtie and Carolyn Quinn have come under fire along with other young presenters across radio and television. Broadcasters are said to make mistakes such as mixing up singulars and plurals and using 'may' instead of 'might'. One of the most common mistakes cited by language campaigners is the incorrect use of the word 'refute'. They point out that the word means to disprove, not deny. On one broadcast about the death of Pakistan cricket coach Bob Woolmer, the presenter said Woolmer's 'wife Gill refutes speculation that her husband may have taken his own life following Pakistan's exit from the World Cup'.

But it is not all bad news. According to signatory James Cochrane, whose book *Between You and I, A Little Book of Bad English* has an introduction by the broadcaster John Humphrys, one man never makes mistakes. 'You do not hear them on the Terry Wogan show because he is a well educated man of a certain age,' argued Cochrane. He said he was supporting the campaign because 'the BBC ought to be a defender of good English'.

It is likely to be a tough battle. A BBC spokeswoman admitted there was no regular monitoring of correspondents. 'Grammar guidance is currently available to our staff on the corporation's intranet,' she said. 'It is only there for guidance; there are no set rules on grammar.'

Others said the critics should accept language was fluid. 'Language evolves and we should evolve with it,' said Adam Jacot de Boinod, author of *The Meaning of Tingo*, which highlights the weaknesses of English by listing foreign words for which there is no English equivalent.

He said once people reached 40, they often felt nostalgic for what they were taught as children – and if the call for a language adviser was simply 'to be pedantic and yesteryear', he would oppose it.

Figure C4.3.1 Anushka Asthana and Vanessa Thorpe, *The Observer*, 28 October 2007

 C5   **FURTHER ELEMENTS OF GRAMMAR IN EARLY MODERN ENGLISH**

In B5 we looked at some of the grammatical characteristics of Early Modern English. In this section we will consider some more of these and investigate some of the developments that have occurred over time.

C5.1 More on pronouns

In Early Modern English the second-person pronoun was socially marked (read B5.2 if you haven't already done so), as well as having different forms depending on whether it was first-, second- or third-person, singular or plural. Over time, however, the practice of marking social status through pronouns stopped. Why do you think this happened? It might help you to think through the issues if you imagine what it would be like if Present Day English still had socially marked pronouns. What problems might you encounter when using these? Would the mode of communication (speech or writing) influence your decision as to what forms to use? What might be the consequences of choosing the 'wrong' form? Can you see any advantages to this system? (If your first language is a language that marks status in pronouns – e.g. French or German – you will already have an insight into this.) Consider these issues and, if possible, discuss them with another student before reading the comments below.

Comments

Leith (1983: 107) points out that pronouns are directly associated with social interaction and suggests that because of this, we are perhaps especially sensitive to their effect in conversation. Although it is probably impossible to state definitively the reasons for the decline in the use of socially marked pronouns in English, we can at least speculate on some likely explanations. One likely problem, of course, is that you would not necessarily have always known which pronoun was the right one to use. Embarrassment or even offence might be caused if you referred to someone as *thou* and they were expecting *you*. Leith (1983) suggests that this might have been a particular concern for the middle classes. Whereas the upper-classes were sure of their position in society, the middle class was more fluid (having money often bought you a place among the middle classes, even if you were of more 'humble' origins). Consequently, it was not always easy to tell who was deserving of the more polite *you*. A safer option was to use the polite form regardless of the social status of the person you were talking to. Notice that this explanation relates to the sociolinguistic notion of the middle-classes being the major drivers of change in language (see A4.1). A further explanation is suggested by Barber (1997: 155) who explains how the Quakers (a religious group) favoured the use of *thou* rather than *you* owing to their egalitarian ideals. Leith (1983: 110) suggests that this may have led to *thou* becoming stigmatised as the pronoun of choice for the religious fanatic, resulting in non-Quakers favouring *you*.

When the tendency in the historical development of English has been towards regularisation, why do you think the pronoun system has not been regularised more than it has been?

C5.2 Gradable adjectives

Adjectives modify nouns – that is, they express the attributes of a noun. They can appear before the head noun of a noun phrase ('A *silent* film') or they can follow a verb and relate back to the noun phrase that is the subject of the sentence ('The film was *silent*'). Gradable adjectives are those that have comparative and superlative forms. For example, *big* (base form), *bigger* (comparative form), *biggest* (superlative form).

Activity ✪

In Present Day English what are the grammatical rules that govern the formation of the comparative and superlative forms of the adjectives *small*, *heavy*, *light* and *friendly*? What about adjectives such as *beautiful*, *unpleasant*, *reckless*, *complicated*, *good* and *bad*? When you have worked this out, read through the following examples of Early Modern English. Identify the adjectives and then note the differences that you can see in how the comparative and superlative forms of the adjective were formed in EModE.

O yes, but I forgot. I have, believe it,
One of the treacherousest memories, I do think,
Of all mankind.

(Ben Jonson, *The Alchemist*)

Brutus shall lead; and we will grace his heels
With the most boldest and best hearts of Rome.

(William Shakespeare, *Julius Caesar*, Act III, Scene I)

Arise faire Sun and kill the enuious Moone,
Who is already sicke and pale with griefe,
That thou her Maid art far more faire then she:

(William Shakespeare, *Romeo and Juliet*, Act II, Scene II)

In Belmont is a lady richly left,
And she is fair and, fairer than that word,
Of wondrous virtues.

(William Shakespeare, *The Merchant of Venice*, Act I, Scene I)

O, the most affablest creature, sir! so merry!
So pleasant!

(Ben Jonson, *The Alchemist*)

. . . transformed into the most uncleanest and variablest nature that was made under heaven;

(Hugh Latimer, *Sermons on the Card*, 1529)

'Tis very true. O wise and upright judge,
How much more elder art thou than thy looks!

(William Shakespeare, *The Merchant of Venice*, Act IV, Scene I)

> . . . there grew of necessity in chief price and request eloquence and variety of discourse, as the fittest and forciblest access into the capacity of the vulgar sort;
>
> (Francis Bacon, *The Advancement of Learning*, 1605)
>
> This cannot be, except their condition and endowment be such as may content the ablest man to appropriate his whole labour and continue his whole age in that function and attendance;
>
> (Francis Bacon, *The Advancement of Learning*, 1605)
>
> . . . the grave is more easy for me than this dungeon.
>
> (John Bunyan, *The Pilgrim's Progress*, 1678)

Comments

There are two ways of forming comparative and superlative adjectives in Present Day Standard English. For adjectives of one syllable (or those of two syllables which end in <y>, <ow> or <er>, e.g. *friendly, narrower, cleverer*), the practice is to add an inflectional morpheme: <-er> for comparatives and <-est> for superlatives. Hence, *small, smaller* and *smallest*; *heavy, heavier* and *heaviest*; *light, lighter* and *lightest*; *friendly, friendlier* and *friendliest*. This, of course, is a relic of English's past as a synthetic language. In Old English, for instance, the comparative and superlative forms of the adjective *glæd* ('happy') were *glædra* and *gladost*. (Note that a few adjectives are irregular, such as *good, better, best* and *bad, worse, worst*.) For polysyllabic adjectives we don't add an inflection but rather use an adverb – *more* for comparatives and *most* for superlatives. Hence, *beautiful, more beautiful* and *most beautiful*; *unpleasant, more unpleasant* and *most unpleasant*. If you deviate from these grammatical rules – for example, by saying *more small* or *complicatedest*, prescriptivists would accuse you of being wrong and descriptive linguists would note that you were using non-standard forms. What you should have noticed from the EModE examples above, however, is that the rules governing the formation of comparatives and superlatives in Present Day Standard English do not appear to hold for Early Modern English. Instead, we find polysyllabic superlatives formed with <-est> (*treacherousest* and *variablest*), monosyllabic comparatives formed with the addition of an adverb (*more fair*) and double superlatives (*most affablest*). We might note that in some circumstances, the use of the double superlative is perhaps employed by the **iambic pentameter** of the verse. Very briefly, iambic pentameter verse consists of ten syllables with every other syllable stressed, as in the line from *Julius Caesar*, 'With the most boldest and best hearts of Rome'. Using the double superlative in this example makes the line fit the ten syllable structure (even though in performance the grammatical words *the, and* and *of* are unlikely to be stressed). However, the fact that double comparatives and superlatives were used in literary writing suggests that they were not seen as ungrammatical (at least, not to the point of impairing meaning). Furthermore, we also find them in non-literary prose ('the most uncleanest and variablest nature'). Barber (1997:

147) suggests that there may have been a stylistic difference between the *<-er/est>* and *more/most* forms. He suggests that *<-er/est>* forms may have been considered colloquial whereas *more/most* forms might have been deemed more formal. Nonetheless, he admits that, in general, Early Modern English writers were pretty much free to decide which form to use.

Activity ✪

> Read through the following list of adjectives (some are taken from Barber 1997: 146) and discuss them with some other students. How would you form the comparative and superlative of each? Do you all agree with each other? What factors might determine the form you choose to use? What do your answers suggest about the future development of English?
>
> ❏ pleasant ❏ gentle
> ❏ unhappy ❏ friendly
> ❏ subtle ❏ simple
> ❏ common ❏ cruel
> ❏ stupid ❏ cloudy

C5.3 What did *do* do?

Activity ✪

> Read through the following PDE sentences and decide what the function of the auxiliary verb *do* is in each case.
>
> 1 I do like coffee!
> 2 Do you like tea?
> 3 I like coffee but I do not like tea.

Comments

The first sentence would be grammatically complete even without the verb *do*. The function of *do* in this example is to add emphasis to the speaker's assertion that he/she likes coffee.

In contrast, without *do* the second sentence would be grammatically incomplete (at least, in Standard British English). Generally speaking, yes/no questions are formed by inverting the subject and the verb from the position they would be in if we were making a statement. For example, to form a yes/no question out of the statement 'She is writing a letter' we invert the subject *she* and the verb *is* (that is, we swap them around). This gives us 'Is she writing a letter?' However, if the statement from which the question is derived does not contain an auxiliary verb (*be* or *have*), or if the main verb is not *be* or *have*, then we need to insert *do*. For example, the statement 'They enjoy hiking' does not contain an auxiliary verb and so in PDE we cannot simply invert the subject and verb to form a question. 'Enjoy they hiking?' is ungrammatical in Standard English. In such a case we don't invert the subject and verb, we simply insert *do* before the subject, as in 'Do they enjoy hiking?' In this respect, *do* is often referred to as a 'dummy' auxiliary.

In the third sentence, *do* is used to form a negative statement. Again, without *do* the statement would be ungrammatical.

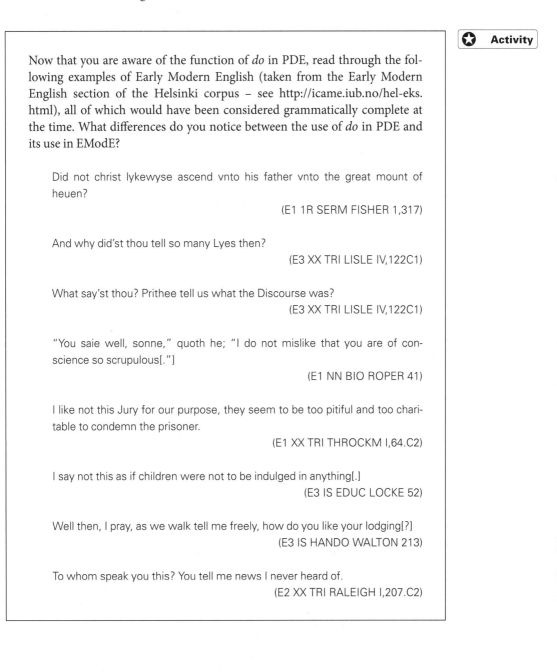

⭐ **Activity**

Now that you are aware of the function of *do* in PDE, read through the following examples of Early Modern English (taken from the Early Modern English section of the Helsinki corpus – see http://icame.iub.no/hel-eks.html), all of which would have been considered grammatically complete at the time. What differences do you notice between the use of *do* in PDE and its use in EModE?

Did not christ lykewyse ascend vnto his father vnto the great mount of heuen?

(E1 1R SERM FISHER 1,317)

And why did'st thou tell so many Lyes then?

(E3 XX TRI LISLE IV,122C1)

What say'st thou? Prithee tell us what the Discourse was?

(E3 XX TRI LISLE IV,122C1)

"You saie well, sonne," quoth he; "I do not mislike that you are of conscience so scrupulous[."]

(E1 NN BIO ROPER 41)

I like not this Jury for our purpose, they seem to be too pitiful and too charitable to condemn the prisoner.

(E1 XX TRI THROCKM I,64.C2)

I say not this as if children were not to be indulged in anything[.]

(E3 IS EDUC LOCKE 52)

Well then, I pray, as we walk tell me freely, how do you like your lodging[?]

(E3 IS HANDO WALTON 213)

To whom speak you this? You tell me news I never heard of.

(E2 XX TRI RALEIGH I,207.C2)

Comments

As with the formation of comparative and superlative adjectives, there was a greater freedom of choice for Early Modern English writers in how they formed negative statements and yes/no questions. In some of the examples above the auxiliary *do* is used exactly as it is in PDE. Sometimes, though, it is not used at all, leading to sentences that would be considered grammatically incomplete in PDE. For example, the syntactic structure of the question 'And why did'st thou tell so many Lyes then?' would be acceptable in Present Day Standard English (even though some aspects of morphology, spelling and lexis would be different). On the other hand, the statement 'I like not this Jury for our purpose' would be considered grammatically non-standard or, at least, archaic.

C6 ENGLISH IN THE NEW WORLD

As English developed in North America it was subject to contact with the languages of other settlers and with those languages of the Native Americans. Inevitably, these other languages had an influence on how American English developed. And as American English progressed into the eighteenth and nineteenth centuries, it became a powerful vehicle for the expression of national identity.

C6.1 Loanwords in American English

Contact with other languages inevitably led to the borrowing of words into the varieties of English spoken by the colonists. A selection of loanwords (drawn from Marckwardt 1980) includes vocabulary taken from the following languages:

French

pumpkin, brioche, chowder, praline, caribou, gopher, bayou, crevasse, flume, levee, rapids, cent, dime

Spanish

alfalfa, marijuana, mesquite, cockroach, coyote, mustang, chaparral, lasso, ranch, rodeo, stampede, enchilada, frijole, taco, tequila, tortilla, poncho, sombrero, canyon, sierra

Dutch

coleslaw, cookie, waffle, caboose, sleigh, stoop (meaning 'porch'), *boss, Yankee, dumb* (meaning 'stupid')

German

delicatessen, hamburger, pumpernickel, sauerkraut, schnitzel, pretzel

Activity ✪

What semantic fields do the words above come from? Does this tell you anything about the nature of contact between the early settlers in America?

Comments

What is interesting about these loanwords is, as Marckwardt (1980) points out, that so many come from the **semantic field** of food. Marckwardt (1980: 62) hypothesises that this suggests 'pleasant but commonplace social contacts', though it is difficult to arrive at this conclusion solely from examining loanwords. We would be on safer ground simply to acknowledge that food played an important part in the contact between different cultures in the early years of the American colonies.

The loanwords listed above are from immigrant groups within America at the time. Another group of people who contributed significantly to the lexicon of American English were the native inhabitants of the country: the Native American Indians. A selection of American Indian loanwords (again, from Marckwardt 1980: 30) is as follows:

Trees, plants, fruits
catalpa, hickory, pecan, persimmon, sequoia, squash

Foods
hooch, pemmican, succotash, supawn

Animals
chipmunk, moose, muskrat, opossum, raccoon, skunk, terrapin, woodchuck

Amerindian culture
powwow, totem, papoose, squaw, moccasin, tomahawk, kayak, tepee (tipi), wigwam

---

★ **Activity**

What reason would the early settlers in America have had for borrowing these words into English?

Comments

Marckwardt (1980) notes that these loanwords vary in the extent to which they have been absorbed into American English. Some words, like *moccasin* and *kayak*, are used internationally, while others are known only in particular areas of America. Others have little reference beyond the American Indian culture they are taken from (e.g. *tomahawk*). It is likely that such words were borrowed by early settlers to describe foods, plants and animals that they had no experience of in their own cultures. It should also be noted that these words were not borrowed in the form that they now take. Most have been spelled differently, often to reflect early settlers' struggles to pronounce the original forms. For example, Marckwardt (1980: 33) explains that *squash* is a shortened form of the Narrangansett word *askutasquash*, while *racoon* is a corruption of *arakunem*.

C6.2 The politics of spelling

As English continued to develop during the nineteenth century in America, so too did the attitudes towards its usage. In D5 you can read about the attempts in England during the Early Modern period of such literary luminaries as Jonathan Swift to 'fix' the English language – that is, to formulate a system of rules for so-called 'correct' usage. At the beginning of the nineteenth century, the American lexicographer Noah Webster took an opposing view to Swift and his companions and was more interested in radically changing the language rather than preserving it in the way that Swift and others had proposed. Webster's main concern was with the spelling system of English and his efforts to reform this sprang from his concern that there was an increasing divide between the spoken and written forms of the language (Simpson 1986: 58). In his *Compendious Dictionary of the English Language*, Webster expressed his views as follows:

> Every man of common reading knows that a living language must necessarily suffer gradual changes in its current words, in the signification of many words, and in pronunciation. The unavoidable consequence then of fixing the orthography of a living language, is to destroy the use of the alphabet. This effect has, in a degree, already taken place in our language; and letters, the most useful invention that ever blessed mankind, have lost and continue to lose a part of their value, by no longer being the representatives of the sounds originally annexed to them. Strange as it may seem, the fact is undeniable, that the present doctrin [*sic*] that no change must be made in writing words, is destroying the benefits of an alphabet, and reducing our language to the barbarism of Chinese characters in stead of letters.
>
> (Webster 1806: vi, quoted in Simpson 1986: 58)

Notwithstanding his extreme and somewhat erroneous view of the Chinese writing system, Webster was clearly a man with strong opinions. Indeed, his desire for reform was political as much as linguistic. He saw his efforts as contributing to the development of a growing American national identity, and the lengths to which he went are testament to how important language can be in expressing identity. Webster's suggested reforms included an overhaul of the spelling system and his efforts in this sphere gave rise to some of the differences that still exist today between spelling in American and British English. Carney (1994: 475–6) summarises some of Webster's initial proposals for spelling reform as follows:

❏ Superfluous vowels, such as word-final <*e*>, should be removed – e.g. *definit, disciplin, doctrin, granit, imagin, maiz, nightmar, vultur*.
❏ Superfluous consonants should be removed, e.g. *chesnut, crum, diaphram, ile, thum*.
❏ Vowel digraphs should be simplified, e.g. *fether, lepard, cloke, juce*.

Some of Webster's proposals, such as those above, even he considered too radical to be accepted and when he published his *American Dictionary of the English Language* in 1828, he was careful not to make any proposals that might have been deemed too outlandish (after all, he would not want to have put people off buying his dictionary).

Among the reforms that did become accepted in American English are the following (again drawn from Carney 1994: 475–6):

❏ Mass nouns spelt with *<our>* in British English are spelt *<or>* in American English, hence *armor, behavior, color, favor, honor, labor, odor, vapor, vigor.*
❏ British English *<-re>* endings become *<-er>* in American English, hence *theater, center, fiber, liter, meter.*
❏ The British English suffix *<-ise>* become *<-ize>* in American English, hence *capitalize, organize, naturalize, dramatize, analyze, paralyze.*
❏ British English *<c>* in nouns such as *defence, offence, licence, pretence, practice* is replaced in American English with *<s>*, giving rise to forms such as *defense, offense, license, pretense, practise.*
❏ The digraphs *<ae>* and *<oe>* in Greek and Latin loanwords are replaced in American English by *<e>*, e.g. *anaemia/anemia, anaesthetic/anesthetic, diarrhoea/diarrhea, encyclopaedia/encyclopedia, mediaeval/medieval.*
❏ Double consonants in unstressed syllables in British English are often single in American English, e.g. *traveler, counselor, worshiping.*

In addition to the above 'rules', American English also makes use of distinctive spellings of certain words. Carney (1994: 475–6) lists the following (British English examples are given first, American English equivalents second): *gaol/jail, tyre/tire, whisky/whiskey* (though note that in Irish English, the latter spelling is used), *plough/plow, cheque/check, draught/draft, kerb/curb.*

✪ **Activity**

What is your opinion of Webster's spelling reforms? What advantages can you see to his simplified spelling system and what disadvantages? With regard to the future development of English, what potential problems can you see with attempting to reform spelling? (Think about the relationship between sound and spelling, and also the various different 'users' of English.)

Comments

On the surface, it is easy to see why a reformed spelling system seems an attractive idea. We have seen how English spelling often represents older pronunciation (see B4.3) and how, consequently, there sometimes seems to be little connection between the spelling of a word and its pronunciation. We might quibble and say that, for instance, Webster's simplification of *cheque* to *check* makes the noun ambiguous with the verb ('to check'), but such ambiguities are easily resolved in context (plus we have no difficulty in interpreting the meaning of these terms in speech, despite the fact that they sound alike). The more important issue with spelling reforms such as Webster's is that the rules suggested are often as inconsistent as the existing practices. Carney (1994: 53) points out, for example, that if we are going to simplify the spelling of nouns that in British English end in *<-re>* (e.g. *theatre* becomes *theater*) then, logically, we ought also to change the spelling of those nouns that end in <-le> (e.g. *battle* should be spelt *battel*). This, though, has not happened. An even more important issue is the fact that accents vary and one person's pronunciation of a word can be very different to another's. For example, in some accents of American English, <r> following a vowel is pronounced whereas in other accents it is not – so *car* may be pronounced [ka:r] or [ka:]. It is not possible to represent all these accentual variations in the spelling of a word – this would require a different spelling for some accents, a practice which would contradict the purpose of having a standardised spelling system. Any spelling system, then, is always likely to favour some accents and disadvantage others.

C6.3 Early African American English

In B6.4 we considered the possibility of African American English having developed from creoles spoken by African slaves in America. Dillard (1992) sees this as a strong possibility:

> Slaves coming to virtually any part of the East Coast in the eighteenth century are very likely to have known some version of Pidgin English. From the evidence we have, what was spoken in West Africa and at sea was rather similar to what was being used in the American colonies, and not just in the south.
>
> (Dillard 1992: 65)

Krapp (1925) quotes the following extract from John Leacock's play of 1776, *The Fall of British Tyranny*, as an example of one of the earliest written representations of the speech of African slaves:

> [Context: On board a British man-of-war near Norfolk, Virginia. The scene comprises a conversation between Lord Kidnapper and Cudjo, an escaped slave.]
>
> *Kidnapper*: How many are there of you?
> *Cudjo*: Twenty-two, massa.
> *Kidnapper*: Very well, did you all run away from your masters?
> *Cudjo*: Eas, massa Lord, eb'ry one, me too.
> *Kidnapper*: That's clever; they have no right to make you slaves. I wish all the Negroes wou'd do the same. I'll make 'em free – what part did you come from?
> *Cudjo*: Disse brack man, disse one, disse one, disse one, come from Hamton, disse one, disse one, come from Nawfok, me come from Nawfok too.
> *Kidnapper*: Very well, what was your master's name?
> *Cudjo*: Me massa name Cunney Tomsee.
> *Kidnapper*: Colonel Thompson – eigh?
> *Cudjo*: Eas, massa, Cunney Tomsee.
> *Kidnapper*: Well then I'll make you a major – and what's your name?
> *Cudjo*: Me massa cawra me Cudjo.
> *Kidnapper*: Cudjo? – very good – was you ever Christened, Cudjo?
> *Cudjo*: No, massa, me no crissen.
> *Kidnapper*: Well then I'll christen you – you shall be called major Cudjo Thompson . . .
> *Cudjo*: Tankee, massa, gaw bresse, massa Kidnap.
>
> (Leacock 1776, quoted in Krapp 1925: 255)

Activity

> What evidence is there in the speech of the character Cudjo to suggest that the author is attempting to represent a pidgin? (You may find it useful to read B7.3 if you haven't already done so). How reliable is data of this kind for tracing the development of African American English?

Comments

Clearly there are attempts in the above extract to represent a non-standard form of speech via non-standard spellings. For example, the spelling of *every* as *eb'ry* suggests a pronunciation of /v/ as /b/ and the apostrophe suggests the elision of the middle syllable. *Eas* appears to be a rendering of *yes* and suggests a pronunciation of this word that begins with a diphthong (/əa/ perhaps?) rather than the palatal approximant /j/. In terms of grammar we can note the use of the object pronoun *me* rather than the standard *I*. The line 'Me massa name Cunney Tomsee' lacks a gentive inflection on *massa* and the verb *is* is missing before *Cunney Tomsee*. The line *me no crissen* lacks a verb and is a simplified form of negation. No doubt you will be able to spot other examples of this kind. There is, then, the suggestion of the simplification and mixing that is a feature of pidgins. Of course, we need to exercise caution in drawing conclusions from such data, since it is fiction as opposed to naturally occurring language and it is a representation of a variety rather than a phonetic transcription. However, the choices the writer has made in representing the speech of an African slave do at least give a suggestion as to what might have been some common features of this variety.

PRESENT DAY ENGLISHES   C7

In B7 we considered the development of international Englishes, or World Englishes as they are often called. Each variety of English has its own particular characteristics, as well as its own sub-varieties such as regional dialects, social dialects that are seen as particularly prestigious, etc. When English first began to spread beyond the shores of the British Isles the movement was very much one way. English went out into the world and developed in many different ways (see B7). But now that there are so many international varieties of English in existence it no longer makes sense to think of the development of English as being a one-way process. It is no longer the case that all varieties of English are developments of British English. Some varieties of English, for example, have developed from American English, thus their connection with British English is indirect at most. This has consequences not just for the development of the variety in question but also for the sense of ownership that native speakers have about their language. For a person growing up in India, with no connection to the UK, and speaking Indian English as a first language, their Indian English variety is the norm by which they will judge other varieties. It makes no sense anymore to take an Anglo-centric view and see British English as a base form and all other varieties as deviations from this. And because the development of English worldwide is no longer a one-way process, it is also the case that the many international varieties can affect each other's development – in terms of lexis, grammar, pronunciation, orthography, norms of usage, etc. In this unit we will look at some of the ways in which English has developed in recent years. We will concentrate particularly on lexical developments, though in unit D7 you can also read about some of the recent grammatical changes in English. As you read through this section, think about the issues raised in relation to your own variety of English.

C7.1 Unknown words from Australian English?

Activity ✪

The following is a list of colloquialisms in Australian English taken from Trudgill and Hannah (2002: 22). The authors state that these colloquialisms are 'not known in EngEng' (i.e. English English). Read through the list. How many of the words and phrases do you recognise? How many of them do you use or are used in the variety of English that you speak? If you are a speaker of British English, do you agree with Trudgill and Hannah that these words are 'not known' in your variety? If you are familiar with any of these words, think about *how* you became familiar with them.

to chunder	to vomit
crook	ill, angry
a dag	an eccentric person
a drongo	a fool
to rubbish	to pour scorn on
a sheila	a girl
tucker	food
a spell	a rest, break
to shout	to buy something (e.g. a round of drinks)
an offsider	a partner, companion
a chook	a chicken
to fine up	to improve (of weather)
beaut	very nice, great
uni	university

Comments

Despite what Trudgill and Hannah claim, I would be very surprised if you are a native speaker of British English and have not heard of at least some of these colloquialisms. An informal straw poll among my students revealed that the only item on the list that they were not familiar with was *an offsider*. Of the others, some were commonly used (e.g. *to chunder, shout, uni*), while some were known but not used (e.g. *sheila, tucker, chook*). In response to the question of how you might be familiar with these words, there are a variety of potential explanations. Some are obvious contractions – e.g. *uni* and *beaut* – which even if you don't use them yourself are not difficult to interpret. Some are, in fact, common in British English, if not in exactly the same form. *Tuck* for instance, is a colloquialism for food in some contexts (did your school have a *tuck shop*?) and is clearly related to *tucker*. Some words, on the other hand, have entered British English as a result of contact with Australian English. This is unsurprising given the popularity of Australian television shows in Britain over recent years. In this respect, international varieties of English are influencing British English (which, of course, should itself be considered just another international variety). And in this way English will continue to develop. It would seem that, at the very least, Trudgill and Hannah are confusing 'not known' with 'not used', but even so we would need to qualify this by saying something like 'not used in standard written British English'. The issue of usage is particularly important since although international varieties may share words, where they often vary is in how such words are used. For example, the short form *beaut* may sometimes be used in British English, though only as a noun (e.g. 'That's a beaut!'). In contrast, the Australian Corpus of English shows how it is common in Australian English for *beaut* to be used as an adjective (e.g. 'It's beaut, isn't it?'; 'he made my brother a real beaut dingo').

C7.2 Enlarging the lexicon

Throughout the twentieth century the lexicon of English developed substantially. Contact between languages, such as that alluded to above, is one means by which this occurred. We have seen, for instance, that borrowing words is a popular way of introducing new vocabulary into English. Over time English has borrowed from many languages – Latin, Norse, Danish, French, German, Italian, Spanish, to name but a few. But there are other means by which new words can enter the language. They can, for instance, be created from the existing word-stock. One way of doing this is through compounding, which we saw in B1.2 was greatly used in Old English. There are, though, numerous other types of word formation. Read through the list below and as you do so, try to think of your own examples for each category.

Acronyms

Acronyms are formed from the initial letters of some or all of the words in a particular phrase. Typically, the acronym is then pronounced as a word in its own right (as opposed to pronouncing each constituent initial letter). Acronyms are often found as names of organisations, for example, *NATO* (North Atlantic Treaty Organisation), *HESA* (Higher Education Statistics Agency), *BAAL* (British Association for Applied Linguistics) and *PALA* (Poetics and Linguistics Association). It is also common to find acronyms developing in institutions, where they are used as a form of shorthand among people familiar with the full terms. Examples from my own university include *CAB* (Course Assessment Board), *MAMEL* (MA in Modern English Language), *ASIS* (Applicant and Student Information) and *CATS* (Credit Accumulation and Transfer Scheme). Note too how acronyms can be used to deliberately make it difficult for people to understand what you are talking about . . . Acronyms you might encounter in everyday life include *WYSIWYG* (what you see is what you get) and *BOGOF* (buy one, get one free). Some acronyms become so well-used that they are no longer recognised as acronyms – especially if in written language they are spelled using lowercase letters. Examples include *radar* (radio detection and ranging), *scuba* (self-contained underwater breathing apparatus), *laser* (light amplification by stimulated emission of radiation), *AIDS* (acquired immune deficiency syndrome), *RAM* (random access memory) and *PIN* (personal identification number). In the case of the last, the fact that its status as an acronym is often forgotten can be seen in the way that people often use the phrase 'pin number' – the word *number* is, of course, technically redundant since this is what the <*n*> of *PIN* stands for.

Derivation

Words are made up of **morphemes**, which are the smallest units of language that carry semantic information – i.e. information about meaning. Morphemes can be either **free** or **bound**. A free morpheme is a morpheme which can stand alone. For example, *book-case* is a compound noun that is made up of two free morphemes – *book* and *case* – both of which are words in their own right. A bound morpheme is one which must always be attached to a free morpheme. The <*-s*> ending on third-person singular verbs ('he walk**s**') is a bound morpheme, as is the <*-ed*> that we put on the end of regular past tense verbs ('They walk**ed**'). These are examples of inflectional morphemes. Adding inflectional morphemes to the root of a word indicates a grammatical change (e.g. present tense to past tense) but it does not change the meaning of the word or the class that it belongs to. To do this we need to use derivational morphemes – or **affixes**. Affixes are another type of bound morpheme and affixation (the process of adding affixes) is a particularly common word formation process. In English, affixes can be sub-divided into **prefixes** and **suffixes**. Prefixes are found at the beginning of words and suffixes at the end. For example, the prefix <*un-*> can be added to the adjective *happy* to form *unhappy*. If we then add the suffix <*-ness*> we get a noun, *unhappiness*. If we add the suffix <*-er*> to the verb *research* we get a noun, *researcher*. Affixation is responsible for the creation of a vast number of words in English, many of which become absorbed into Standard English. An example of the creative use of affixation can be seen in the words that arose out of the negative criticism that the fast-food chain *McDonald's* has received over recent years. As a result of this, the prefix *Mc* has come to be interpreted in some contexts as meaning 'low prestige' and it is common to hear people talk about *McJobs* (i.e. low-skilled jobs which afford little opportunity for career advancement) and *McDegrees* (i.e. university degrees considered to be of little worth).

Back-formation

Back-formation refers to the process of removing an affix from an existing word in order to create a new word. For example, the verb *televise* was created by removing the suffix from *television*. Similarly, the verb *burgle* was created by removing the suffix from *burglar*, *laze* was created from *lazy*, and *word-process* from *word-processor*.

Blending

Blends are formed by taking elements from two existing words and combining them to form a new word – in effect, 'blending' two existing words together. For example, *netiquette*, a blend of *internet* and *etiquette*, is sometimes used to refer to appropriate linguistic behaviour when communicating online. Not far from where I live there is an entertainment complex consisting of restaurants, cinemas, a bowling alley, etc., that styles itself *Centertainment*, a blend of *centre* and *entertainment*. A nearby shopping centre advertises itself as 'the land of *shoppertunity*', a blend of *shopper* and *opportunity*. These are blends that are not in common usage, but some blends do get absorbed into Standard English – e.g. *smog* (*smoke* + *fog*), *motel* (*motor* + *hotel*) and *chortle* (*chuckle* + *snort*). *Boxercise* (*box* + *exercise*) as the name of a sport now appears to be fairly common, and has perhaps become well-established because it seems appropriate that a blend of two activities should be described using a blend of the names of these activities.

Clipping

Clipping involves the deletion of syllables from a polysyllabic word. Examples include *prof* (*professor*), *lab* (*laboratory*), *flu* (*influenza*), *uni* (*university*), *doc* (*doctor*), *pub* (*public house*), *bike* (*bicycle*), *phone* (*telephone*), *exam* (*examination*) and *wig* (*periwig*). *Advertisement* can be clipped to *advert* or the even shorter *ad*. Some clippings become so well established that we often don't realise that they are shortened forms of longer words. *Bus*, for instance, is a clipping of *omnibus* and *taxi* is a clipping of *taximeter cabriolet*. *Pram* (a clipping of *perambulator*) is an interesting example in that it loses the final three syllables and also the unstressed schwa that follows the initial consonant.

Coinage

Coinage is the creation of an entirely new word (i.e. a word with no relation to any existing word) and is a particularly rare type of word formation. Most coinages tend to be product names. Examples include *Kodak*, *Teflon* and *Xerox*. O'Grady and de Guzman (2006: 160) point out in relation to *Teflon* that the <*-on*> suffix potentially makes the word sound more scientific because of the fact that this suffix is used in existing words like *phenomenon* and *automaton*. This may have been an influencing factor in its coinage.

Conversion

Present Day English words are remarkably versatile as can be seen in the process of conversion. Conversion refers to the practice of changing the word class of an existing word to generate a new word. For example, we can use the noun *holiday* as a verb ('They holidayed abroad'), or the verb *ask* as a noun ('that's a big ask'). Conversion is a common process of word formation in Present Day English though it was not possible in Old English, since changing word classes in an inflectional language usually involves the addition of inflectional morphemes.

Onomatopoeia

Onomatopoeic words are lexical representations of particular sounds. A recent story in *The Times* newspaper about the return of the ITV news programme *News at Ten* began with the sentence 'The bongs are back'. The word *bong* in this context is onomatopoeic and represents the sound of Big Ben (the clock at the Houses of Parliament in London) striking, a sound heard at the beginning of every broadcast of *News at Ten*. Other examples include *buzz*, *crash*, *sizzle*, and *cuckoo*.

Gorno (*gore* + *porno*) is currently popular as a term to describe the kind of films that consist primarily of graphic torture scenes intended to shock the audience. Also from the film industry, *threequel* (*three* + *sequel*) is used to describe the third in a series of films. These blends are often used in a tongue-in-cheek way (for example, by film critics), but are they ever likely to become established in Standard English? Or are they more likely to fall out of usage? In what circumstances are blends absorbed into Standard English?

Here are some PDE words, along with their original forms. Can you explain why the initial <*n*> was lost in each case? (Hint: which form of the indefinite article would you use before the PDE forms?)

adder	(from OE *nǣdre*)
nickname	(from ME *ekename*)
umpire	(from Old French *nonper*)

Sometimes more than one word-formation process can be identified in the development of a word. For example, the word *blitzkrieg* ('lightening war') was borrowed into English from German during the Second World War to describe the bombing raids on London. It was then clipped to *blitz* and has since widened in meaning so that it can now mean 'an intense campaign', as in this recent example from a news story on the Cheshire County Council website: 'Some 3,000 road signs and posts have recently been removed from highways in Cheshire as part of a blitz on unwanted signage'. *Blitz* has also undergone conversion to other word classes and can now be used as a verb ('to blitz' someone or something – i.e. to carry out a blitz) and as an adjective, in which case it has acquired a further meaning ('we were blitzed' – i.e. drunk). What new words have entered your variety of English recently? Which type of word formation was used to create them? Why were they created and how likely is it that they will survive to become an established part of the lexicon? Which type of word formation process seems to be most common?

Semantic change

In addition to the word-formation processes described above, existing words can take on new meanings. Sometimes semantic **broadening** can occur, as a result of which a word's meaning becomes more general that it originally was. In Old English, for example, *hāligdæg* (PDE *holiday*) was a compound noun meaning 'holy day', though over time it has come to mean any period of rest from work. *Window* once meant simply an opening in a wall to let in light and/or air, whereas in PDE it also means a period of time ('a window of opportunity') and a work-area on a computer screen. Another example of widening can be seen in the verb *to dial*. The verb is a conversion from the noun *dial*, which was borrowed from the Latin *diale* and was in use in Middle English to refer to a flat plate or disc marked with a scale of measurement (*sundial*, for example). Following the invention of the telephone in the nineteenth century, *dial* came to refer to the movable disc that telephones used to have and which callers would move in order to make a connection to another number. The verb form *to dial* came into use to refer to the practice of moving this rotating disc. Notice, though, that we still talk about *dialling* a number even though nowadays most phones have touch-button keypads rather than a movable dial.

The converse of widening is **narrowing**. Just as some words take on more meanings, the meanings of some become more specific over time. *Liquor* originally meant liquid of any kind (see the extract from *The Canterbury Tales* in C3.2) though it now refers specifically to alcohol. The verb *to starve* which comes from Old English *steorfan* originally meant simply 'to die', though over time its meaning has narrowed so that it now means 'to die through lack of food', though in the Middle English period it meant 'to die as a result of cold'. (The Middle English sense is still used in some dialects of Present Day English.) Narrowing explains some seemingly odd uses of words in PDE. In the UK it is common at Christmas to eat *mince pies*, which are small round cakes filled with *mincemeat*. *Mincemeat*, though, is dried fruit, not meat as we would understand the word today (i.e. animal flesh). The use of the word *meat* to refer to a foodstuff that doesn't contain flesh stems from an earlier meaning of *meat* that meant food in general. This earlier sense also explains the EModE word *sweetmeat*, meaning 'confectionery'.

Motivations for semantic change

Why do the meanings of particular words change over time? Williams (1975: 174) notes the influence of contact between languages in causing semantic change. He explains, for example, how OE *deer*, which originally meant 'animal', changed to mean a specific type of animal as a result of the French word *beast* entering English. *Beast* also referred to animals generally but was viewed as more prestigious than the OE term, thus forcing *deer* to take on a narrower meaning. Blank (1999: 61) points out that in tracing semantic change there are two aspects to consider. The first is the motivation that causes a speaker to innovate – that is, to change the meaning of a word. The second is the motivation that other speakers have for adopting the change. Some potential motivating factors for semantic change suggested by Blank (1999) are:

New concept

Technological innovation caused the semantic widening of *mouse* so that it now refers to the device used for moving a cursor on a computer (the motivation for using the word *mouse* no doubt stems from a physical similarity).

Sociocultural change

Concepts shift when we change society in some way. As a result, meanings of words may change too, e.g. when periods of exemption from work ceased to coincide solely with religious festivals, *holiday* (OE *hāligdæg*, 'holy day') broadened in meaning.

Close conceptual or factual relation

Close links between particular concepts can result in changes of meaning. For example, it is common for people to use the word *infer* when they mean *imply* (e.g. *My teacher *inferred that my essay was pretty bad*). *To imply* is 'to suggest without stating explicitly' whereas *to infer* is 'to draw a conclusion based on an implication'. In cases such as the above, the meaning of *infer* thus takes on the meaning of *imply*, especially if the context makes it clear which meaning is intended.

Emotionally marked concepts

Blank (1999) notes that certain emotionally marked domains such as death, sex, bodily functions, etc., are marked as taboo. As a result, euphemisms are often used in place of potentially embarrassing alternatives – hence, the phrase 'he's passed away' uses the conceptual metaphor LIFE IS A JOURNEY to avoid using the verb *die*.

C7.3 Tok Pisin

In B7.3 we considered the development of pidgin and creole forms of English using examples from West African varieties. There are, of course, many other pidgins and creoles in existence. Tok Pisin ('talk pidgin') is the name of New Guinea Pidgin English. According to Romaine (1988: 122), it is likely that non-English speakers hearing Tok Pisin for the first time actually thought that what they were hearing was English – in fact, it is a combination of English (the lexifier) and a number of indigenous South Pacific languages (Sebba 1997: 25).

| Activity ⭐ |

Below is an example of Tok Pisin taken from Romaine (1988: 122). The speaker is answering a question from Romaine about what his impressions of Tok Pisin were when he first heard it spoken. How much of the extract can you understand? Can you identify the words that are derived from English? When you have thought about this, read Romaine's translation.

> Mipela ting em tok bilong waitman ia. Mipela ting tok bilong waitpela. Bihain ol i tok em i tok insait long namel i tasol. I no bilong waitman. Mipela askim kiap ol kiap mipela askim kiap. Mi tok, 'Em tok ples bilong yu?' Em tok, 'Nogat'. Disfela tok pisin em i bilong yupela bilong Niu Guini. Mipela longlong. Mipela ting em bilong kiap ia bilong gavman, tok ples bilong en, nau. Nogat.

The Standard English translation would be:

> We thought it was the white man's language. We thought it was the language of white people. Then they said that there's only a little bit [of English] inside of it [i.e. Tok Pisin]. It's not the white man's. We asked the kiaps [Australian administrative officials]. We asked the kiap. We said, 'Is this your native language?' He said, 'No. This pidgin language is your language, a New Guinean language.' We were wrong. We thought it was the kiap's language, the government's language, their native language, but it wasn't.

★ **Activity**

> Look back at the Tok Pisin extract. Using the translation, can you work out what some of the unfamiliar words mean? What does the suffix *pela* mean? What about the morpheme *yu*? What typical pidgin characteristics do you notice? (It may be useful to re-read B7.3 on the characteristics of pidgins.)

Comments

Some of the vocabulary may initially look unrecognisable but on closer inspection is clearly derived from local pronunciations of English words – for example, *ting* ('think'), *tok* ('talk'), *nogat* ('no good'), *gavman* ('government'), *ples* ('place'), *bilong* ('belong'). In this respect we can see how English is acting as a lexifier language. Romaine's Standard English translation also allows us to work out the grammatical function of some of the Tok Pisin words. The word *waitpela* is translated as Standard English 'white people', suggesting that *pela* is a suffix meaning 'people'. In fact, a literal translation of *pela* is 'fellow' (deriving from a localised pronunciation of the word), but since *waitman* is translated as the singular 'whiteman', we can work out that *pela* can act as a plural marker – so *waitpela* means 'white people' and we can note that *pela* has undergone semantic widening. From this we can work out that while *yupela* is translated as 'your', the literal translation is 'you people' (the natural-sounding translation takes into account the preceding verb *bilong*). This in turn suggests that *yu* is likely to be a second person pronoun. Indeed, *yu* turns up in the phrase *Em tok ples bilong yu?* Because we know that *yupela* divides into two morphemes, we know that *mipela* must divide this way too (i.e. *mi–* and *–pela*). And because this is translated as 'people', we can work out that *mi* on its own is likely to be a singular first-person pronoun (literally *me*, i.e. *I*). In fact, Romaine translates *Mi tok* (literally 'me talk') as 'we asked', though this is likely to be because her translation takes account of the situational context of the speaker's story (i.e. a group of people hearing Tok Pisin for the first time) to provide a more natural-sounding translation. No doubt you will be able to work out more of the Tok Pisin words using a similar deductive process, though the pidgin characteristics of the language should already be clear. The majority of the vocabulary is taken from English. Simplification is evident in the way that the pronoun system uses a minimum number of forms and marks plural pronouns by compounding the singular form with the suffix *pela*. Past tense forms of the verb are avoided – for example, *Em tok* ('him talk') translates as 'he said'. Note too how the simplification extends to the avoidance of irregular forms – *Em tok*, despite being a third-person present tense form, has no third-person marker on the verb (i.e. *tok* as opposed to **toks*). We therefore see both regularisation and a loss of redundancy (since the pronoun indicates the third person there is no need to indicate this again on the verb). Mixing is apparent in the way that phonological characteristics of the substrate languages of Tok Pisin influence the pronunciation of the English words that Tok Pisin makes use of. For instance, the long vowel in *talk* is short in Tok Pisin (the spelling *tok* suggests /tɒk/) and the labio-dental /f/ of *fellow* becomes bilabial /p/ in *pela*. Note how this short account of a small extract from a pidgin illustrates the variety of ways in which English can develop once it comes into contact with other varieties in a specific sociocultural setting.

C8 **THE FUTURE OF ENGLISH**

The rise of English as a global language raises many interesting questions concerning its future and the future of those languages that it comes into contact with and, in some cases, displaces. In this final unit we will consider some of the possible future developments for English.

C8.1 The cost of global English

The global spread of English is not without controversy. While English often brings economic advantage it can also affect the relative status of other languages. In the case of English being used as an official language in countries where it is not (or was not traditionally) a native language (e.g. Ghana), this can create numerous problems. Some of these are discussed by Phillipson (1992: 35–6). Below is a summary of his main points:

❏ In countries where English is established as an official language, speakers of the indigenous languages of that country can become alienated as their national identity is threatened by the dominance of English.

❏ The dominance of English in former British colonial countries can lead the colonised people to 'internalize the norms of the colonizers' (Phillipson 1992: 36) – that is, to absorb the social, political and cultural views of the colonial power. This can result in the loss of local cultures and customs.

❏ The use of English in such countries sustains the dominance of the usually small governing elite.

Added to these problems, of course, are the issues discussed in section B8.1 – such as the fact that English often leads to the dying out of many of the world's lesser known languages.

Activity ✪

What might be done to alleviate the potentially damaging effects of the global spread of English? Is it possible to regulate the use of English across the world? If you had the power, what policies could you put in place to prevent English displacing local languages? What chance of success might such policies have? If possible, debate these issues in a group.

C8.2 Scare stories: declining standards

From time to time stories arise in the press about the threat to literacy caused by the characteristics of text-messaging and online communication. The implication is often that English is becoming debased because people no longer know how to use it 'correctly' (you can investigate the issue of prescriptivism in C4.3). A story in the British newspaper *The Daily Telegraph* a few years ago reported that a thirteen-year-old girl had handed in a piece of schoolwork written entirely in the shorthand associated with text-messaging. Here is what she supposedly submitted:

My smmr hols wr CWOT. B4, we usd 2go2 NY 2C my bro, his GF & thr 3 :- kds FTF. ILNY, it's a gr8 plc.

(http://www.telegraph.co.uk/news/main.jhtml?xml
=/news/2003/03/03/ntext03.xml)

✪ Activity

Can you 'translate' the text into Standard English? Are the abbreviations purely arbitrary or do they follow particular patterns? What techniques of word-formation can you identify? Now consider the following questions. How likely is it that text-messaging will affect the future development of English? What factors do you need to take into consideration in order to make an informed decision? Should we be concerned about this?

Comments

The translation of the text offered in the newspaper that reported the story is: 'My summer holidays were a complete waste of time. Before, we used to go to New York to see my brother, his girlfriend and their three screaming kids face to face. I love New York, it's a great place.' Scare stories such as that above are fairly common in the press. Whether or not the text-message quoted above was really submitted as a piece of schoolwork is of less importance than the fact that stories such as this one generate a moral panic concerning falling standards in literacy. However, to believe that the techniques of text-messaging are likely to affect the development of both the English language and literacy is to ignore the fact that, as we saw in A8.3, technological innovations do not necessarily affect every *variety* of the language. Added to this is the fact that within each variety of English are a series of different **registers** – that is, language variations caused by particular social circumstances. For instance, in a job interview we tend to use a fairly formal register, whereas talking in the pub with friends will involve a much more informal style. In the former situation we would also tend to use Standard English (because of the 'prestige' that people cannot help but attribute to particular varieties) while in the latter situation we might be more likely to revert to a regional dialect, especially if this is shared with the other speakers. Prescriptivists tend to forget that we change the way we write and speak depending on the circumstances we find ourselves in. Using text-message shorthand is inappropriate for writing an academic essay because it is not versatile enough to be able to handle complex ideas and arguments, and because the extensive use of acronyms and abbreviations relies on the reader understanding all of these, which may not necessarily be the case. However, for the purposes of communicating quickly with someone who you know will understand the short forms that are commonly used, text-message shorthand is obviously appropriate. Similarly, while dialect forms are perfectly appropriate when talking in an informal situation with people from the same speech community as you, Standard English is much better when addressing, say, a group of people for whom English is a second language, because it is a variety that is commonly known internationally. So, the first mistake that prescriptivists make when bemoaning such forms as text-message shorthand is to forget that people are able to handle many different registers and varieties and that changes to one of these does not necessarily affect the others. If schoolchildren are handing in essays written in text-message shorthand then the issue is not so much that text-messaging is affecting the development of English (for this to happen the changes would need to affect other groups of people too), rather that such students need help in mastering the more appropriate registers of English available to them. A second reason why the conventions of text-messaging and e-discourse are unlikely to find their way into Standard English is that the current technology for communicating via phone and email is likely to be superseded. Indeed, to some extent this is already happening. Text-messaging shorthand arose because of the difficulties of trying to communicate quickly using a fairly primitive mobile phone keypad. Predictive texting solves some of these problems and removes the need for many of the short forms in the example above.

C8.3 Future developments in English

Activity ✪

One of the common features of the development of English over time has been its tendency towards regularisation (for example, the regularisation of plural inflections so that most nouns are pluralised by the addition of <-s> or <-es>). Make a list of as many features of English as you can think of that have become regularised over the course of English's development. Think about this in relation to the structural levels of language described at the beginning of section C and the other elements of language that we have considered throughout this book:

structure – phonology, morphology, lexis, syntax
shape – graphology, orthography
meaning – semantics, pragmatics.

Would you expect the process of regularisation to continue? What other aspects of English may become regularised? Which varieties of English would be likely to be affected?

✪ Activity

Another important issue in the development of English has been language contact. We have seen how English has been affected to a greater or lesser extent by all the languages it has come into contact with during the course of its history. As English continues its global spread, how might contact with other languages influence its continued development and how is contact with English likely to affect *other* languages? What might be the social, political and cultural consequences of such contact?

✪ Activity

In what other ways might the development of English be influenced by the growth of new technologies? Consider this issue in relation to both written and spoken language.

Section D
EXTENSION

D

READINGS IN THE HISTORY OF ENGLISH

If you have already read sections A, B and C of this book you will be well aware that the history of English is long and complex. This relatively short book spans over 1500 years of linguistic, social and political history. Not surprisingly it is impossible for it to cover every aspect of the development of English throughout this time. Indeed, I have not attempted to do this. Instead I have tried to provide enough of an overview of the language at each of its stages of development for you to be able to grasp the major aspects of its history, and to give you enough background knowledge so that you can go off and explore the history of English in more depth for yourself. To do this you will need to read widely. The nine readings in this section are intended to supplement the information contained in the rest of this book and to provide a springboard for exploring the topics covered in more detail. The readings vary in terms of type, length and complexity. Some are extracts from books and some are extracts from articles published in scholarly journals. Some deal with aspects of linguistic structure while others are concerned with wider social events and how these impacted on English. In each case I have tried to choose readings that complement and expand on the material covered in sections A, B and C, and which also give a flavour of the wide range of approaches to the study of the history of English.

D1 **VOCABULARY IN OLD ENGLISH**

This first reading follows up specifically on the introduction to the linguistic features of Old English outlined in B1 and C1. In it, the eminent Anglo-Saxon scholar Bruce Mitchell suggests that Old English syntax is actually not as radically different from the syntax of modern English as we might initially think, and that in terms of understanding Old English, vocabulary poses much more of a problem than grammar.

D1.1 Other differences between Old English and Modern English

Bruce Mitchell
Mitchell

Bruce Mitchell (reprinted from *An Invitation to Old English and Anglo-Saxon England*. Oxford: Blackwell, 1995: 25–30)

Introduction

Apart from spelling and pronunciation, there are three differences between Old English and Modern English which I would characterise as major: Old English statements can have one of three word-orders, all of which still appear in Modern German, whereas

Bruce
Mitchell

Modern English statements have a fixed order; Old English largely relies on inflexions (changes in, or additions at, the end of words, as in the possessive <*s*> in 'the ship's mast' and the plural <*s*> in 'three ships') to indicate relationships which we tend to express today by the word-order and by prepositions; and the vocabulary of Old English is mostly native Germanic, with some borrowings from Latin and from the Scandinavian languages, which were also Germanic, whereas Modern English has borrowed with brilliant ruthlessness from all the languages with which its speakers have made contact, thereby widening its capacity for the expression of new ideas, increasing its richness by the addition of synonyms, and replacing many Old English words with borrowings. As a result, less than 20% of the words which can be used in English today come down from Old English, though to be sure these are the everyday words which occur with great frequency. Even so, it may seem a startling thing to say but I have come to believe that the factor which above all makes Old English seem a foreign language to those trying to read it today is neither its inflexions nor its word-orders nor its syntax but its vocabulary.

The standard books on Old English devote much space to phonology, inflexions, and syntax, but little to vocabulary. They rarely point out, as they should, that the Old English inflexions were already much reduced and frequently reinforced by prepositions or that English syntax as we now know it has been very little influenced by contact with foreign languages. So, before we examine the differences in vocabulary between Old English and Modern English, let me demonstrate what I call the 'Englishness' of Old English syntax by quoting, first in Old English and then in a literal translation which preserves the order and lineation of the original, a passage written by Ælfric *c.* 1000:

> Sum swȳþe ġelǣred munuc cōm sūþan ofer sǣ fram sancte Benedictes stōwe on Æþelredes cyninges dæġe to Dūnstāne ærċebisceope þrim ġēarum ǣr hē forþfērde and se munuc hātte Abbo. þā wurdon hīe æ sprǣċe sprċe oþ þæt Dūnstān rehte be sancte Ēadmunde swā swā Ēadmundes swurdbora hit rehte Æþelstāne cyninge þā þa Dūnstān ġeong mann wæs and se swurdbora wæs forealdod mann. þā ġesette se munuc ealle þā ġereċednesse on ānre bēċ and eft þā þā sēo bōc cōm to us binnan fēam ġēarum þā āwendon wē hit on Englisc swā swā hit hēræfter stent. Se munuc þā Abbo binnan twǣm ġēarum ġewende hām tō his mynstre and wearþ sōna tō abbode ġesett on þǣm ylcan mynstre.

> A very learned monk came from the south over [the] sea from St Benedict's place in Æthelred's king's day to Dunstan archbishop three years before he died and the monk was called Abbo. Then were they in conversation until Dunstan told about St Edmund just as Edmund's swordbearer it told Æthelstan king then when Dunstan [a] young man was and the swordbearer was [an] aged man. Then set the monk all the account in a book and afterwards then when the book came to us within [a] few years then turned we it into English just as it hereafter stands. The monk then Abbo within two years went home to his monastery and was soon to abbot appointed in that same monastery.

(In both passages, I use only the point (.))

The differences in syntax are minimal: tautologic 'then when' twice; one definite article 'the' and three indefinite articles 'a/an' unexpressed; the different pattern for what today would be 'in King Æthelred's day'; and six or seven differences in word-order. Let us now examine wherein the differences in vocabulary between Old English and Modern English lie.

Vocabulary

As I have already said, the Old English language is predominantly Germanic. [. . .] [S]ome Old English words are recognizable from their Modern English [MnE] counterparts, although the meanings may have changed, e.g. *dēor* means '(any) wild animal' not 'deer'; *fugol* means 'bird', as in 'the fowls of the air', not 'fowl'; *lǣwede* means 'lay, as opposed to cleric' not 'lewd'; and *sellan* means 'to give' not 'to sell'. Other words differ in spelling and pronunciation as a result of changes in Middle English and Modern English. But the correspondences in the table which follows will help you to recognise the Old English forms of some of these words.

OE spelling	MnE spelling	Vowels	Consonants
lang	long	an on	
fæt	vat	æ a	f:v
hāliġ	holy	ā: o	
hām	home	ā: o.e	
āc	oak	ā: oa	c: k
hlāf	loaf		hl: l
ecg	edge		cg: dge
dēman	deem	ē: ee	
frēosan	freeze		s : z
ċild	child		ċ:ch
miht	might	ih: ī	h:gh
scip	ship		sc : sh
līf	life	ī.e	
ġiellan	yell	ie: e	ġ: y
ġiefan	give	ie: i	ġ: g
dōm	doom	ō: oo	
mūs	mouse	ū: ou.e	
nū	now	ū: ow	
synn	sin	y: i	
mȳs	mice	ȳ: i.e	

Some words from the passage can perhaps be guessed, e.g. *munuc* 'monk', *cyning* 'king', *swurdbora* 'swordbearer', and *ġear* 'year'. But some are less easy to recognise. Examples from the same passage include *ġelǣred* 'earned', *forþferde* 'forth went, died', and *ġereċednesse* 'narrative'. To these we can add *stent* which means 'stands' and which is a form *of standan* 'to stand', a word you can recognise. Here we see the same phenomenon as in MnE 'man' plural 'men' (not 'mans'). There are inevitably exceptions to the correspondences given above, e.g. OE *hāt* is 'hot' and OE *fȳlþ* is 'filth'. I shall try to help you with these more opaque words as you meet them.

Bruce Mitchell

To do this, I have now to ask you to follow me for a short distance into what Dr Johnson, the eighteenth-century lexicographer, called 'the dusty deserts of barren philology'. I have just mentioned the variation 'man/men'. These two forms descend directly from OE *mann/menn*. Such variations are common in Old English. At one time the form which has changed ended with an unstressed syllable containing the sound [ɪ] (as in 'music') or [j] (which is the symbol for the initial sound in 'year'); for *mann* the original plural was probably *manniz*. These sounds [ɪ] and [j] are made with the tongue high up in the front of the mouth and it would seem that speakers began to prepare for this high front sound before they had finished the vowel of the stressed syllable. As a result they pronounced the stressed syllable higher and/or further forward than they should have done. The unstressed syllable then disappeared, as in *menn*, or was changed in form, as we shall see later. Grammarians call this change '*i*-mutation'.

'But why should I bother about it?' The answer to this natural question is that an understanding of *i*-mutation will help you to recognise many more Old English words. If you consider the following pairs of words, you will notice that some pairs display the singular/plural variation seen in *mann/menn* but that in others the mutated form is a new word based on the non-mutated form, as in MnE 'strong/strength'.

Non-mutated		Mutated	
lang	long	*lengþ*	length
fōt	foot	*Fēt*	feet
dōm	doom	*dēman*	to deem
cuss	kiss	*cyssan*	to kiss
full	full	*Fyllan*	to fill
heorte	heart	*hiertan*	to hearten

The variation *standan/stent* above shows the same vowel relationship as *lang/lengþ* above.

Our detour has demonstrated that some Old English words were formed from others by the addition of a suffix which caused *i*-mutation, e.g. *lang/lengþ* and *fūl/fȳlþ* (in these two, the suffix was <-*iþ(u)* >) and *cuss/cyssan* and *full/fyllan* (in which the suffix was <-*jan*>). Other suffixes, which do not affect the vowel of the stressed syllable or stem, include <-*hād*>, as in *ċildhād* 'childhood'; <-*iġ*> (originally <-*æġ*>, so no *i*-mutation), as in *hāliġ* 'holy'; <-*lic*>, as in *heofonlic* 'heavenly'; and <-*sum*>, as in *hīer-sum* 'hear-some, obedient'. Words containing these suffixes present no problems to present-day speakers of English. Nor do words formed by the addition of prefixes, e.g. *beodan* 'to command', *forbeodan* 'to forbid, prohibit'; *bindan* 'to bind', *onbindan* 'to unbind'; and *drifan* 'to drive', *tōdrifan* 'to drive apart, scatter'.

The formation of words by the addition of affixes (prefixes or suffixes) was one of three main ways in which the Old English language formed new words. A second was by making compounds of two (or more) words already existing in the language. A third was by borrowing from other languages. Modern English shows a strong preference for borrowing rather than for making compounds, although we can still make compounds today, e.g. 'no-go area', 'space shuttle', 'drop-out', 'guesstimate', 'do-gooder', 'non-starter', and 'skyscraper', a word which has been used of sails, horses, and men, as well as of buildings; whoever coined it had the imagination of a Shakespeare. But the Germanic habit of compounding was much more common in Old English.

Ordinary everyday compounds like *niht-waco* 'night-watch', *hēahclif* 'high-cliff', *folc-lagu* 'folk-law', *ǣr-dæg* 'early-day', and *wīn-druncen* 'wine-drunk', present no problem. Compounds with an inflected first element include *Engla-lond* 'land of the Angles'. But the Anglo-Saxons were often faced with the problem of expressing new ideas, especially when translating from Latin texts. In such situations, they either borrowed words (see below) or made new compounds. Sometimes the elements of a foreign word were represented by Old English equivalents, e.g. *wel-willend-ness* for *benevolent-ia* 'benevolence', *fore-set-ness* for *prae-posit-io* 'preposition', and *prīness* for *Tri-nitas* 'Trinity'. But sometimes the elements of a compound were based on a meaning of a Latin word. Thus the Pharisees were seen as men professing, and rigidly bound by, the law (Matthew 23: 13–29) – hence *ǣ- lārēowas* 'law-teachers' – or as men who stood apart and thought themselves holier than other men (Luke 18: 10–14) – hence *sundor-hālgan* 'apart-holies'. That these processes are now less natural for speakers of English can be seen in various ways. First, the language now tends to prefer borrowed words rather than compounds, e.g. 'benevolence' and 'preposition' above. Second, many native compounds such as *tungol-cræft* 'star-craft' for 'astronomy' and *lār-hūs* 'lore-house' for 'school' have disappeared from the language. Third, proposed native replacements like the sixteenth-century 'hundreder' for 'centurion' or the nineteenth-century 'folk-wain' for 'bus' seem to us ridiculous, whereas to Germans *Fernsprecher* 'far-speaker' for our Greek-derived 'telephone' is not unnatural, though they do, of course, use *Telephon*.

[. . .]

We turn now to borrowed words in Old English. The largest foreign element is the contribution from Latin; over one hundred survive today. It is not always possible to know exactly when a word was borrowed. But some decisions can be made. Early borrowings include words such as *camp,* Latin *campus,* 'field, open space, battle', from which were derived *campian* 'to fight' and *cempa* 'a warrior'; *mīl* 'mile' from Latin *mille passum* 'a thousand paces'; *wīn* 'wine' from Latin *vinum*; and *mangere* '(fish)monger' from Latin *mango* 'a dealer in slaves and other wares'. These have corresponding forms in other Germanic languages. Other early borrowings include *strǣt* 'street' from Latin *strata via* and *butere* 'butter' from Latin *butyrum*. These were borrowed before <t> became <d> between vowels in Vulgar Latin between *c.* 400 and 700; compare Italian *strada* 'street, road'. A third group of early borrowings comprises words which show Germanic or early Old English sound changes that did not take place in words with the same sound which were borrowed later, e.g. *nǣp* 'neep, turnip', Latin *napus* (compare the later borrowing *pāpa* 'pope', Latin *papa*), and *munt* 'mount(ain)', Latin *montem* (compare the later borrowing *font* 'font', Latin *fontem*).

The coming of Christianity naturally led to many ecclesiastical borrowings, including the Old English equivalents of 'altar', 'deacon', 'dean', 'epistle', 'litany', 'mass', 'prior', 'stole', and 'tunic'. We find *Pharisei* 'Pharisees' and *Fariseisc* 'of or belonging to the Pharisees'. More general borrowings include *cantere* 'cantor, singer', *plaster* '(medical) plaster', *paper* 'papyrus', and *comēta* 'comet'.

Most of the Scandinavian borrowings (or loans) are found in the Anglo-Saxon Chronicle or in the Laws. About thirty appear in writing before *c.* 1016, the date of the accession of King Cnut. Examples which still survive today are: *feolaga* 'fellow, colleague', *hūsbonda* 'householder', *hūsting* 'court, assembly, tribunal' (MnE 'hustings'), *lagu* 'law', *ūtlaga* 'outlaw', and *pǣl* 'servant, slave'. Another group of thirty-three recorded after 1016 includes twelve words which are very common today: 'crooked', 'die', 'knife', 'haven', 'hit', 'root', 'sale', 'score', 'skin', 'snare', 'take', and 'they'. These everyday borrowings reflect the existence of mixed communities of Anglo-Saxons and Scandinavians. But it is very probable that most of them were in the spoken language in the tenth century. Scandinavian loans continued into the Middle English period and (more spasmodically) thereafter.

Borrowings from other languages are rare. A few words such as *engel* 'angel', *ćiriće* 'church', and *deofol* 'devil', may have reached the Germanic languages directly from Greek. Celtic elements occur mostly in place names, e.g. *torr* 'rock, rocky peak'. An early borrowing appears in Old English as *rīċe* 'kingdom'. It is parallel with Modern German *Reich* and survives as the second element in 'bishopric'. Other possible Celtic words include *assa* 'ass', *bannoc* 'piece (of cake or loaf)', *binn* 'bin, manger', and *brocc* 'badger'. The most interesting is undoubtedly OE *ambeht*, *ombeht,* which means both 'office, service' and 'servant' and was borrowed into Germanic probably direct from Celtic but possibly through Latin *ambactus*, the ultimate source of MnE 'ambassador'. It is recorded in Middle English but ultimately disappeared – only to be reborrowed in the twentieth century from Swedish as 'ombudsman'.

There are a few words which might be derived from either Latin or French, e.g. *capun* and *castel*. But we are told by Alistair Campbell [(1959)] that 'in OE no loan-words which can certainly be regarded as French occur in manuscripts older than 1066, *except prūd*, *prūt* "proud", whence are derived *prȳt*, *prȳte* "pride"'. This may well reflect the impression made by the visiting Normans on their Anglo-Saxon hosts.

D1.2 Issues to consider

❏ In the above extract, Mitchell explains how English has gained a substantial amount of its vocabulary by borrowing words from other languages. Indeed, such is the extent of its borrowing that it has been suggested that English does not so much borrow words as pursue 'other languages down alleyways to beat them unconscious and rifle their pockets for new vocabulary'! (The quotation is attributed to James D. Nicoll, who posted it on an internet discussion forum in 1990.) The joke, of course, is that while we may talk about English 'borrowing' words from other languages, a more realistic view would be to say that it steals them, since there is little sense in which it ever gives the borrowed words back to the donor languages (though, of course, such words can subsequently be borrowed *from* English *into* other languages; a more accurate description would be to say that words are copied from one language to another). In the Old and Middle English periods many words were borrowed from Latin and French. But why is it that comparatively few words were borrowed into English from Celtic and Norse? What explanation might there be for this, and what does it tell us about the factors that underlie the development of English over time?

❏ What other plurals in English can you think of that have come about as a result of *i*-mutation?

❏ While *i*-mutation explains irregular plurals such as *feet* and *mice* (cf. **foots* and **mouses*), it does not explain such irregular plurals as *oxen*, *children* and the now

D1

archaic *brethren*. What explanation might there be for why these latter type don't simply form their plural by the addition of <-*s*> or <-*es*>? (Hint: re-read section B1.4!)

D2 **OLD ENGLISH DIALECTS**

In the extract below, Joseph Crowley explains the various types of evidence – linguistic and non-linguistic – that we have for the differences between the Old English dialects, as well as the extent to which we can rely on such evidence. He suggests that looking at place-names (which you can explore in more detail for yourself in C2) is a particularly useful way of corroborating evidence about dialectal differences that have been gleaned from the analysis of Old English texts. He also discusses the Ruthwell Cross (an Anglo-Saxon cross from the early eighth century that has part of the Old English poem 'The Dream of the Rood' carved on it in runes) and the Franks Casket (a casket from the early seventh century that also has runic inscriptions in Old English), two famous artefacts and exemplars of OE dialect. Crowley also mentions the existence of an Old English **koiné**. (A *koiné* is a mixture of two or more mutually intelligible varieties – as opposed to two or more varieties that are *not* mutually intelligible) which involves some linguistic simplification of the varieties involved.) Crowley's article provides an insight into the various techniques that can be employed in the study of Old English dialects – an exercise which is made difficult by the relative scarcity of data and by the fact that the data we do have is solely written language.

D2.1 The study of Old English dialects

Joseph P. Crowley

Joseph P. Crowley (reprinted from *English Studies* 67: 97–104 (1986))

Our picture of the Old English dialects is derived from a complex of scholarship in various disciplines and scattered library locations: Old English linguistics (both descriptive and historical), Middle and Modern English dialect geography, comparative Germanic grammar, place-name studies, textual criticism, paleography, archaeology and history. Based on an investigation of much of that scholarship, this paper develops some generalisations about Old English dialects and the study of them. These generalisations specifically concern the historical context of the dialects, the linguistic evidence of them, and the linguistic criteria for distinguishing them. [. . .] These generalisations are based on many, various, and sometimes fragmentary particulars, and in making them it has sometimes been difficult to see or define overall patterns. Nevertheless, the points and examples should introduce and clarify something of what is known, and also what is not known, about Old English dialects.

Historical factors
In the genesis of the Old English dialects, post-migration factors appear to have been more important than pre-migration factors. For the most part, the dialects were not

Joseph P.
Crowley

brought over from the continent. While there is historical and archaeological evidence to support Bede's statement that the principal peoples in the settlement were the Angles, Saxons, and Jutes (cf. Myres 1970), there is even more evidence, archaeological, documentary, and onomastic, to indicate that more tribes than these three took part in the migration and that the settlement groups were heterogeneous – that there were rarely coherent, homogeneous, separate areas of settlement exclusively for the Angles or Saxons or Jutes. Though it is a fact that certain distinct regional groups in sixth-century Anglo-Saxon jewelry correspond to particular cultures of the continental Angles and Saxons respectively, this proves nothing about the *dialect* divisions of Old English in that period. The linguistic features which differentiate Old English dialects [. . .] seem to have developed in England after the migration and primarily because of isolative geographical and political conditions. The invaders probably spoke various dialects of Germanic, but the differences between those dialects were not [. . .] those that by *c.* 750 AD (the time our witness documents begin) distinguished the Old English dialects. Most of the divisions between the continental tribes were probably lost in the mixing and social reorganisation of the migration and settlement.

The chief factors, then, in shaping the attested Old English dialects seem to have been forces in post-migration England: physiography, military and political history, Christianity and education, and contacts with other languages – in order of descending importance. In the formative stages of the Old English dialects, *c.* 450–*c.* 700, isolative mountain ranges, rivers, fenlands, and vast forests probably determined the crucial divergences between speech groups. Dialect boundaries as well as the boundaries of the early kingdoms often reflect the basic physiographical factors. For example, topographical features separate the Northumbrian region from the Southumbrian; the Ribble, the Derwent, and the Severn seem to define some isoglosses distinguishing West Midland dialect from Central Midland; if data for the dialect geography of East Anglia and of Sussex were available, we would expect isoglosses shaped by the fenland and the Weald respectively. Moore, Meech, and Whitehall (1935: 27) found physiographic factors to be the most important in the shaping of Middle English dialect boundaries – which developed largely from Old English boundaries. Once regional differences in phonology and inflections developed during the proto-Old English period, the spoken dialects were probably not radically modified by later political and educational changes, for such factors directly affected the speech of only a minority of the population.

Military and political history is second to physiographical factors as a shaper of Old English dialects. The four attested Old English dialects represent the four successively dominant kingdoms in the course of Anglo-Saxon history: Kent, Northumbrian [sic], Mercia, Wessex. The dialects of the minor kingdoms do not survive, presumably because they were not used in writing nearly so much as the attested dialects were, if at all. As a kingdom prospered and led, it prompted writings in its own dialect in the scriptoria of the land. The early Bretwaldas of Kent and Northumbria, for instance, supported the church and its monasteries and funded their works, including manuscript production. The great Mercian kings of the eighth and ninth centuries and Alfred's dynasty in Wessex did likewise and also authorised many charters. Offa and Cenwulf established Mercian sub-kings, Mercian bishops, and Mercian clerics in the Southeast, a fact which helps explain the Anglian forms in southeastern texts of the eighth and ninth centuries. The fact that West Saxon dialect predominates in Old English texts is

**Joseph P.
Crowley**

much the result of the military, administrative, and educational vigor of Wessex under Alfred, Edward, Aethelstan and Edgar. The educational program begun by Alfred produced the texts of Early West Saxon; the monastic reform, which spread rapidly and widely with the support of King Edgar and the centralised administration of a united kingdom of England, produced the principal texts in Late West Saxon and indeed most of our corpus of Old English texts, for Late West Saxon had become a standard written language of England.

Less important in forming the dialects but crucial in transmitting them was Christianity. The monasteries of England and the education that came with them directly or indirectly caused practically all the principal witnesses of the Old English dialects. The teachers in the schools and scriptoria of the minsters and monasteries served as principal teachers, scribes, and shapers of written language, though they probably had little or no effect on the dialects of spoken English. The men they educated produced the writings which evidence dialects: the Bibles, glosses, charters, chronicles, saints' lives, homilies, and even elegics, riddles, and heroic epic. The most productive centers of writing were ecclesiastical centers like Wearmouth-Jarrow, Lindisfarne, York, Malmesbury, Exeter, Worcester, and especially Winchester and Canterbury. Furthermore, in certain of these centers, distinctive spellings, special types of handwriting (cf. Ker 1957: lvii–lix; Bishop 1971: xxi–xxiii), standardised vocabulary, and other scriptorial conventions were established. During the Anglo-Saxon period, there developed at least one and perhaps three standard written languages: a Late West Saxon variety, and perhaps an eighth- and ninth-century Mercian variety and a tenth-century Southeastern *koiné* for prose.[1] These standard written languages were sometimes used by clerks far beyond the bounds of the spoken dialect. For example, Mercian appears to have been written at Canterbury; Late West Saxon was used at York.

Largely as a result of the work of clerical scribes, the evidence of dialects comes to us, and it comes in writing. Its nature as writing includes certain limitations: it is subject to scribal interference and scriptorial convention. Furthermore, the evidence – written mostly by literate males in religious houses – gives no indication what was probably the range of distinctive varieties of Old English according to sociolinguistic variables such as age, education, occupation, sex, or social class.

And, incidentally, the Church preserved for us in the boundaries of its medieval dioceses an outline of the boundaries of the eight or ten early Anglo-Saxon kingdoms which existed when the various dioceses were created in the seventh century. These kingdom boundaries have been used as indicators of Old English dialect boundaries – especially where they are supported by ethnic and/or physiographical divisions. [. . .] It should be cautioned, however, that mapping of dialect areas is questionable because the primary evidence of the dialects is written language from a few, particular centers, some of which are not localised. Whether the written language of such a center was used throughout the kingdom in which the center was located is not known, nor is the exact relationship between that written language of a center and the spoken dialect of that locality (nor for that matter is the relationship between a given scribe and the conventional language of the scriptorium in which he works). (Cf. Campbell 1959: 19–20; Cameron 1982: 957.)

Contact with foreign speech groups is the least important factor shaping the Old English dialects as we know them because it has the fewest observable effects. One possible example of the influence of a foreign language is that trading contacts may account

Joseph P.
Crowley

for the parallel development of certain unique, innovative sound changes in the Kentish dialect of Old English and in Frisian. Coins, runes, place-names, and documents attest to extensive commercial contact between Kent and Frisia throughout the Middle Ages, especially between *c.* 450 and *c.* 900 when the Old English dialects were shaped (cf. Nielsen 1981; Kufner 1972: 89–90; Loyn 1962: 81–3).

The Old English dialects in texts of the period, however, were not much affected by either the Celtic of the natives or the Scandinavian languages of the Vikings. In the northern and western Anglo-Saxon territories where Celtic-speaking peoples survived, some Celtic influence is reflected in early personal and place-names, in a few orthographic conventions that occasionally appear in the earliest Anglo-Saxon manuscripts, in early Northumbrian social institutions, and in themes and motifs of literature and art. Nevertheless, Celtic had no observable effect on the basic structures of the English language or its dialects. One might speculate whether spontaneous sound changes peculiar to western England could have been influenced by Celtic [. . .]. But this cannot be demonstrated; as far as we can tell, the Celtic influence on Old English dialects was negligible.

Scandinavian influence on Old English dialects in the areas of heavy Scandinavian settlement – the Danelaw and the Northwest – must have been considerable. Many Scandinavian elements show up in the Middle and Modern English dialects of those regions, and a few structurally important items such as the personal pronouns *they/their/them* make their way into general English. But the Scandinavian influence on English dialects, which began after *c.* 850 and outside the tradition of writing, does not show up in any significant way in the records of Old English. The substantial pre-1066 texts from the Danelaw areas show either the local Old English dialect without Scandinavian influence or standard Late West Saxon. So, despite the circumstantial evidence and Middle English attestation of a significant Scandinavian influence, not much can be made of it for Old English.

Linguistic evidence

Two general sorts of linguistic evidence for Old English dialects survive: textual (glosses, poetry, and prose) and non-textual (coins, inscriptions, and names). The textual evidence is primary and fundamental. The non-textual is supplementary; it may corroborate the textual evidence or help locate the isoglosses for the distinctive features found in the textual evidence but, with the exception of the inscriptions on the Ruthwell Cross and the Franks Casket, cannot substitute for it.

The textual foundation for our knowledge of Old English dialects other than Late West Saxon is provided by a rather small number of texts, for only about twelve contain substantial amounts of English, are fairly well dated and localised, and are linguistically consistent. [. . .] A few more texts are fairly substantial and consistent but poorly localised, and a few others are substantial and localised but linguistically inconsistent (showing dialect mixture). Almost all poetic texts are so mixed dialectally as to be of little use as primary witnesses.

[. . .]

The textual evidence attests four dialects: West Saxon, Northumbrian, Mercian, and Kentish (with evidence for Kentish in texts of mixed dialectal character). Documents in West Saxon, mainly Late West Saxon, far outnumber all the non-West Saxon

Joseph P.
Crowley

witnesses put together, and they are normally better preserved, more substantial, more consistent, and more precisely dated and localised. The available data do not support a further classification into subdialects, except possibly for late Northumbrian. The evidence is fragmentary. There is no evidence for Northumbrian of the ninth century and the early tenth; for Mercian before *c.* 750, or of the later two-thirds of the eleventh century; for Kentish before *c.* 800 and after *c.* 1000; and for West Saxon before *c.* 850. Relatively few witnesses date before 950. Those that do are quite important, because texts after 950 are usually affected by the standard Late West Saxon literary language.

[. . .] The attestation for a Kentish dialect is particularly shaky. Not only are all the witnesses of mixed dialectal character, but many of the significant monuments are from only one tenth-century manuscript (British Museum MS. Cotton Vespasian D. vi.) from Canterbury. Furthermore, there is historical and manuscript evidence to indicate the use of a *koiné* in Canterbury scriptoria of the tenth and eleventh centuries (Campbell 1959: 21).

Three non-textual sources – coins, inscriptions, and names – provide supplemental linguistic evidence of Old English dialects. Coins are at present of little use, and the same is true of most inscriptions. Aside from the Ruthwell Cross and the Franks Casket, the dialect evidence of inscriptions is fragmentary, and usually inadequately localised because many of the inscribed items are portable pieces. The dating of inscriptions is likewise imprecise. The Ruthwell Cross and Franks Casket inscriptions, however, are important witnesses of early Northumbrian dialect. No other inscriptions add so appreciably to our knowledge of Old English dialects.

Place-names have made a much more significant contribution, for they provide precisely localised phonological and lexical elements. Place-name evidence is more numerous and more widely and densely distributed than are texts and also provides evidence for areas not otherwise attested. Place-names are available for various parts of almost all counties and sometimes are dense to suggest a subcounty isogloss for a feature frequently exhibited in the place-names. Place-names, furthermore, may show sound changes or dialectal vocabulary elements not common in prose or poetry. To be reasonably sure that the name elements are local and indeed represent the development of the sound being studied, name evidence must be carefully and comparatively studied.

[. . .] Names alone are insufficient to establish dialect criteria for Old English, partly because most name evidence is from later periods. Yet names are the best evidence for corroborating dialect characteristics already established in the textual evidence and for indicating isoglosses.

Note

1   For an examination of the scholarship pertaining to these standard written languages, cf. Crowley's 1981 dissertation: pp. 129–32, 197–209. Specifically for the Mercian variety cf. Vleeskruyer 1953; for West Saxon cf. Gneuss 1972; on Southeastern cf. Campbell 1959: 21.

D2.2 Issues to consider

❑   Why is it that topographical features are so important in the preservation of dialectal differences in the Old English period? (Hint: think about why regional dialectal difference is not as marked in contemporary Britain.)

❏   How might a knowledge of topographical features be helpful when studying place names in English?

❏   Crowley mentions the existence of an Old English *koiné* (defined above in my introduction to his article). What kind of simplification would you expect to find in such *koinés*?

THE INFLUENCE OF FRENCH   D3

It may initially seem strange to be reading an extract about French in a book on the history of English, but if you have already read sections A3 and B3 you will be aware that French played an important role in the development of English in the Middle English period. The extract below, from Douglas Kibbee's book, describes the kind of people who would have spoken French in England following the Norman Conquest of 1066. Knowing a little about this should help you to understand the impact of French on English during this period.

D3.1 Who spoke French in England?

Douglas Kibbee (reprinted from *For to Speke Frenche Trewely. The French Language in England, 1000–1600: Its Status, Description and Instruction*. Amsterdam: John Benjamins, 1991: 8–11, 186–8)

Douglas Kibbee

The Royal Court

Emma of Normandy married Æthelred in 1004 (or perhaps 1002, according to the *Dictionary of National Biography*), introducing the first significant French influence on English affairs (see Arnould 1958 for full treatment of pre-conquest contacts). Her son, Edward the Confessor moved to Normandy at the age of 9, when his father died and his mother remarried (to Canute, second son of the King of Denmark). Thereafter Edward was raised in Normandy, but he retained some proficiency in English. On a hunting trip, Edward is said to have called out in English to a countryman who was in his way (Clover 1888: 25). Edward apparently dealt with his subjects without an interpreter. In England, Edward is said to have given preferential treatment to his Norman cousins, although he owed his succession to the English Earl Godwin. A dispute between Eustace de Boulogne and the citizens of Dover (within Godwin's earldom), led to Godwin's exile and even stronger Norman presence at the court, at least temporarily. William, setting the stage for a conquest still 15 years off, came to visit his cousin Edward during Godwin's exile. Upon Godwin's return the next year, many of these Norman counselors fled. From the flight of the Normans in 1052 until Edward's death in 1066, Norman presence at the court was not strong, although at Edward's deathbed he was attended by Robert FitzWimark. However, the number of Normans in England was sufficient to merit special mention in the laws of William I, who refers to '*omnis Francigena qui, tempore regis Eadwardi propinqui mei, fuit in Anglia*' (cited in Wilson 1939: 9).

Douglas
Kibbee

The aristocracy

William of Malmesbury's statement that no Englishman was earl, bishop or abbot, which seems to corroborate the plaint of the *Anglo-Saxon Chronicle* that '[William] gave away everyman's land' (cited in Shelly 1921: 25), must be tested by the facts as we know them. The invasion of England was not a national migration, but rather a military conquest. While some (e.g., Vising and most recently Iglesias-Rábade) have postulated the movement of some 200,000 Normans to England during the reign of William I, Berndt (and with him most other modern scholars) has placed the number of invaders at about 5,000 men, and the total number of immigrants at no more than 20,000 (including the army). The knight service of Normandy a century later was less than a thousand men, so the higher estimates of troop strength seem far out of line with reality. The lists of French participants in the battle of Hastings such as the Battle Abbey lists include no more than 500 names (Smyser 1948), and some of these were later additions to elevate the status of more recent arrivals. The population of England at this time has been estimated at 1.5 million, making the Norman portion of the population roughly 1.3% (Berndt 1965). In 1072 one of twelve earls was English (Waltheof of Northumberland). In 1070 two of fourteen bishops were English (Wulfstan of Worcester and Siward of Rochester). In 1072, seven of the twelve abbots who signed the Canterbury Privilegium were English. In the *Domesday Book* there are large English landholders, some of whom have Norman tenants (Shelly 1921: 32–3).[1] In the royal charters of William I clear references are made to English sheriffs (e.g., Swegn, sheriff of Essex) and English thanes and barons in Kent (Shelly 1921: 33). Not only were English sheriffs sometimes able to retain their positions, but in some instances English sheriffs succeeded Norman sheriffs (see Green 1982).

In the first century after the Conquest, many of the larger landholders in England were absentee landlords, maintaining their homes in Normandy and only rarely visiting their English territories (Berndt 1965: 152). In 1086 the 190 lay barons of England, of whom only five or six were of English origin, held some 40% of the wealth of the land. Many of these contracted their marriages on the continent and continued to reside there. The lower gentry, however, along with the middle and lower classes that had come from France were quickly assimilated, often through intermarriage (as we see from the parentage of Orderic Vitalis, whose father was a native of Orléans and whose mother was English). As proof of rapid assimilation, Shelly (1921: 44) cites numerous instances in which the term 'Angli' is applied indiscriminately to Norman and English residents of the island.

At the higher levels of society, there seems to have been no compunction about mixing with the native English stock, as we see from the parents of Orderic Vitalis, one of our principal sources for information about this period. Orderic reports that Robert d'Oily and Miles Crispin married daughters of Wigod of Wallingford (cited in Shelly 1921: 61), while at the same time reporting less welcome relationships, claiming that many English women entered convents to avoid being dishonored (cited in Shelly 1921: 26).

The lower classes

Berndt (1965: 148, citing the *Cambridge Medieval History*, V, p. 513) claims that the peasantry made up 85–90% of this Anglo-Saxon population. Although the *Domesday Book* reveals that some Normans were farming, and a portion of those farming as tenants for

English landholders, the number of farmers listed as *francigenae* was less than 0.35% of the total in nine West Midland shires (Berndt 1965: 148). In the countryside, and this was an overwhelmingly rural society, there was little Norman presence, and therefore little reason to know or to use French.

Douglas
Kibbee

As for the skilled tradesmen and the merchants, we have no firm information on the ethnic breakdown of these segments of the population, but Shelly (1921: 72) alludes to the mass importation of French stonemasons to construct the castles, churches and monasteries. The numbers of French natives reported living in the major cities do not indicate total French domination of commercial activity. Furthermore, we see in the vocabulary of the building trades, as reported in Rothwell 1983 (citing Salzman 1967) a north–south division (described below). In another piece of linguistic evidence, one may wonder why, if there was such an influx of Norman craftsmen at this time, there are no words relating to crafts taken into English from Norman French. The first attested use of *mason* in an English text is from 1165 (Mackenzie 1939, II: 51).

Geographic distribution of the French-speaking population

The Normans were never more than a minute part of the rural population, and in the towns they never constituted a majority. In some towns, *novi burgi* sprung up, to house the Norman soldiers and the Norman craftsmen who came later. In 1086, according to the *Domesday Book*, 160 *francigenae* lived in Norwich, and 145 owned houses in York. Although Berndt does not consider geographic distribution (except for a rural/urban division), Rothwell (1983) offers interesting evidence for a north-east to south-west line dividing those areas where French influence penetrated more deeply and for a longer time (south of this line) from those areas in which French had little impact (north of the line). Shelly (1921: 33) notes that in the *Domesday Book* there is considerable regional variation in the numbers of English and Norman landholders. He speculates that the death, in defence of Harold, of many of the major landholders in the south-eastern counties led to a stronger Norman influence there than we find in the more peripheral areas (Devonshire, Cornwall, Wiltshire, Nottinghamshire, Lincolnshire, Yorkshire). The geographic proximity to Normandy must also have been a factor.

[. . .]

Conclusions

The study, practical or theoretical, of a language, native or second, cannot be divorced from the cultural context in which that study takes place. Furthermore, the nature of that study, down to the very language used to express it, is further evidence of the complex relationship between language, language study, and the central currents of intellectual discourse of any period.

That the French language was the object of study in England in the Middle Ages and Renaissance is the result of political, social, commercial and technological conditions which in turn determined the way in which French would be studied. Norman influence before and after the Conquest was limited consciously in an attempt to maintain an air of legitimacy. In Period I [1004–1152] therefore we have no evidence that French was the object of formal instruction to anyone. On the contrary, William tried to learn English. With Henry II and the Angevin empire came a new wave of French immigration, and the crowning period of Anglo-French literature. Still, Latin was the

**Douglas
Kibbee**

language of record in Period II [1152 – 1258], and there is still no evidence that French was formally taught: no textbooks, no student copies, no mention in literature or chronicle of such instruction.

Period III [1258–1362], starting almost two centuries after the Conquest, is decisive for the fate of French in England, and for the nature of the instructional materials that were to develop. This is the time when French became the language of English legal record, and increasingly the language of administration in a progressively more centralised government. At the same time, technological and economic developments encouraged the use of paper over wax tablets as the method of taking notes, and written record took the place of oral witness in the legal system. Commercial ties with Flanders (under a French-speaking count) and with Gascony furthered the interest in French among a broader portion of the English population. At this time, reflection on French and instruction in French began. In its initial stages French may not have been an entirely foreign language to its students, but it was further from that status than it would be at any subsequent time. Knowledge of French was required for participation in the most important aspects of government. French was the vernacular language of culture all over Europe, but its cultural appeal did not lead to adoption as an official language in Germany or Italy. In Period III, the impetus for the study of French in England was not primarily cultural but practical. This is reflected by the order of appearance of the teaching materials. First came the vocabularies, vocabularies not based on famous authors but on everyday needs. Interspersed in these vocabularies are some hints of grammar – pronominal declension and the identification of gender in nouns. The latter has always posed a particular problem for the English speaker, so its inclusion as one of two grammatical facts demonstrates not only the fact that the learners were native speakers of English but also that French was being taught independently of Latin (where the importance of gender would already be understood). In the study of the lexical items, we observe, in addition to the practical nature of the vocabulary, also the frequent distinction of homonyms, with somewhat less frequent distinction of synonyms. Homonyms are important because they present the different graphic representations of identical or similar phonetic realisations, and thus an emphasis on the oral nature of the language and the instruction; the student is learning through a process of dictation the skills that are part of secretarial use of language: copying down the words of those speaking (in private correspondence, in court of law, or in administrative record). Synonyms are important because they confirm the direction of instruction: all the synonyms are in fact translational equivalents of a single English word (e.g., 'red', or 'break'). Therefore, the language of the student and of the teacher must be English. These same grammatical and lexical facts are inserted in the orthographic treatises which appear at about the same time, confirming the interaction between these two types of texts. The orthographic treatises further demonstrate the interest in correct presentation of official documents. The elaboration of instructional materials in French is thus directly or indirectly tied to technology (replacement of temporary wax records by more permanent paper records); to politics (the creation of a more centralised administrative and judicial system dependent on written record); to the structure of society (that French rather than English became the vernacular language of written record depends on the use of French as a native language in the highest levels of the aristocracy); to commerce (the interest in certain dialects of continental French – Picard, Walloon, Gascon as well as *François* – rather than insular French); and to culture (French was assuming the role of vernacular language of culture throughout Europe). This peculiar combination of circumstances helps to explain why orthographic and lexical treatises preceded dialogues and grammars (dictation as a means of learning as well as the goal of learning; correctness of official records).

As Period III progressed, and through Period IV [1362–1470s], commerce with French-speaking people in Flanders, Anjou, and Aquitaine, as well as war-time contact between French and English populations encouraged oral production in addition to written notation of French. In this period were produced the dialogue collections of French and finally, only at the time when French was losing its grip on administrative function, a grammar of French (Barton's *Donait françois*). French became the object of serious reflection, of detailed description according to the Latin model, only when the main function of French in English society had been reduced to a social one. At this point Law French had become its own language, for which the study of continental French had no relevance. That legal language depended primarily on the mastery of verbal morphology, pronominal declension, and a number of legal and epistolary formulae. Commercial French called for similar morphological knowledge combined with a different vocabulary, one that emphasised more give-and-take, a vocabulary presented in the dialogues. In all other official functions where the vernacular was used, English replaced French. Outside of legal and commercial circles, therefore, French was more a social and intellectual exercise than a practical one.

Note

1   Shelly (1921: 78) recounts the story of a wealthy English landowner, Ligulf, who had given two bells to the new monastery at St. Albans (governed by a Norman abbot). Upon hearing the bells for the first time, Ligulf is quoted as saying, in English, 'How sweetly bleat my goats and sheep'.

D3.2 Issues to consider

❑   The extract from Kibbee's book emphasises the importance of considering how social and political factors influence the development of a language. Kibbee makes the point that the death in the Battle of Hastings of many south-eastern English landowners resulted ultimately in greater Norman influence in this part of England than elsewhere (since William the Conqueror subsequently replaced many of these men with Normans). What sort of effect might this have had on the development of English during the Middle English period? (Think about this issue in relation to the advice at the end of section A8.3.)

❑   It is sometimes suggested that Middle English emerged as a result of the creolisation of Old English (read section B7.3 if you are not familiar with the term *creolisation*). What problems can you see with this hypothesis? (Hint: think about the necessary conditions for creolisation and the effect that creolisation has on a language.)

D4 **CHANGES IN PRONUNCIATION**

Section B4 contains the background detail you need in order to grasp what happened during the Great Vowel Shift of the Early Modern period. The readings below provide more descriptive and explanatory detail. The extract from Dick Leith's book presents a description of the Great Vowel Shift to add to that found in B3, as well as a consideration of the importance of social factors as a cause for change. An extract from Jean Aitchison's book follows, in which she focuses particularly on outlining the chain shift.

D4.1 The Great Vowel Shift

Dick Leith

Dick Leith (reprinted from *A Social History of English*. London: Routledge, 1983: 145–9)

During the fifteenth and sixteenth centuries, it seems that there were radical changes in southern pronunciation. The vowels in words such as *tide* and *house*, originally long ones, became diphthongised. Those in words like *meet* and *moot* were raised to the position formerly occupied by *tide* and *house*. Many words with *ea* spellings like *meat*, whose pronunciation had been kept separate from those spelt *ee*, were raised to the same /i:/-type vowel as in words like *meet*. And other words with *a* spellings, like *mate*, were at first raised, and then diphthongised. This generally upward movement among the vowels occurred too late for the changes to be recorded in spelling. The decisions of the printers had been made, so that our modern spellings preserve the patterns of 500 years ago.

The details of the shift are notoriously difficult to work out. We often have to contend with the puzzling, even contradictory, observations of contemporary scholars. Recent attempts to reconstruct the chronology of the changes have often, moreover, disagreed among themselves. And only in very recent times have linguists tried to suggest a motivation for the shift that is rooted in a social context. Scholars in the past have been content to attribute the changes to some inherent tendency within the language itself, as though it possessed some mysterious predisposition towards the raising and diphthongisation of front vowels. Here, however, we shall look for an explanation that takes account of social stratification and the desire to mark social identity through language.

The sixteenth- and early seventeenth-century observers whose contemporary accounts we have to interpret were men who lived and worked in the south-east of England. We shall accordingly locate the origins of the Vowel Shift in Tudor London, as different dialects mixed, and as self-consciousness about class and status intensified. As a new prestige pronunciation emerged in London as a result of the shift, it gradually spread outwards and downwards in the social scale, affecting the sound-systems of other dialects. As we shall see, regional pronunciation today often preserves sound-patterns that characterise earlier stages of the shift, or even sounds that pre-date it entirely. If we look again at dialects of the extreme north of England, we find pronunciations that may help us to understand the *phonetic* basis of the shift.

Until well into the present century, a traditional pronunciation of words like *house* and *mouse* has been preserved by speakers in rural areas north of the Humber. This vowel is not a diphthong, as in RP, but a long vowel, more like the stereotyped *hoose*

Dick Leith

of Scottish pronunciation. As such, it is closer to the vowel in RP *moon* and *soon* than *house* and *mouse*. Historians of English have assumed that a vowel of this northern type existed in words like *house* over most of England, at least up to the time of Chaucer. The *oo* vowel, then, pre-dates the Vowel Shift.

The diphthongisation of this long back vowel – /u:/ – may have proceeded in the following way. Instead of the back of the tongue remaining at a constant height in the articulation of the /u:/ sound, raising began at the centre of the tongue. A glide developed, therefore, from a central vowel, /ə/, towards the /u:/ vowel. We shall call this stage one of the process. A diphthong of this type can be heard in Cockney speech today, in words like *spoon*, which sounds a bit like *spur-oon*. Gradually the tongue movement involved in the articulation of *house* became more pronounced. The initial /ə/ element in the diphthong lost its neutral quality and took on a back vowel resonance, as in modern RP, or a front vowel quality, as in many south-eastern dialects (sounding, for instance, like *heouse*, with the initial vowel similar to *bet*). We shall call this stage two. *The Linguistic Atlas of England* (Orton et al., 1978) shows over a dozen distinctive pronunciations of the diphthong which have evolved in the dialects; and the sound is particularly susceptible to regional variation in the United States.

The vowel of *house* was not the only one to be diphthongised. Words like *tide* may once have sounded like /ti:d/, with a long, high front vowel similar to that found in RP *bee* and *feed*. As in *house*, a glide from the centre (but moving frontwards) may have characterised the first stage of diphthongisation. Gradually the diphthongisation has spread through all words of this class, except in certain cases. For instance, words like *night* and *right* in many northern counties retain the earlier *ee* sound, as in *it'll be reet* (right). This is because the *gh* in the spelling registers the presence of an earlier velar fricative /x/, which in these areas has been lost relatively recently, as is explained above. The fricative kept the preceding vowel short, but when it was lost, the vowel was lengthened long after other /i:/ words had been diphthongised.

We assume that a process of diphthongisation such as we have described took place in words like *house* and *tide* in southern England. The origins of the process may be sought in a casual, informal style of speech, perhaps involving the development of a 'lax' pronunciation of the diphthongs as a means of economising on articulatory energy. Alternatively, the conditioning effect of following consonants, perhaps in a set sequence (nasals, say, before fricatives, before plosives, etc.) may afford the explanation: it has been claimed that dialect maps of northern England show that in certain areas diphthongisation is still in process of occurring before certain consonants. The fortunes of *tide* and *house* are summarised in Table D4.1.1.

Table D4.1.1 Process of diphthongisation in *house* and *tide*

	Front		Back
High	/ti:d/	monophthong	/hu:s/
Mid	/tərd/	Stage one: first element of diphthong is /ə/	/həus/
Low	/tard/ in present RP	Stage two: first element of diphthong is a low vowel	/haus/ in present RP

D4

Dick Leith

Once the vowels of *house* and *tide* had been diphthongised, there was room for the other long vowels to move upwards. Originally, the vowel of *meet* may have been pronounced with a vowel like the *é* in the French taught in school. We can symbolise this as /e:/. The vowel in words like *moot* would have been a long back vowel of similar tongue height, /o:/. By about Shakespeare's time, it is probable that the vowels in these words were much the same in quality as they are in contemporary RP.

So far, we have described only that part of the shift where high vowels are concerned. While it is conceivable that the process began at the 'top end', it is now more usually thought that it was the raising of low vowels that triggered it. To illustrate this, we shall need to look more closely at the long front vowels, which at this time were much more numerous than is the case with contemporary RP. The vowel in *meat*, as the spelling suggests, was different from that of *meet*. It may have been like that *of met*, but with a longer vowel (/ɛ:/). Finally, there was *mate*, with a low, fairly front vowel, a bit like northern *mat*, only lengthened (/a:/). Our illustration now appears as shown in Table D4.1.2.

Table D4.1.2

	Front	
High	tide	/i:/
Mid-high	meet	/e:/
Mid-low	meat	/ɛ:/
Low	mate	/a:/

It was the pronunciation of words like *mate* that seems to have been crucially important in sixteenth-century London. At first this was a short vowel, which was lengthened as the final *e* (a relic of the obsolescent inflexional system in the grammar) ceased to be pronounced; its phonetic quality would have differed from region to region. In some south-eastern dialects, notably those of Kent and Essex, it seems to have developed a relatively high pronunciation. Such a raising may be associated with forceful styles of speech, since it has been found that increased articulatory energy tends to raise front vowels. We do not have any knowledge of other sounds in these dialects at this time, but it is possible that if *mate* had a fairly high vowel, then either it had merged with *meat*, or *meat* had been raised to merge with *meet*. We can see here, then, the possibility that the Great Vowel Shift involved the 'pushing upward' of the long front vowels by the development of words like *mate*.

If we compare our diagram above with [. . .] modern RP [. . .] we find that *meet* has been raised to the high front position formerly occupied by *tide*, and *meat* now has the same vowel as *meet*. The vowel in *mate* has been raised, to the position formerly occupied by *meet*, but has since (by about 1800) been diphthongised. In regional pronunciations, however, we find different patterns. Some dialects of the north midlands have a diphthongal pronunciation of *meat* (sounding like *mate* to RP ears) which keeps it distinct from *meet*. And in many regional accents of the north, the vowel in words like

Dick Leith

mate is not diphthongised, but retains the character of the vowel in the south before diphthongisation.

We have now outlined most of the changes involved in the shift. But we have yet to suggest the mechanism. As we have seen, a relatively high variant of the vowel in *mate* was associated with the speech of Essex and Kent, and [. . .] Kentish was a stigmatised dialect. The London bourgeoisie, then, would want to distance its own pronunciation from that of the lower class, which was constantly being swelled by immigrants from these areas. One way of doing this was to raise the vowel of *mate* even higher than that of the lower-class variant; and raising of the lowest vowel in the system would necessitate raising all the vowels above and, ultimately, pushing the vowel of *tide* into a diphthong. It seems that in the speech of the bourgeoisie, the vowel of *mate* was raised to a height close to that of *meat*, so that some observers actually recorded a merger of the two sounds. It is arguable whether this actually occurred; but what the contemporary observers in the sixteenth century seem to have recorded is a picture of enormous complexity, with three competing systems in this area of long front vowels. The aristocracy, now no longer able to distance itself with the use of French, seems at first to have kept *mate*, *meat*, and *meet* distinct. At the other extreme, a third system had merged *meat* and *meet*. It appears that this was the lower-class pattern: and the fact that it is this that eventually formed the pattern for the future prestige accent need not surprise us. As is often the case, the unacceptable yesterday becomes the acceptable today.

D4.2 The Mad Hatter's tea-party

Jean
Aitchison

Jean Aitchison (reprinted from *Language Change: Progress or Decay?* 3rd edition. Cambridge: Cambridge University Press, 2001: 183–93)

Sometimes changes affect languages in a relatively minor way. Natural tendencies, exaggerated by social factors, cause disruptions, then the language restores the equilibrium again. The situation is reminiscent of day-to-day house cleaning or simple weeding in a garden, when minor problems are quickly eradicated.

At other times, however, the problem is not so easily remedied. An apparent therapeutic change can trigger off a set of wholesale shifts in which the various linguistic elements appear to play a game of musical chairs, shifting into each other's places like the participants at the Mad Hatter's tea-party. Sound shifts are better studied than syntactic shifts. In this chapter, therefore, we shall begin by looking at sound shifts.

Shifting sounds

A [. . .] well-known musical-chair movement is one which occurred in the English long vowels. It started around the fifteenth century, and is generally known as the Great Vowel Shift (see Figures D4.2.1 and D4.2.2 overleaf). [. . .] In this, all the long vowels changed places – though there is still considerable controversy as to which vowel was the 'Mad Hatter' which started this general shift.

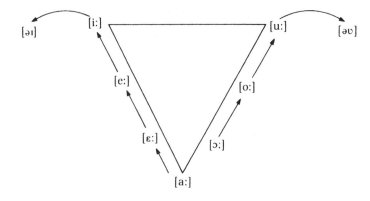

Figure D4.2.1 The Great Vowel Shift

Great Vowel Shift							
Middle English		became	Early Modern English		became	Modern English	
[a:]	[na:mə] 'name'	⟶	[ɛ:]	[nɛ:m]	⟶	[eɪ]	[neɪm]
[ɛ:]	[mɛ:t] 'meat'	⟶	[e:]	[me:t]	⟶	[i:]	[mi:t]
[e:]	[me:t] 'meet'	⟶	[i:]	[mi:t]	⟶	[i:]	[mi:t]
[i:]	[ri:d] 'ride'	⟶	[əi]	[rəid]	⟶	[ai]	[raid]
[ɔ:]	[bɔ:t] 'boat'	⟶	[o:]	[bo:t]	⟶	oʊ/əʊ	(boʊt/bəʊt)
[o:]	[bo:t] 'boot'	⟶	[u:]	[bu:t]	⟶	[u:]	[bu:t]

Figure D4.2.2 The Great Vowel Shift: examples

These dramatic shifts totally altered the appearance of the languages concerned within the course of perhaps a couple of centuries. How and why did they occur?

Push chains or drag chains?

The biggest problem, with any chain shift, is finding out where it starts, Suppose we noticed that the guests at the Mad Hatter's tea-party had all moved on one place. After the event, how could we tell who started the shift? The Mad Hatter, Alice or the March Hare? Essentially, we need to know the answer to one simple question. Were most of the sounds dragged, or were they pushed? Or could they have been both dragged and pushed? The terms **drag chain** and **push chain (chaîne de traction**, and **chaîne de propulsion)** are the picturesque terms coined by André Martinet, a famous French linguist, who in 1955 wrote a book, *Economie des changements phonétiques*, [. . .] which attempted to account for these types of shift. According to him, in a drag chain one sound moves from its original place. and leaves a gap which an existing sound rushes to fill, whose place is in turn filled by another, and so on. In a push chain, the reverse happens. One sound invades the territory of another, and the original owner moves away before the two sounds merge into one. The evicted sound in turn evicts another, and so on (see Figure D4.2.3).

Jean
Aitchison

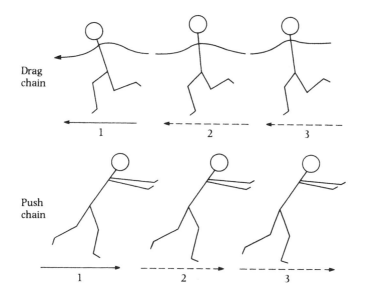

Figure D4.2.3 Drag and push chains

The question as to whether we are dealing with a drag chain or a push chain, or even both together, may seem trivial at first sight. But since these chains have a more dramatic effect on the language structure than any other kind of change, it is of considerable importance to discover how they work. In recent years, there has been some doubt as to whether both types of chain really exist.

Most linguists are happy with the notion that one sound can fill a gap left by another, but they are less happy with the notion that one can actually push another out of its rightful place. Unfortunately, we cannot solve this problem by looking at [. . .] the Great English Vowel Shift. [. . .] [A]s far as the Great Vowel Shift is concerned, there seems to have been so much fluctuation and variation in the vowel system from around 1500 onwards, that the exact chronological order of the changes is disputed. Let us therefore examine some better-documented musical-chair shifts in order to see if both types of chain are in fact possible. This may shed light on Grimm's Law and the Great English Vowel Shift.

Sure examples of drag chains are relatively easy to find. A notable example occurs in German around AD 500, in the so-called High German or Second Consonant Shift, illustrated in Figure D4.2.4. [. . .] This is called the second shift because Grimm's Law, outlined in the previous section, is generally known as the first shift. It was not nearly as sweeping as the earlier shift, however, and appears to have petered out before completing itself. Essentially, [θ] became [d], [d] became [t], and [p] [t] [k] became [pf] [ts] [kx] (see Figure D4.2.4).

Jean
Aitchison

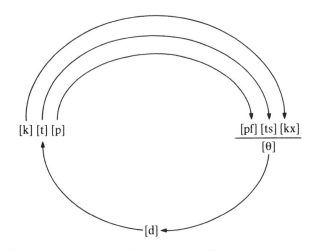

Figure D4.2.4 High German or Second Consonant Shift

Second Consonant Shift			Modern German			English
[p]	⟶	[pf]	[pf]/[f]	[pfefə]	*Pfeffer*	'pepper'
[t]	⟶	[ts]	[ts]/[s]	[tsuŋə]	*Zunge*	'tongue'
[k]	⟶	[kx]	[kx]/[x]	[brexən]	*brechen*	'break'
[d]	⟶	[t]	[t]	[tu:n]	*tun*	'do'
[θ]	⟶	[d]	[d]	[drai]	*drei*	'three'

Figure D4.2.5 High German or Second Consonant Shift: examples

The chronology of this change has been relatively well established: [p] [t] [k] were the first to change, around AD 500. [d] changed in the seventh century, filling the empty space left by [t]. Some time after, [θ] moved into the space left by [d]. So we have a clear example of a drag chain, with sounds apparently being dragged into filling gaps in the system. English, incidentally, did not undergo this second shift, so the English translation of the examples in Figure D4.2.5 shows the unshifted sounds.

The shift described above is a particularly clear example of a consonantal drag chain, though numerous others exist, from a wide variety of languages, including one in Chinese which performed a complete circle, in the sense that each of three varieties of *s* changed into another, while the overall inventory of sounds remained the same. [. . .]

Drag chains involving vowels are also fairly easy to find. A change which has been relatively firmly dated is one in the Yiddish dialects of northern Poland (see Figure D4.2.6). [. . .] Here, [u:] changed to [i:], followed by [o:] to [u:].

Let us now go on to consider push chains. Examples of these are harder to find. and some people have denied their existence altogether on the grounds that if [e] became [i], it could not then push [i] out of the way, because it would already *be* [i]. [. . .] In other

Jean
Aitchison

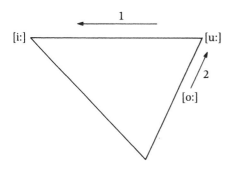

Figure D4.2.6 Drag chain in Yiddish dialect of northern Poland

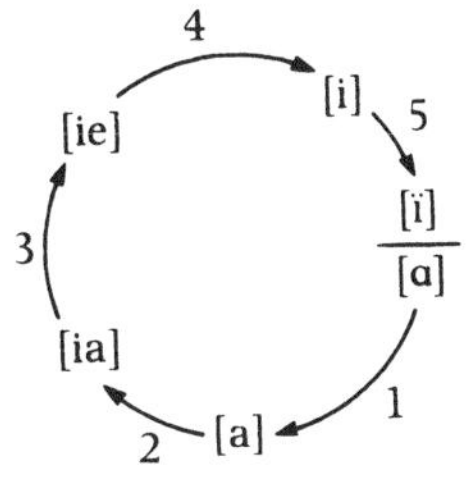

Figure D4.2.7 The Great Vowel Shift of Late Middle Chinese

words, sounds could merge together, it was claimed, but not push one another out of the way. But this objection only holds if sounds change in sudden leaps. Since there is now plenty of evidence that vowels move gradually, it is possible for [e] to move partially towards [i], and for [i] to move away a little in response. It is less easy to see how consonants could behave in this way, and there is not (to my knowledge) a convincing example of a push chain involving consonants. However, a good case has been put forward for a push chain involving vowels in the so-called Great Vowel Shift of Late Middle Chinese, which began in the eighth century AD. [. . .] The basic movement is shown in Figures D4.2.7 and D4.2.8. There is fairly firm evidence that the changes occurred in the sequence shown in Figure D4.2.7 and over the time scale indicated in Figure D4.2.9 (overleaf).

We may conclude, then, that drag chains and push chains both exist, though drag chains appear to be commoner than push chains. This raises the possibility of whether both types can be combined into one chain shift. Could a chain shift perhaps start in the *middle*, so that it dragged some sounds and pushed others, as in Figure D4.2.10? Could [e] in Figure D4.2.10 be the villain of the piece and *both* push [i] *and* drag [a]? The answer is unclear, though it is possible that the answer is 'yes', since if Chaucer's rhymes are genuine rhymes, and not near misses, there is some evidence that he sometimes made [e:] rhyme with [i:]. If this spelling reflects the genuine pronunciation, then

Late Middle Chinese			became	Standard Mandarin	
[ɑ]	[ɣɑu]	'symbol'	⟶	[a]	[xau]
[a]	[ɣau]	'piety'	⟶	[ia]	[ɕiau]
[ia]	[kia]	'street'	⟶	[ie]	[tɕie]
[ie]	[kiei]	'chicken'	⟶	[i]	[tɕi]
[i]	[tsi]	'purple'	⟶	[ï]	[tsï]

Figure D4.2.8 The Great Vowel Shift of Late Middle Chinese: examples

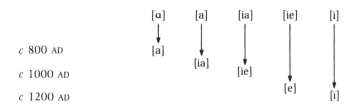

Figure D4.2.9 Chronology of the Great Vowel Shift of Late Middle Chinese

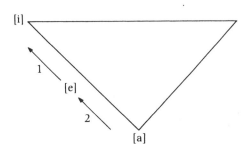

Figure D4.2.10 Combined push and drag chain

his work contains the earliest hints of the English Great Vowel Shift, indicating that it perhaps began in the *middle* of the chain – and some work on the topic supports this suggestion. [. . .]

The situation may soon be clearer. Two new English vowel shifts are taking place at the current time, one in Great Britain, the other in the USA. These will be outlined below. They indicate that drag chains and push chains can indeed be mixed. They also show that language retains its ability to maintain its equilibrium even in the modern world, where speakers come into contact with a confusing mix of different pronunciations.

Estuary English vowels

The current British shift is a feature of so-called 'Estuary English', the area around the Thames Estuary. [. . .] The Estuary English accent is somewhere between the pronunciation thought of as the educated standard, and a London Cockney one:[. . .] traditionally, a Cockney is someone born within earshot of the bells of Bow, an area in East London. Recently, Estuary English has begun to spread far beyond its original homeland.

Superficially, the most noticeable feature of Estuary English is possibly the extensive use of a glottal stop in place of [t] [. . .], as in 'Be'y 'ad a bi' of bi'er bu'er' for 'Betty had a bit of bitter butter.' Yet the vowel changes may cause more problems for outsiders, since each vowel appears to be moving into the slot originally occupied by a neighbour. These changes are taking place in British diphthongs, or 'gliding vowels', sounds in which one vowel slides seamlessly into another, as in 'How now brown cow' which contains the diphthong [au] in most older pronunciations.

Now consider the following words:

D4

Jean
Aitchison

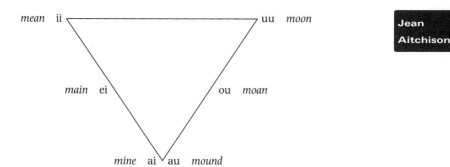

Figure D4.2.11 English diphthongs: conventional (older) pronunciation

mean [miin]   *moon* [muun][. . .]
main [mein]   *moan* [moun]
mine [main]   *mound* [maund]

On a vowel triangle, the first part of each diphthong would be placed as in Figure D4.2.11 in a conventional (older) pronunciation (slightly simplified).

But listen to a schoolboy or schoolgirl pronouncing these words today. The phrases in the first column (below) would probably sound somewhat like those in the second:

Don't be *mean*	→	Don't be *main* [mein]
The *main* road	→	The *mine* [main] road
It's *mine*	→	It's *moyne* [moin]
See the *moon*	→	See the *moan* [moun]
Don't *moan*	→	Don't *moun* [maun]
A little *mound*	→	A little *meund* [meund]

The slip-sliding vowels can be represented in a (simplified) diagram as in Figure D4.2.12. [. . .]

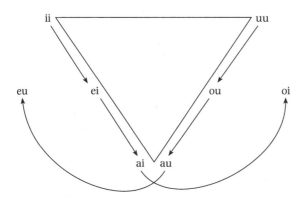

Figure D4.2.12 Estuary English vowels

Jean Aitchison

No wonder, perhaps, that the older generation has trouble comprehending the younger, even though this shift has now spread far beyond teenagers. 'The prime minister descended into estuary English in an attempt to reach out to the masses', complained a newspaper article, 'Should our leaders be "plumbing down" in this estuarine way?'[. . .]

D4.3 Issues to consider

❑ As should be apparent from the extract from Jean Aitchison's book, the Great Vowel Shift that affected the long vowels of Middle English was not an isolated occurrence. The shift in vowels that has given rise to Estuary English is a recent example of a sound shift in English. What external factors might have been instrumental in causing this shift? Think about the possible external influences that caused the Great Vowel Shift of the Early Modern period. Might the same influences have caused the more recent 'Estuary English' shift, or would you put this recent change down to other factors?

❑ Aitchison suggests that Estuary English was developed by teenagers. Why do you think it was this age group particularly who were responsible for the change, and what factors have caused its spread to other social groups and geographical areas?

D5

'FIXING' THE LANGUAGE

The French have a formal institution called the *Académie française*, which was founded in 1635 for the purpose of 'protecting' the French language. It continues today and, according to its website, 'The principal function of the academy is to work with all care and all possible diligence to give definite rules to our language and to render it pure, eloquent and capable of being used to discuss the arts and the sciences'. It should be clear from C4 that this is an overwhelmingly prescriptive organisation. There has never been an equivalent academy for the English language, though the establishment of one was debated in the Early Modern period. In the reading below, Baugh and Cable explain the background to the proposals for an English Academy.

D5.1 The appeal to authority, 1650–1800

Albert C. Baugh and Thomas Cable

Albert C. Baugh and Thomas Cable (reprinted from *A History of the English Language*, 5th edition. London: Prentice Hall, 2002: 280–7)

An English Academy

There can be little doubt that the vital incentive to the establishment of an academy in England came from the example of France and Italy. The suggestion of an English Academy occurs early in the seventeenth century. Indeed, learned societies had been known in England from 1572, when a Society of Antiquaries founded by Archbishop Parker began holding its meetings at the house of Sir Robert Cotton and occupied itself with the study of antiquity and history. It might in time have turned its attention to the improvement of the language, but it languished after the accession of James I. A

Albert C.
Baugh and
Thomas Cable

proposal that promised even more was made about the year of Shakespeare's death by
Edmund Bolton, an enthusiastic antiquary. It was for a society to be composed of men
famous in politics, law, science, literature, history, and the like. Those proposed for
membership, beside the originator, included such well-known names as George Chap-
man, Sir Edward Coke, Sir Robert Cotton, Sir Kenelm Digby, Michael Drayton, Ben
Jonson, Inigo Jones, John Selden, Sir Henry Spelman, and Sir Henry Wotton, all men
with scholarly tastes and interests. But the project died with James I.

In time, however, the example of the French Academy began to attract attention
in England. In 1650 James Howell spoke approvingly of its intentions to reform French
spelling, and in 1657 its history appeared in English, translated from the French of Pel-
lisson. With the Restoration, discussion of an English Academy became much more
frequent. In the very year that Charles II was restored to the throne, a volume was published with the title *New Atlantis . . . Continued by R. H. Esquire* (1660) in which, as a feature of his ideal commonwealth, the author pictured an academy 'to purifie our Native
Language from Barbarism or Solecism, to the height of Eloquence, by regulating the
termes and phrases thereof into constant use of the most significant words, proverbs,
and phrases, and justly appropriating them either to the Lofty, mean, or Comic stile'.[1]

Shortly thereafter the idea of an academy received support from several influential persons, notably from Dryden and John Evelyn. In the dedication of the *Rival Ladies*
(1664) Dryden says, 'I am Sorry, that (Speaking so noble a Language as we do) we have
not a more certain Measure of it, as they have in France, where they have an Academy
erected for the purpose, and Indow'd with large Privileges by the present King'. A few
months later the Royal Society took a step that might have led it to serve the purpose of
an academy. This society, founded in 1662, was mainly scientific in its interests, but in
December 1664 it adopted a resolution to the effect that as

> there were persons of the Society whose genius was very proper and inclined to
> improve the English tongue, Particularly for philosophic purposes, it was voted
> that there should be a committee for improving the English language; and that they
> meet at Sir Peter Wyche's lodgings in Gray's-Inn once or twice a month, and give
> an account of their proceedings, when called upon.

The committee was a large one; among its twenty-two members were Dryden, Evelyn,
Sprat, and Waller. Evelyn, on one occasion, unable to attend the meeting of the committee, wrote out at length what he conceived to be the things that they might attempt.
He proposed the compilation of a grammar and some reform of the spelling, particularly the leaving out of superfluous letters. This might be followed by a

> lexicon or collection of all the pure English words by themselves; then those which
> are derivative from others, with their prime, certaine, and natural signification;
> then, the symbolical: so as no innovation might be us'd or favour'd, at least, 'till
> there should arise some necessity of providing a new edition, & of amplifying the
> old upon mature advice.

He further suggested collections of technical words, 'exotic' words, dialect expressions,
and archaic words that might be revived. Finally, translations might be made of some of

the best of Greek and Latin literature, and even out of modern languages, as models of elegance in style. He added the opinion in conclusion that

> there must be a stock of reputation gain'd by some public writings and compositions of ye Members of this Assembly, and so others may not thinke it dishonor to come under the test, or accept them for judges and approbators.

Evelyn's statement is important not so much for the authority that attaches to his words as for the fact that his notions are quite specific and set out at length. Whether because the program he outlined appeared too ambitious or for some other reason, nothing was done about it. The committee seems to have held only three or four meetings. The Royal Society was not really interested in linguistic matters.

It is quite likely, as O. F. Emerson thought,[2] that the moving spirit in this gesture of the Royal Society was John Dryden. Though he was certainly not a pioneer in suggesting the creation of an English Academy, he was the most distinguished and consistent advocate of it in public. Later he seems to have joined forces with the Earl of Roscommon. Horace Walpole, in his life of the earl, says

> we are told that his Lordship in conjunction with Dryden projected a society for refining and fixing the standard of our language. It never wanted this care more than at that period; nor could two men have been found more proper to execute most parts of that plan than Dryden, the greatest master of the powers of language, and Roscommon, whose judgment was sufficient to correct the exuberances of his associate.[3]

Thus the movement for an academy did not lack the support of well-known and influential names.

But at the end of the century the idea was clearly in the air. In 1697, Defoe in his *Essay upon Projects* devoted one article to the subject of academies. In it he advocated an academy for England. He says

> I would therefore have this society wholly composed of gentlemen, whereof twelve to be of the nobility, if possible, and twelve private gentlemen, and a class of twelve to be left open for mere merit, let it be found in who or what sort it would, which should lie as the crown of their study, who have done something eminent to deserve it.

He had high hopes of the benefits to be derived from such a body:

> The voice of this society should be sufficient authority for the usage of words, and sufficient also to expose the innovations of other men's fancies; they should preside with a sort of judicature over the learning of the age, and have liberty to correct and censure the exorbitance of writers, especially of translators. The reputation of this society would be enough to make them the allowed judges of style and language; and no author would have the impudence to coin without their authority. Custom, which is now our best authority for words, would always have its original here, and

not be allowed without it. There should be no more occasion to search for derivations and constructions, and it would be as criminal then to coin words as money.

**Albert C.
Baugh and
Thomas Cable**

Swift's Proposal, 1712

By the beginning of the eighteenth century the ground had been prepared, and the time was apparently ripe for an authoritative plan for an academy. With the example of Richelieu and the French Academy doubtless in his mind, Swift addressed a letter in 1712 to the Earl of Oxford, Lord Treasurer of England. It was published under the title *A Proposal for Correcting, Improving, and Ascertaining the English Tongue.* After the usual formalities he says

> My Lord, I do here in the name of all the learned and polite persons of the nation complain to your Lordship as *first minister*, that our language is extremely imperfect; that its daily improvements are by no means in proportion to its daily corruptions; that the pretenders to polish and refine it have chiefly multiplied abuses and absurdities; and, that in many instances it offends against every part of grammar.

He then launches an attack against the innovations he had objected to in his paper in the *Tatler* two years before, observing, 'I have never known this great town without one or more *dunces* of figure, who had credit enough to give rise to some new word, and propagate it in most conversations, though it had neither humour nor significancy'.

The remedy he proposes is an academy, though he does not call it by that name.

> In order to reform our language, I conceive, my lord, that a free judicious choice should be made of such persons, as are generally allowed to be best qualified for such a work, without any regard to quality, party, or profession. These, to a certain number at least, should assemble at some appointed time and place, and fix on rules, by which they design to proceed. What methods they will take, is not for me to prescribe.

The work of this group, as he conceives it, is described in the following terms:

> The persons who are to undertake this work will have the example of the French before them to imitate, where these have proceeded right, and to avoid their mistakes. Besides the grammar-part, wherein we are allowed to be very defective, they will observe many gross improprieties, which however authorised by practice, and grown familiar, ought to be discarded. They will find many words that deserve to be utterly thrown out of our language, many more to be corrected, and perhaps not a few long since antiquated, which ought to be restored on account of their energy and sound.

And then he adds the remark which we have quoted in a previous paragraph, that what he has most at heart is that they will find some way to fix the language permanently. In setting up this ideal of permanency he allows for growth but not decay:

> But when I say, that I would have our language, after it is duly correct, always to

Albert C. Baugh and Thomas Cable

last, I do not mean that it should never be enlarged. Provided that no word, which a society shall give a sanction to, be afterwards antiquated and exploded, they may have liberty to receive whatever new ones they shall find occasion for.

He ends with a renewed appeal to the earl to take some action, indulging in the characteristically blunt reflection that 'if genius and learning be not encouraged under your Lordship's administration, you are the most inexcusable person alive'.

The publication of Swift's *Proposal* marks the culmination of the movement for an English Academy. It had in its favor the fact that the public mind had apparently become accustomed to the idea through the advocacy of it by Dryden and others for more than half a century. It came from one whose judgment carried more weight than that of anyone else at the beginning of the eighteenth century who might have brought it forward. It was supported by important contemporary opinion. Only a few months before, Addison, in a paper in the *Spectator* (No. 135) that echoes most of Swift's strictures on the language, observed that there were ambiguous constructions in English 'which will never be decided till we have something like an Academy, that by the best Authorities and Rules drawn from the Analogy of Languages shall settle all Controversies between Grammar and Idiom'.

Apparently the only dissenting voice was that of John Oldmixon, who, in the same year that Swift's *Proposal* appeared, published *Reflections on Dr. Swift's Letter to the Earl of Oxford, about the English Tongue*. It was a violent Whig attack inspired by purely political motives. He says, 'I do here in the Name of all the Whigs, protest against all and everything done or to be done in it, by him or in his Name'. Much in the thirty-five pages is a personal attack on Swift, in which he quotes passages from the *Tale of a Tub* as examples of vulgar English, to show that Swift was no fit person to suggest standards for the language. And he ridicules the idea that anything can be done to prevent languages from changing. 'I should rejoice with him, if a way could be found out to *fix our Language for ever*, that like the *Spanish* cloak, it might always be in Fashion. But such a thing is impossible.'

Oldmixon's attack was not directed against the idea of an academy. He approves of the design, 'which must be own'd to be very good in itself'. Yet nothing came of Swift's *Proposal*. The explanation of its failure in the Dublin edition is probably correct; at least it represented contemporary opinion. It says

> It is well known that if the Queen had lived a year or two longer, this proposal would, in all probability, have taken effect. For the Lord Treasurer had already nominated several persons without distinction of quality or party, who were to compose a society for the purposes mentioned by the author; and resolved to use his credit with her Majesty, that a fund should be applied to support the expence of a large room, where the society should meet, and for other incidents. But this scheme fell to the ground, partly by the dissensions among the great men at court; but chiefly by the lamented death of that glorious princess.

This was the nearest England ever came to having an academy for the regulation of the language. Though Swift's attempt to bring about the formation of such a body is frequently referred to with approval by the advocates of the idea throughout the century, no serious effort was made to accomplish the purpose again. Apparently, it was felt that

Albert C.
Baugh and
Thomas Cable

where Swift had failed it would be useless for others to try. Meanwhile, opposition to an academy was slowly taking shape. The importance of the *Proposal* lies in the fact that it directed attention authoritatively to the problems of language that then seemed in need of solution.

[...]

Substitutes for an Academy

Since the expectation of those who put their hopes in an academy must have been considerably lessened by the failure of Swift's *Proposal*, the only means left to them was to work directly upon the public. What could not be imposed by authoritative edict might still win adoption through reason and persuasion. Individuals sought to bring about the reforms that they believed necessary and to set up a standard that might gain general acceptance. In 1724 there appeared an anonymous treatise on *The Many Advantages of a Good Language to Any Nation: with an Examination of the Present State of Our Own*. This repeats the old complaints that English has too many monosyllables, uses too many contractions, and has no adequate grammar or dictionary. But what is of more importance is that it seeks to stir up popular interest in matters of language, calls upon the public to take part in the discussion, and proposes the publication of a series of weekly or monthly pamphlets on grammar and other linguistic topics. In 1729 one Thomas Cooke published 'Proposals for Perfecting the English Language'.[4] The reforms he suggests extend to the changing of all strong verbs to weak, the formation of all plurals of nouns by means of <-s> or <-es>, the comparison of adjectives only with *more* and *most*, and the like. Cooke was both an idealist and an optimist, but he did not put his faith in academies. The change in attitude, the belief that a standard was to be brought about not by force but by general consent, is revealed in the words of Sheridan:

> The result of the researches of rational enquirers, must be rules founded upon rational principles; and a general agreement amongst the most judicious, must occasion those rules to be as generally known, and established, and give them the 8,1 force of laws. Nor would these laws meet with opposition, or be obeyed with reluctance, inasmuch as they would not be established by the hand of power, but by common suffrage, in which every one has a right to give his vote: nor would they fail, in time, of obtaining general authority, and permanence, from the sanction of custom, founded on good sense.[5]

The two greatest needs, still felt and most frequently lamented, were for a dictionary and a grammar. Without these there could be no certainty in diction and no standard of correct construction. The one was supplied in 1755 by Johnson's *Dictionary*, the other in the course of the next half-century by the early grammarians.

Notes

1   Edmund Freeman, 'A Proposal for an English Academy in 1660', *MLR* 19 (1924), 291–300. The author of this article plausibly suggests Robert Hooke as the R. H. Esquire.
2   O. F. Emerson, *John Dryden and a British Academy* (London, 1921; *Proceedings of the British Academy*).

3 *Catalogue of the Royal and Noble Authors of England* (2nd edition, 1959). The statement is echoed by Dr. Johnson in his *Lives of the Poets.*

4 As an appendix to his *Tales, Epistles, Odes,* etc.

5 T. Sheridan, *British Education,* pp. 370–1.

D5.2 Issues to consider

❏ Bearing in mind what you know about the historical development of English over time, what is the underlying problem with the notion of setting up an academy to regulate language use? (Hint: think about the causes of linguistic change.)

❏ When the supporters of an English Academy were making their proposals, what might have motivated them to do so?

❏ Baugh and Cable note that with regard to the French Academy, 'James Howell spoke approvingly of its intentions to reform French spelling'. It is highly likely that the supporters of an English Academy viewed English spelling as also badly in need of reform. From the perspective of being a twenty-first-century speaker of English, how would you go about reforming the system of spelling in English (if you are a speaker of English as a second language you may have particularly strong view about this!). And why would such an activity be ultimately not worth doing? (Think about the relationship between sounds and spellings; you might find it useful to re-read section B4 on sound change in Early Modern English.)

D6 THE DEVELOPMENT OF AMERICAN ENGLISH

H. L. Mencken's book, *The American Language: An Inquiry into the Development of English in the United States,* was very popular when it was first published in 1919. In the extract below, Mencken outlines the development of a number of 'American' words, paying particular attention to conditions which caused them to come into use, as well as the relationship of American English to British English.

D6.1 The beginnings of American

H. L. Mencken (reprinted from *The American Language: An Inquiry into the Development of English in the United States.* One volume abridged edition. New York: Alfred A. Knopf, 1967: 136–42)

Changed meanings

The early Americans [. . .] made many new words by changing the meaning of old ones. *To squat,* in the sense of to crouch, had been sound English for centuries, but they gave it the meaning of to settle on land without the authority of the owner, and from it the noun *squatter* quickly emanated. Of *lot* Krapp says

> The method of portioning out the common lands to the townsmen of the first New England communities has led to the general American use of *lot* to designate

a limited section of land . . . In the Norwalk Records (1671) the agreement is recorded that 'all those men that now draw *lots* with their neighbors shall stand to their *lots* that they now draw'.[1]

Other examples of the application of old words to new purposes are afforded by *freshet* and *barn*. A *freshet*, in eighteenth century-English, meant any stream of fresh water; the colonists made it signify an inundation. A *barn* was a house or shed for storing crops; in America it became a place for keeping cattle also. The process is even more clearly shown in the history of such words as *corn* and *shoe*. *Corn*, in orthodox English, means grain for human consumption, and especially wheat, e.g., the *Corn Laws*. Our corn is *maize;* as the staple grain of the New World, it soon became known as *Indian corn*, to distinguish it from *corn* in the English sense; but by the middle of the eighteenth century simple *corn* usually sufficed. Such derivatives as *corn field*, *-husk*, *-fed*, *-starch* and *-whiskey* all relate to *maize*,[2] and so does the familiar American phrase *to acknowledge the corn*. The DA traces *corn field* to 1608, *-stalk* to 1645, *-land* to 1654, *-crib* to 1687, *sweet-* to 1646, *-house* to 1699, *-hill* to 1616, *-row* to 1769, *-patch* to 1784, *-bread* to 1775, *-flour* to 1674, *pop* to 1819, *-barn* to 1780. Most of these are probably older. The American colonists borrowed not only the Indian method of growing corn by planting a fish in every row, for fertilizer, but also some of the Indian ways of preparing it for the table, e.g., by making hominy. But the English at home did not like it;[3] nor do they like it yet.

Shoe, in England, meant (and still means) a topless article of footwear, but the colonists extended it to varieties covering the ankle, thus displacing the English *boot*, which they reserved for foot coverings reaching at least to the knee. This distinction between English and American usage still prevails; such Americanisms as *bootblack* (1817) and *to bootlick* (1845) originally referred to the American *boot*, not the English. *Bureau*, to an Englishman, means an article of furniture including a writing desk – what we ordinarily call a *secretary*; in the United States it means a chest of drawers for holding linens, usually with a mirror attached. The English use it occasionally in our sense of a government or other office, but they prefer *office*. But they use *bureaucrat* and *bureaucracy* just as we do.

In colonial America, *shop* originally designated a small retail establishment, as it still does in England. But *store* had come in by 1721; by 1741 it had yielded *storekeeper*. In England, even yet, *store* means primarily a large establishment, like what we call a *warehouse*,[4] but the word in the American sense has been used for a cooperative retail store since about 1850, and recently there has been some currency for *department store*. Contrariwise, the English *shop* has been reintroduced in the United States, often in the elegant form *shoppe*. The DA traces *bookstore* to 1763, *grocery store* to 1774, *to keep store* to 1752 and *store book* to 1740, but most of the other familiar derivatives of *store* came later.

Rock to an Englishman, commonly signifies a stone of large size, and the Pilgrims so used it when they named *Plymouth Rock* in 1620. But the colonists applied it to small stones during the eighteenth century, and in 1816 Pickering remarked that 'in New England we often hear the expression of *heaving rocks* for throwing stones'. Webster omitted the American sense from his dictionaries and Sherwood denounced it in his 'Gazetteer of the State of Georgia'. [The English preference for *stone*, as something to throw, is maintained in New England and its western dependencies; but from Pennsylvania south, *rock* is preferred.]

Cracker for what the English commonly call a *biscuit* is traced by the DAE to 1739. In recent years *biscuit*, in the English sense, has been borrowed in America, as in *National Biscuit Company*, and the English have made increasing use of *cracker*, which first appeared in England in 1810. The word seems to come from the verb *to crack*, and probably was suggested by the cracker's crispness. *Block*, in the Northern United States sense of a group of houses, is sometimes used in England, as in *block of shops*, but perhaps only as a conscious Americanism.[5] The first American example is dated 1796, but the OED does not report the form in English use until fifty-five years later. In the sense of the whole territory or mass of buildings between four streets it goes back to 1815 in the United States, and is still exclusively American, as also in the sense of the distance from one street to the next, as in 'a *block* further on', and 'He walked ten *blocks*'.

Creek in England, means a tidal inlet of the ocean or of some large river, but in American it began to designate any small stream so long ago as 1622. It is still used along the Atlantic coast in the English sense, as in *Curtis Creek* (Maryland) and *Deep Creek* (Virginia), but the English never use it in the more usual American sense. The use of *spell* in various familiar phrases, e.g., *spell of sickness*, is apparently indigenous to America. *Spell of work* is old in English, but the first known examples of *spell of weather*, *cold spell*, *rainy spell* and *hot spell* are American, and so is the first recorded use of *spell* standing alone, as an indicator of 'a time or while'. *Lumber*, in England, means articles left lying about and taking up needed room, and in this sense it survives in America in a few compounds, e.g., *lumber room;* in the sense of timber it is an Americanism, traced by the DAE to the seventeenth century. Its familiar derivatives, e.g., *lumberyard*, *lumber-man*, *lumberjack*, greatly reinforce this usage. *Dry goods*, in England, means 'non-liquid goods, as corn' (*i.e.*, wheat); in the United States the term means 'textile fabrics, cottons, woolens, linens, silks, laces, etc.' The difference had appeared by 1725.

In England *college* ordinarily means one of the constituent corporations of a university, though sometimes it is also applied to a preparatory school, e.g., *Eton College;* in the United States, since the seventeenth century, it has been applied to any degree-giving institution short of university rank,[6] (to say nothing of such citadels of *Kultur* as *barber colleges*, *beauty colleges* and *colleges* of *mortuary science*). In England *city* is restricted, says Horwill, to 'a large and important town, or one that contains a cathedral'; in America it has long been applied to much smaller places.[7]

Many English zoological and botanical terms were applied by the colonists to species generally resembling what they had known in England, but actually different. In America since colonial times *partridge* has been used to designate not only the true partridge but also the ruffed grouse, the common quail and various other tetraonid birds. So with *rabbit*: zoologically speaking, there are no native rabbits in the United States; they are all hares. But *hare* to an American normally means the so-called Belgian hare, which is not a hare at all, but a true rabbit. The American *robin* is really a thrush, second cousin to the mockingbird. In England *bay* is used to designate the bay tree (*Laurus nobilis*)*;* in America it designates a shrub, the wax myrtle (*Myrica cerifera*), whose berries are used to make the well-known *bayberry* candles. Other botanical and zoological terms to which the colonists gave new significances are *blackbird*, *beech*, *hemlock*, *lark*, *laurel*, *oriole*, *swallow* and *walnut*.

The impact of a new landscape caused the early colonists to abandon several English topographical terms, e.g., *moor*, and use others that were rare or dialectal in England, e.g., *run* and *branch*. They also invented new ones, usually by giving familiar English

D6

words new meanings, e.g., *divide* and *bluff*. *Bluff*, the first Americanism to be denounced in England, was apparently borrowed from the Dutch in the seventeenth century, as an adjective describing blunt and nearly vertical ships' bows. (In the Savannah Valley it was made a noun, and by the nineteenth century it had spread west. It has been legitimised in England by Lord Tennyson (1830) and by the geologist Sir Charles Lyell (1842).) The other American *bluff*, in the sense of bluster or pretense, probably owes something to both adjective and noun. Records do not tell us whether it originated as a poker term, but it has been in general use for more than a century.)

Archaic English Words

The notion that American English is fundamentally an archaic form of British English has been propagated both by Americans who seek to legitimise our English by identifying it with Shakespeare's, and by Englishmen who deny Americans any originality whatsoever in speech by showing that every new Americanism was used centuries ago. The latter enterprise has been carried to such extravagant lengths that one might find a correspondent of the London *Times* reporting that he had found *duck soup* and *hitchhike* in a state paper of Henry VII. But despite all this absurdity there is a certainly recognizable substratum of archaic English in the American vocabulary, including many terms that Englishmen have denounced as American barbarisms. Ready examples are *to guess*, *to advocate*, *to notify*, *to loan* and *mad* for *angry*.

[. . .] The American use of *to notify*, as in 'The police were *notified*,' has been in English use since 1440, though it has been rare since about 1700. *To loan*, in American use since 1729, strikes Englishmen as a typical Americanism, but the OED traces it to *c.* 1200, and it appears in one of the acts of Henry VIII. Since 1750, however, the English have preferred *to lend*. So with *sick* for *ill*, which the OED traces to the King Alfred translation of Boethius's *De Consolatione Philosophiae*, *c.* 888. It began to be displaced by *ill* in the fifteenth century, and the English now regard the latter as more chaste and elegant, and have given *sick* the special sense of nauseated. In many compounds the original (and now American) sense survives, e.g., *sickness*, *sick bed*, *sick bay*, *sick leave* and *sick* (noun).

The list of such old English terms still alive in American would include many other words and phrases that have been denounced by English purists as abominable Americanisms, e.g., *patch* (of land), *druggist*, *gotten*, *gap* (a break in a range of hills), *to wilt*, *deck* (of cards), *shoat* and *fall* (for autumn). But, as Krapp argued, it is easy to overestimate the size and importance of this archaic element in American speech. It is largest in the dialect of certain remote communities, notably the Maine coast, Delmarva (*i.e.*, the eastern shore of Chesapeake Bay), eastern North Carolina and the southern Appalachians, but even in such communities it is smaller than is commonly assumed. The theory that the English brought by the early colonists underwent a sort of freezing here was first propagated, according to Krapp, by A. J. Ellis,[8] analogising from the fact that the Old Norse of *c.* 1000 has survived with relatively little change in Iceland. But Ellis was densely ignorant of the history of the English settlements in America, and ascribed to them a cultural isolation that never existed. Krapp goes on:

> The American community has not been segregated, unadulterated, merely self-perpetuating. Relations with the parent country have never been discontinued . . .

**H. L.
Mencken**

The absurdity of describing American English as the archaic speech of an isolated community may be realized by considering what might have happened if the conditions favoring isolation had been present. If migration to New England had ceased in the year 1700, if New England had remained after that time a separate state, severed not only from Europe but from the rest of America, it is not improbable that something approximating the language of Dryden might still be heard in New England. But Dryden's speech is forever lost in the medley of later voices that sound more loudly in our ears.[9]

The argument for the archaic quality of American English did rest upon certain observable facts. In most of the colonies, e.g., New England after 1640,[10] Virginia after 1660, Pennsylvania after 1700, the population growth was mainly from natural increase and from non-English immigration: Ulster Scots, Germans, Welshmen [sic], Highlanders, Huguenots, Moravians and Sephardic Jews. Moreover, few of the colonists visited the mother country, for a sea voyage was long and dangerous and expensive. Furthermore, the centers of colonial literacy were not centers of interest in belles-lettres; neither the New England Puritan nor the Philadelphia Quaker patronised the theater, nor, when one of them did venture to England, did he find himself at home in the amiable profligacy of eighteenth-century London society. Benjamin Franklin admitted modeling his prose style on that of Addison and Steele, but Franklin was exceptional, and even he seems not to have quoted or mentioned Shakespeare despite having access to his works.[11] Few of the traditional masterpieces of English literature were to be found in institutional, much less private, libraries; the works most often read were those that catered to the practical needs of the colonists: manuals of religious instruction, law books, arithmetics, treatises on surveying, and – as the agitation grew that led to the Revolution – works of political theory, especially those of the French encyclopedists.[12] And, finally, the expanse of the Atlantic and the practical business at hand kept the colonists from falling prey to the eighteenth-century movement in England to petrify the language as insurance against the corruption of time. Johnson thundered against such novelties as *fun*, and read the death warrants of many archaisms that were not really archaisms at all, e.g., *glee*, *jeopardy* and *to smoulder*. The Americans, largely cut off from this double policing, went on making new words and cherishing old ones.

But it would be a mistake to assume that the colonists were simple children of nature. The wilderness was close at hand, to be sure, but in the wilderness the colonists had built an urban society that compared favorably with anything in Europe outside the major centers. In 1775 Philadelphia and Boston were the second and third most important cities under the British flag, and the sons of Southern planters often attended the English universities and the Inns of Court; even earlier, the library of William Byrd, of Westover, excelled that of most English gentlemen. The distinctiveness of American English developed with American political independence, and with the new cultural independence, not only of the frontier but of the cities that had been established in colonial times.[13]

Notes

1 Krapp, Vol. I, pp. 85–6.
2 Says Edgar J. Goodspeed in his preface to *The Goodspeed Parallel New Testament: the*

American Translation and the King James Version (Chicago, 1943): 'Differences of meaning have . . . grown up in different parts of the English-speaking world since Tyndale's day. What he called a *corn-field* we call a *wheat-field*, and his account of the disciples plucking the ears of *corn* conjures up a wholly false picture before the American mind, they were picking ears of wheat. King James's *corn of wheat*, of course, means a grain of wheat. Neither of them ever saw what we understand by a *corn-field.*' *Corn*, as a general term, would of course include not only wheat and maize but oats, barley, rye and rice.

3 In John Gerard's *Herball*, or *Generall Historie of Plants*, enlarged and amended by Thomas Johnson (London, 1638), it was denounced as unfit for human food: 'The bread which is made thereof is meanly white, without bran; it is hard and dry as bisket is, and hath in it no clamminess at all; for which cause it is of hard digestion, and yieldeth to the body little or no nourishment; it slowly descendeth and bindeth the belly, as that doth which is made of millet or panick [an Italian variety of millet].'

4 'In England', says H. W. Horwill (*Dictionary of Modern American Usage*), '*store* has normally much the same meaning as storehouse'. He quotes the following from *Some Impressions of the United States*, by E. A. Freeman; London, 1883, p. 63: 'In the early settlements a shop was really a *store* in a sense in which it hardly is now on either side of the ocean.'

5 The more usual term seems to be *parade of shops. Business block* is unknown to the English.

6 There is an interesting discussion of its early uses in America in *On the Use of the Words* College *and* Hall *in the United States*, by Albert Matthews, DN, Vol. II. Pt. II, 1900, pp. 91–114.

7 Not infrequently it is embodied in their names (as in *Ellicott City*, Md., with 2,109 inhabitants in 1950, *Dow City*, Iowa, with 524 and *Filer City*, Mich., with 320).

8 In his *Early English Pronunciation*, brought out at intervals from 1869 to 1889. (A century of scientific dialectology has demonstrated that the problem is far more complicated, anyhow, than Ellis realised: the focal areas in a speech community may preserve relics, while isolated areas may undergo radical changes. See William M. Austin, The Scientific Method and Historical Linguistics, *Journal of the American Oriental Society*, Vol. LXV, January–March 1945, pp. 63–4.)

9 Is American English Archaic? *Southwest Review*, Summer 1927, pp. 292–303.

10 Prescott F. Hall, *Immigration*; 2nd edition, New York, 1913, p. 4. See also *The Founding of New England*, by James Truslow Adams; Boston, 1921, pp. 221 *ff*.

11 'No allusion to Shakespeare has been discovered in the colonial literature of the seventeenth century, and scarcely an allusion to the Puritan poet Milton'. Bliss Perry, *The American Spirit in Literature*; New Haven, 1918, p. 61.

12 See *The Cambridge History of American Literature*, Vol. I, p. 110.

13 See Carl Bridenbaugh, *Cities in the Wilderness: The First Century of Urban Life in America, 1625–1743*; New York, 1938; and *Cities in Revolt: Urban Life in America, 1743–1776*; New York, 1955.

D6.2 Issues to consider

❑ The title of Mencken's book – *The American Language* – has attracted criticism from linguists (e.g. Marckwardt 1980). The same criticisms might also be applied to the title of the chapter from which this reading is drawn – 'The beginnings of American'. What problems can you see with these titles? What assumptions do they make about the nature and development of English in America?

❑ In one sense, Mencken's book is now a historical document in its own right. Re-read the section 'Changed Meanings' and consider the words that Mencken defines. If you are a speaker of American English, do Mencken's definitions hold for contemporary American usage? If you are a speaker of British English, would you use any of the 'Americanisms'? If you speak another variety of English, has your variety been influenced by American English, British English or both?

❑ What types of word-formation processes have been employed in the words that Mencken discusses?

❑ Re-read the section 'Changed meanings'. What does Mencken's account of word-formation in early American English contribute to our understanding of the motivation for semantic change?

D7 **A CORPUS APPROACH TO LINGUISTIC DEVELOPMENT**

One of the difficulties of studying recent change in English is finding firm evidence for what we might intuitively believe about the nature of change. The differences between Old English and Present Day English are clear, but the differences between Present Day English and that of just forty years ago may seem at first glance to be unremarkable. However, using large electronic corpora (databases of text) can allow us to systematically investigate both form and usage. In the reading below, Geoffrey Leech and Nick Smith use a corpus approach to investigate changes in British and American written English between 1961 and 1992.

D7.1 Recent grammatical change in written English 1961–1992: some preliminary findings of a comparison of American with British English

Geoffrey
Leech and
Nick Smith

Geoffrey Leech and Nick Smith (reprinted from *The Changing Face of Corpus Linguistics* edited by Antoinette Renouf and Andrew Kehoe. Amsterdam: Rodopi, 2006: 185–204)

In recent publications on the Brown family of corpora[1] (Leech, 2003, forthcoming; Smith, 2003a, 2003b) we have presented some grammatical findings from a diachronic comparison, particularly between the LOB and FLOB corpora, of British English (sampled from publications in 1961 and 1991 respectively). The changes that can be observed in these *comparable* corpora separated by the period of a generation are changes only of frequency of use, but nevertheless some notable patterns of increase and decrease emerge from their comparison.

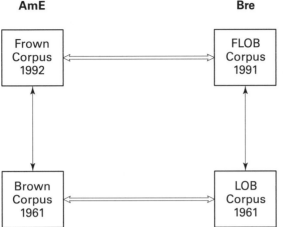

Geoffrey
Leech and
Nick Smith

Figure D7.1.1 The Brown, Frown, LOB and FLOB corpora

Throughout, our focus is on *written*, published English. In most instances, it is likely that any changes observed will have previously been initiated and propagated in the spoken registers of the language variety. However, the present scarcity of suitable spoken BrE [British English] and AmE [American English] corpora from the early 1960s prevents us from carrying out an empirical investigation of the relationship between spoken and written language.

The present paper is a progress report on a further extension of this research, [which] enabled us to use the POS-tagging [marking the part-of-speech (e.g., noun, verb, etc.) of each word in the corpus] in comparing the frequency of occurrence of selected grammatical categories in the American corpora (Brown and Frown) as well as in the British corpora of the same dates.[2] In other words, it was possible to make a four-way comparison, as represented in Figure D7.1.1.

By *comparable corpora* we mean corpora built according to the same principles of design and selection, such as Brown, LOB, Frown and FLOB. In principle, comparisons between such corpora, separated by a period of 30 years in this case, provide a uniquely precise way of tracking historical developments in language use.

[. . .]

The findings we present belong to two major units of grammar: to the verb phrase and to the noun phrase. In discussing these findings, we repeatedly find ourselves referring to colloquialisation and (for British results) Americanisation as likely explanatory factors.

Findings concerning categories of the verb phrase

The verb categories we deal with here are those relating to modality, progressive aspect, passive voice and subjunctive mood. These happen to be categories all showing some striking differences as well as similarities between the AmE and the BrE corpora.

Modal auxiliaries and so-called semi-modals

[. . .] As Table D7.1.1 and Figure D7.1.2 illustrate, there has been a decline in the use of the 'core' class of modals *would, will, can, could, may, should, must, might, shall* plus the

**Geoffrey
Leech and
Nick Smith**

marginal modals *ought (to)*, *need* (+ bare infinitive). In the four corpora overall, these 11 modals occur in the order of frequency corresponding to the order just given, and in fact, the order varies very little among the four corpora. But the decline is much steeper in the case of the middle-order members of the list, *may* and *must*, and particularly the bottom-ranking members, *shall*, *ought (to)* and *need*.

Table D7.1.1 Frequencies of the core modals in AmE and BrE

	American English			British English		
	Brown *(1961)*	*Frown* *(1991)*	*Change* *(%)*	*LOB* *(1961)*	*FLOB* *(1991)*	*Change* *(%)*
Would	3,053	2,868	* −5.9	3,032	2,682	** −11.5
Will	2,702	2,402	** −11.0	2,822	2,708	−4.0
Can	2,193	2,160	−1.4	2,147	2,213	+3.1
Could	1,776	1,655	* −6.7	1,741	1,767	+1.5
May	1,298	878	** −32.3	1,338	1,100	** −17.8
Should	910	787	** −13.4	1,301	1,148	** −11.8
Must	1,018	668	** −34.3	1,147	814	** −29.0
Might	665	635	−4.4	779	640	** −17.8
Shall	267	150	** −43.8	355	200	** −43.7
ought (to)	69	49	−28.9	103	58	** −43.7
Need	40	35	−12.4	76	44	** −42.1
Total	*13,991*	*12,287*	** *−12.1*	*14,841*	*13,374*	** *−9.9*

Note: The figures in the columns headed by Brown, Frown, etc. are frequencies per million word tokens in the corpora; the next column gives the changes in frequency expressed in percentages, i.e. the difference between the two frequencies as a percentage of the first. In addition, a probability value is reported if this is calculated to be statistically significant: * indicates a probability of less than 0.05, ** a probability of less than 0.01, and *** a probability of less than 0.001, of any observed diachronic change. The probability was obtained using the log likelihood test of significance (Dunning 1993).

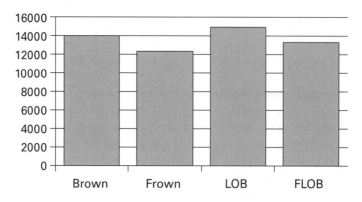

Figure D7.1.2 Declining profile of the core modals in AmE and BrE

D7

Geoffrey Leech and Nick Smith

The frequency decline of individual modals can be observed from Table D7.1.1 [. . .] except that the AmE figures are given on the left. (It makes sense to place the American figures first, as AmE typically shows a tendency to go further, or move faster, in a particular frequency change than BrE.)

The modals show a 'follow-my-leader' pattern, whereby BrE reaches, by 1991, approximately the same frequency pattern as AmE had in 1961. The decline, as shown most graphically in Figure D7.1.2, is considerable – in the region of 10% over the 30 year period – though somewhat higher in AmE (12.2%, as compared with 9.5% in BrE).

The decline in frequency of the modals is countered by an appreciable increase in frequency in both the AmE and BrE corpora of the modal verb idioms often termed 'semi-modals'. Some of these have been widely discussed and investigated (e.g. by Biber et al. 1998: 205–10, Krug 2000) regarding the grammaticalisation thesis that a new generation of modal verbs has been emerging in Modern English, and (more cautiously) that these are in some degree displacing the 'core' modals listed in Table D7.1.2. The negative side of this thesis is most persuasive in the case of *must* and *HAVE to / NEED to*. (Note that the italic capitals indicate the lemma rather than the base form *have* alone.) These apparently competing forms, together with similar verbal expressions of obligation/necessity, have been investigated in LOB and FLOB by Smith (2003b).

Table D7.1.2 Frequencies of some semi-modals in the four written corpora

	American English			British English		
	Brown (1961)	Frown (1991)	Change (%)	LOB (1961)	FLOB (1991)	Change (%)
BE going to	216	332	**+53.9	248	245	−1.5
BE to	344	217	**−36.8	451	376	**−16.9
(had) better	41	34	−17.0	50	37	−26.2
(HAVE) got to	45	52	+15.7	41	27	−34.3
HAVE to	627	639	+2.0	757	825	+8.7
NEED to	69	154	**+123.5	53	194	**+265.0
WANT to	323	552	**+71.1	357	423	*+18.2
BE supposed to	48	55	+14.7	22	47	**+113.1
used to	51	74	*+45.3	86	97	+12.5
Total	1,764	2,109	**+19.7	2,065	2,271	**+9.7

Nevertheless, the overall picture is less than persuasively in favour of the displacement thesis: the increasing use of the semi-modals, significant though it is, still leaves the 'core' modals overall vastly more frequent in our data. (This is further discussed in Leech, 2003: 235–37 and Leech, 2004.) Part of the explanation, apparently, is that most semi-modals are primarily spoken forms and – in spite of colloquialisation – they are still largely avoided in written English.

The category of semi-modals is not well defined. To avoid any particular bias, we

Geoffrey
Leech and
Nick Smith

included in this comparison a broad spread of these verbal idioms, some of which have been declining, whereas others have been increasing dramatically. Those apparently declining or at least not increasing overall are *BE to*, *(had) better* and *(HAVE) got to*, while those apparently increasing are *BE going to* (in AmE), *HAVE to*, *NEED to*, *BE supposed to*, *used to*, and *WANT to*.

Some of the more striking results from the diachronic comparison are:

BE going to:	increase of 54% in the AmE corpora (i.e. from Brown to Frown)
NEED to:	increase of 123% in the AmE corpora and of 249% in the BrE corpora
BE supposed to:	increase of 113% in the BrE corpora
USED to:	increase of 45% in the AmE corpora and of 13% in the BrE corpora
WANT to:	increase of 71% in the AmE corpora and of 18% in the BrE corpora
BE to:	decline of 40% in the AmE corpora and of 17% in the BrE corpora.

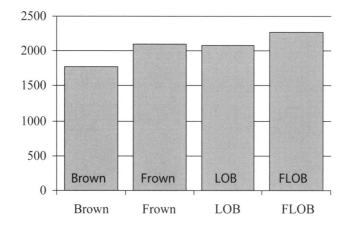

Figure D7.1.3 Overall frequencies of semi-modals

Figure D7.1.3 shows the overall comparison of the AmE corpora and the BrE corpora in the frequency of occurrence of the listed semi-modals. As a class, they show an increase of 19% in the AmE corpora, and of 10% (very similar to the proportional decrease of core modals) in the BrE. Again, we note a more extreme tendency in AmE. However, surprisingly enough, the semi-modals are overall less frequent in the AmE than in the BrE corpora, so in this respect the picture of AmE beating a path followed by BrE is not maintained.

Giving the overall quantitative results, as we have done, does not reveal any detail as to how or why these changes have been taking place. To dig deeper, we need to observe

(a) How the frequency changes pattern in subcorpora (A–C press, D–H general prose, J learned, K–R fiction) and in individual text categories (such as Category B – press editorials; Category D – religion; Category K – general fiction).

(b) How the frequency changes pattern in relation to different senses of the modals.

We cannot do more here than highlight two or three of these more detailed observations.

Geoffrey Leech and Nick Smith

Parallel subdivisions of the corpora yield interesting results in the case of the semi-modals *BE to* and *BE going to* (see also Mair 1997). The press section – particularly the category of news reportage – shows a notable decrease in the occurrence of *BE to*, whereas the same section showed a notable increase in the use of *BE going to* (much higher than in BrE generally). As these semi-modals are both associated with future reference, this suggests a switch from the more formal to the less formal (more colloquial) option in the style of news writing – a variety of written language often considered a bellwether for change, and particularly sensitive to changes coming from the spoken language. Limited evidence from spoken corpora (e.g. Leech, 2003: 232) indicates a strong and increasing tendency to use *going to* for future reference in spoken English, so this switch is not surprising. Puzzlingly, though, in other respects the BrE corpora show a slight (non-significant) decline in the use of *be going to* – perhaps a symptom of some resistance to colloquialisation in other written genres – especially in the subcorpus of General Prose.

To illustrate changing patterns in the use of modal senses, we examined the frequency of epistemic, root and other senses of the three rather sharply declining auxiliaries *may*, *should* and *must*. We conclude that the root senses of *may* of 'permission' (*Please may I finish?*) and of 'root possibility' (*as it may be termed*) have been becoming rare in both AmE and BrE, while relatively speaking, the epistemic 'possibility' sense has been holding its own and becoming by far the most frequent sense of this modal. With *should*, an opposite trend is observed: the root sense, 'weakened obligation', has remained frequent, while the epistemic sense of 'probability' and the remaining senses of 'putative/mandative/quasi-subjunctive' *should* and *should* as a backshift of *shall* have been becoming increasingly rare, perhaps obsolescent. Unlike *may* and *should*, *must* appears to have declined sharply in both root and epistemic senses. From independent corpus evidence (albeit tentative) – see Leech (2003: 232–3) – these trends are paralleled by similar but somewhat more extreme changes in the spoken language. From these findings, there appears to be some trend towards monosemy [singularity of meaning] accompanying the decline of modals, although no such trend is perceptible with *must*.

Progressive aspect

Another verb category of greater frequency in the spoken language is the progressive aspect, which has been broadening its range of application in English since late ME, and is still gaining in frequency (see Mair and Hundt 1995). In the Brown family overall, the use of the progressive has increased by 11.4%, but the picture is highly variable according to grammatical subcategories. The present progressive active is the most common variant of all, and increases by a remarkable +31.8% in AmE and +28.9% in BrE. On the other hand, the past progressive declines slightly, by 1.3% (AmE) and 9.0% (BrE). Other areas of pronounced increase are the combinations modal + progressive and (in BrE) progressive + passive. (Oddly, though, the progressive passive undergoes a decline in AmE [. . .] also frequencies of the modal + progressive combinations rise in BrE, whereas in AmE they remain more or less unchanged, at a lower overall level.) The progressive copula – another construction which like the progressive passive is relatively rare and historically rather recent – increases greatly from 3 to 20 in Brown/Frown and from 8 to 17 in LOB/FLOB, although the numbers are too small for statistical significance. Examples include:

Geoffrey
Leech and
Nick Smith

(1) Maybe my friend, who happens to be white, and I *are being too heartless.* Or maybe we're just *being too jealous.* (FROWN, B)

(2) 'You're *being a pain in the neck,*' John said. (FROWN, L)

[D]etailed examination of the patterns of progressive usage in the LOB/FLOB corpora has failed to reveal any general explanation for the increase of the progressive – for example, extension of its use in certain 'non-progressive' classes of stative verbs. It is worth mentioning a probable increase in the occurrence of the so-called interpretative progressive – where the progressive refers to an underlying psychological interpretation of an overt form of behaviour (particularly verbal behaviour). This usage (see Ljung, 1980 and König, 1980, 1995) appears to be one area showing an extension of progressive meaning in recent years. Examples:

(3) When he speaks of apocalypse, however, he *is* not *speaking* of it in the literal and popular sense. (FROWN, D)

(4) *Am* I *shocking* you? (FROWN, K)

Another atypical usage which shows an increase is the 'matter-of-course' use of the progressive with future-referring modals, particularly *will*:

(5) He *will be standing down* at the next election. (FLOB, B)

(6) Many of you *will be bringing* your camera along to record the weekend. (FLOB, E)

The effect of using the progressive here (as compared with the non-progressive use of *will*) has been variously explained as (a) disclaiming human intention b) expressing a non-immediate consequence of what has already been determined (see Smith, 2003a [. . .]).

Passive voice

There is a consistent fall in the frequency of the passive voice, in both BrE (−12.4%)[3] and in AmE (where it is more extreme at −20.1%). The declining use of the passive may be considered as another case, like the decline of the modals, of AmE leading the way. However, the situation is different: synchronically speaking, whereas the modals are much more frequent in conversation than in written language, the converse is the case for the passive (Biber et al., 1999: 476). This can, therefore, be seen as a negative example of colloquialisation: where the passive, while still strongly entrenched in the more academic varieties of the written language, suffers from a declining popularity consonant with increasing 'oral' influences on writing. Another explanation, however, could be that the sustained attacks on the passive by usage manuals and (most recently) automated grammar checkers have had their effect, especially in AmE.

Geoffrey
Leech and
Nick Smith

Table 7.1.3 Declining frequency of the passive, by subcorpus

| | American English | | | British English | | |
	Brown (1961)	Frown (1991)	Change (%)	LOB (1961)	FLOB (1991)	Change (%)
Press	10,894	7,904	**–27.4	12,992	11,368	**–12.5
Gen. prose	12,691	10,400	**–18.1	14,983	13,126	**–12.4
Learned	19,177	14,180	**–26.1	20,601	17,183	**–16.6
Fiction	5,582	5,290	–5.2	6,113	5,895	–3.6
Overall	*11,588*	*9,254*	***–20.1*	*13,260*	*11,614*	***–12.4*

As Table 7.1.3 shows, the decline in the use of the passive is pervasive in the sense that each subcorpus shows a decline for both AmE and BrE. It is noteworthy, however, that the decline is proportionately high in the Learned subcorpus, where the passive is most frequent, and is low in the Fiction subcorpus, where the passive is least frequent.

Subjunctive mood

In the mid-twentieth century, the subjunctive mood in British English was typically regarded as an obsolete relic of older English, virtually on the brink of extinction. However, by the end of the century a different perspective was being presented: the British use of the mandative subjunctive in that-clauses (as exemplified below) was seen to be making a come-back (e.g. Övergaard, 1995). Examples of the mandative subjunctive are:

> (7) The doctors had suggested Scotty *remain* most of every afternoon in bed until he was stronger. (BROWN, K)

> (8) Hence it is important that the process *be* carried out accurately (FLOB, H)

The mandative subjunctive, in the four corpora under examination, has indeed undergone a modest revival in BrE: rising from the low figure of 14 occurrences in 1961 (LOB) to 33 occurrences in 1991 (FLOB). This corresponds with a decline in the mandative use of *should*, justifiably regarded as the typically British option until recently. In contrast, the figures for AmE show a decline from the relatively high 91 tokens in Brown to 78 tokens in Frown. (However, these figures are too low to be statistically significant and exact exhaustive counts for the later corpora still have to be obtained.)[4]

The unusual pattern of reversal of a pre-twentieth-century decline of the subjunctive appears to be a result of American influence on British usage in the (later) twentieth century [. . .]. Many major grammatical changes seem to be actuated by the growing preference for a more 'oral' style in written language. However, this revival of the mandative subjunctive – a construction associated with formal writing rather than speech – runs counter to the colloquialisation trend, and, as Övergaard discusses in some detail, American influence is the only ready explanation.[5]

Geoffrey
Leech and
Nick Smith

Findings concerning aspects of the noun phrase

[. . .]

Nouns

[A]t this stage we can only indicate roughly what provisionally observed changes invite further research. According to initial research, nouns as a part of speech have increased their frequency of occurrence by more than 4% in the Brown family of corpora (+4.0% in AmE, +5.3% in BrE). Part of this may be due to an increasing popularity of noun + noun sequences (approximately +10 % in AmE, +17% in BrE), also of proper nouns (+12.8% in AmE, +10.0% in BrE,). This higher frequency of nouns again runs counter to the colloquialisation thesis: high noun frequency is associated with high density of information, and is a marked characteristic of informative as contrasted with interactive written styles (Biber 1988: 89). Biber and Clark (2002) found a similar trend across a wider diachronic span.

Genitives and of

The *of*-construction seems to some extent to be giving way to a more frequent use of the equivalent *s*-genitive construction. According to the Brown family of corpora, the increase of the genitive over the 30-year period is remarkable: +41.9% in AmE, +24.1% in BrE. The decrease in the use of *of* over the same period is less remarkable in percentage terms (−10.6% in AmE, −4.7% in BrE), but bearing in mind the very high frequency of this preposition, the decrease is also highly significant. More relevant, though, is a comparison of genitives with *of*-phrases which are semantically equivalent to genitives, or *of*-genitives as we may conveniently call them – e.g. *the common soldiers' letters* compared with *the letters of the common soldiers*. Taking a 2% sample of each corpus, we arrived at tentative figures of –31.9% for AmE and −23.6% for BrE. The loss of *of*-genitives is very roughly commensurate with the gain of *s*-genitives.

[T]he competition between *of*-genitives and *s*-genitives fits into the mould of colloquialisation.[6] [. . .] In the present age, when the spoken medium is asserting itself more powerfully, a resurgence of the *s*-genitive and *th-*/zero relativisation, structures which owe nothing to Romance models, appears to be taking place.

Personal pronouns

One of the puzzling results of the comparison of these corpora is in the frequency changes of 1st and 2nd person pronouns. The pronoun *I* increases its use by +31.2% in AmE, whereas it decreases its use (−10.1%) in BrE. A similar contrast is seen in the plural pronoun *we*: AmE +12.8%, BrE −6.9%. In fact, both pronouns manifest a cross-over phenomenon whereby the frequency in LOB approximates to that in Frown, and the frequency in FLOB approximates to that in Brown[.]

[. . .]

You also shows a large increase in AmE (+18.0%), but is virtually unchanged in BrE (+0.2%). On the face of it, the increase in 2nd person and (especially) 1st person pronouns in AmE is another sign of colloquialisation: these pronouns are strongly associated with the personal style of communication found in conversation. Thus the changes in AmE make sense in terms of the adoption of a more interpersonal, speech-oriented style of address in the written language. But the absence of such changes in BrE, and

Geoffrey
Leech and
Nick Smith

even more so the converse trend in the first person pronoun use, are mystifying. Further research is needed.

More easily interpretable are the changes in third person pronoun use: *HE* loses frequency (−22.9% in AmE, −8.8% in BrE), *SHE* gains frequency (+34.9% in AmE, +8.8% in BrE), yet *SHE* is still less frequent than *HE* in the later corpora. It scarcely needs comment that during the 1961–1992 period, when the women's movement had its major impact, female references gained at the expense of male references, and yet male references still predominated over female in the 1990s. It is also unsurprising that in the written language, the use of *HE* as a gender-neutral pronoun declined, and that non-sexist alternatives such as *HE or SHE* made an (increased) appearance. But the numbers of occurrences of these composite pronouns are small: the increase in the overall count goes from 9 to 56 in AmE, and from 11 to 37 in BrE. Another solution to the problem of gender bias is the use of 'singular *THEY*' in the sense of 'he or she'. We analysed a sample of 6% of the corpus tokens of *THEY*, i.e. roughly 500 instances from each corpus randomly selected, and found an increase from 7 to 9 occurrences of 'singular *they*' in AmE, and of 0 to 9 occurrences in BrE. From an equivalent sample size of *HE*, we found a reduction from 20 to 7 instances of gender-neutral *HE* in AmE, and from 32 to 4 instances in BrE. These numbers are very small, but if we postulate (speculatively) a scaling-up of these results to each pair of corpora as a whole, they point to a pivotal shift from the use of *HE* as a gender-neutral singular pronoun (a hypothetical decrease from 866 to 183 tokens), to the use of alternatives such as *THEY* and *HE or SHE* (the former with a hypothetical increase from 17 to 300 tokens).

Conclusion: Colloquialisation? Americanisation?

Among the frequency changes taking place in the grammar of the noun phrase and the verb phrase between 1961 and 1991/2, it is easy to notice that many show a tendency for spoken language habits to infiltrate the written language: colloquialisation. Perhaps the most conspicuous sign of such an infiltration is the increasing inclination to use of verb contractions (*it's*, etc.) and negative contractions (*wouldn't*, etc.) in the four corpora. The overall increase of these contractions is +63% in AmE, and +25% in BrE. Each class of contractions is represented in Table 7.1.4:

Table 7.1.4 Increasing use of contractions in AmE and BrE

	American English			British English		
	Brown (1961)	Frown (1991)	Change (%)	LOB (1961)	FLOB (1991)	Change (%)
Verb contraction	2,807	5,032	**+79.3	3,126	3,867	**+23.7
Neg. contraction	2,087	2,959	**+41.8	1,940	2,462	**+26.9
Total	*4,894*	*7,991*	***+63.3*	*5,066*	*6,329*	***+24.9*

Geoffrey Leech and Nick Smith

This table also illustrates very clearly another typical trend, whereby AmE shows a more extreme change of frequency than BrE. What is less typical here is that at the starting point (1961) AmE shows a lower frequency than BrE, whereas at the finishing point (1991/2), AmE shows a higher frequency than BrE. In other words, AmE seems to have overtaken BrE in the use of contractions during this 30-year period.

Since colloquialisation appears to be the 'default' trend, if we find a case where an opposite trend takes place, this invites explanation (and further research). For example, the decidedly uncolloquial mandative subjunctive construction discussed above shows an increase in BrE, but this is a change in an opposite direction to colloquialisation. The explanation here appears to be that Americanisation – a trend which often goes hand in hand with colloquialisation, in this case militates against it. It is as if here the usage imperative 'Adopt a more American style' outweighs the imperative 'Adopt a more colloquial style'.

There is not unreasonable scepticism over the interpretation of terms like 'colloquialisation' and 'Americanisation', and certainly these are not uniform trends. They are cases where they appear to operate very clearly (as in the data for contractions in Table 7.1.4) and there are cases where they don't seem to operate at all – as in the declining frequency of *I* and *we* in the BrE corpora. Perhaps the term 'colloquialisation' conceals more than one factor with different effects.

Another argument might be that in a case where AmE 'leads the way' and BrE follows some way behind (as in the case of declining modals), this is not necessarily a case of Americanisation: perhaps it is simply that two regional varieties of the same language follow the same course of change, but that the change is more advanced in one variety than the other. Study of other regional varieties (e.g. Australian, Irish) might throw further light on this. No causative influence of one variety on the other need be implied.

On the other hand, the influence of American usage (like other pervasive American cultural influences we are familiar with) is clear enough, if we examine lexical changes of frequency in the four corpora. For example, *movie(s)* is a noun which in 1961 was almost confined to AmE (67 occurrences in Brown, only 7 in LOB); now it has been catching on in BrE, and this shows up in its increasing frequency in the FLOB corpus (120 occurrences in Frown, 35 in LOB). Another characteristically AmE noun is *guy(s)*, which shows a similar trend: (68 occurrences in Brown, only 6 in LOB; 131 occurrences in Frown, 40 in FLOB). In both these cases the noun has nearly doubled its frequency of occurrence in AmE in 1961–1992; but the increase in BrE is five-to-sevenfold.

But again the trend is not uniform: we find cases where AmE and BrE seem to follow diametrically different paths. The progressive passive [. . .] becomes more infrequent in AmE and more frequent in BrE. This is a tantalising case where competing pressures in the two varieties seem to produce opposite results. The progressive passive is a combination of the progressive (which has been gaining frequency) and the passive (which has been losing frequency). It is also suffers from the double-BE phenomenon, and as a relatively late historical arrival in English (dating from the late eighteenth century) is less thoroughly established than other combinations such as the modal progressive and the perfect progressive. These observations draw attention to the uneasy status of the progressive passive, which might lead it to be inhibited in one variety but not in another. It seems that on the present evidence, AmE, with its more pronounced antipathy to the passive, has been affected by this inhibition whereas BrE has not, but has instead followed the trend of greater use of the progressive in this construction, as elsewhere. [. . .]

Geoffrey
Leech and
Nick Smith

Notes

1   We are using this as a convenient term for Brown, LOB, Frown and FLOB. There is no need to go further, and to consider Frown and FLOB as the children, etc. Pursuing the metaphor, the Brown family might be expanded to include collateral kin such as the Kolhapur corpus of Indian English (Shastri, 1988) and Australian Corpus of English (Collins and Peters, 1988), which are matching corpora in design and sampling, but not of comparable dates to Brown and LOB or Frown and FLOB. We do not consider them here.

2   Although the date of Frown text samples is 1992, we assume this is near enough to 1991 to make little difference to the validity of the comparison.

3   For convenience, we will henceforth use the minus sign with percentages to indicate a percentage decrease, and the plus sign with percentages to indicate a percentage increase.

4   Counts are provided by Serpollet (2003) but based on template searches in XKwic which are probably slight underestimates. Compare Övergaard's frequency data (1995: 14–35).

5   Övergaard's summary (1995: 54) is worth quoting: 'The distribution of the subjunctive variants in mandative sentences in BrE has changed dramatically during the second half of the twentieth century. What appeared to be a unidirectional drift from the non-inflected morphological variant to the periphrastic variant has not only stopped; we are witnessing a reversal of the drift resulting in increased use of the older non-inflected subjunctive, no doubt due to American influence.'

6   Noun-noun sequences (see the discussion of noun frequency) are, like s-genitives, an example of resurgence of native syntactic patterns. Leonard (1968), cited in Leonard (1984: 4), reports that there has been a 'great increase in the occurrences of noun sequences in prose fiction from 1750 to the present day.'

D7.2 Issues to consider

❏   Leech and Smith are careful to point out that they are only reporting the frequencies of the linguistic phenomena that they investigated – that is, in the paper above they do not consider the contextual aspects of usage. Nonetheless, based on these frequencies they are able to make some speculative conclusions about recent trends in British and American English. 'Colloquialisation' appears to be common to both varieties while British English is affected by a process of 'Americanisation'. Bearing in mind the period studied by Leech and Smith (1961–91), can you suggest any external factors that may have been instrumental in these developments?

❏   In their examination of pronouns, Leech and Smith found a decline in the use of *he* as a gender-neutral pronoun (e.g. 'If a student wishes to gain a good degree, he should study hard'). The influence of the feminist movement can clearly be seen here and is an obvious example of external factors affecting usage by promoting conscious change. Can you think of any other examples of how you might have consciously changed the way you use language as a result of external influence? What factors might influence you to change your usage?

D8   **THE FUTURE OF ENGLISH?**

In 1997 David Graddol published a report for the British Council in which he specu-
lated on the future development of English. The report gives a macro-level view of the
development of English and part of the purpose behind this was to encourage debate
about the role of English in the world. As you read through the extract below, consider
how the macro-level issues that Graddol identifies might affect the structure and lexicon of English.

D8.1 English as a transitional phenomenon

**David
Graddol**

David Graddol (reprinted from *The Future of English?* London: British Council, 1997: 60–1)

Will the demand for English in the world continue to rise at its present rate?
Although the position of English seems entrenched, it is possible that the extraordinary
interest in the language in recent years will prove to be a temporary phenomenon associated with the 'first-wave' effects in a period of global change: the transitional nature of
a global economy, the current state of telecommunications networks, the immaturity
of satellite television markets, and educational curricula which lag behind the needs of
workers and employers. These pages examine why the current global wave of English
may lose momentum.

Figure D8.1.1 shows the projections made by the engco model[1] for speakers of
English to 2050. The dotted lines represent speculative curves for second-language and
foreign-language speakers.

There is, as yet, no basis for estimating these groups safely – although it is these
communities who will in practice determine the future of global English. Nevertheless,
the curves are located approximately correctly for the present time (the vertical dashed
line) and the speculative curves demonstrate some ideas developed in this book.

First, L1 speakers of English will soon form a minority group. Second, at some
point the increase in people learning English as a foreign language will level out. This
is a demographic necessity, but may be hastened by a 'leakage' of EFL speakers to L2
status. The key question is, at what point will the numbers of learners decline?

The dotted line, 'market share', indicates a speculative projection of the global ELT
market open to the ELT industries of native-speaking countries, who currently dominate global ELT provision. The curve begins with a notional 50% share, which takes
account of the present closed nature of many national textbook markets. The actual
share of the market taken by publishers and educational providers from Britain, Ireland,
US, Canada, Australia and New Zealand is at present impossible to estimate – but it
is the shape of the curve which is important. Here it shows a declining market share,
as providers from L2 territories become more active. That British and other native-
speaking ELT providers will find the global market much more competitive, will lose
market share and may even experience a decline, is entirely compatible with the idea
that more people in the world are learning and using English.

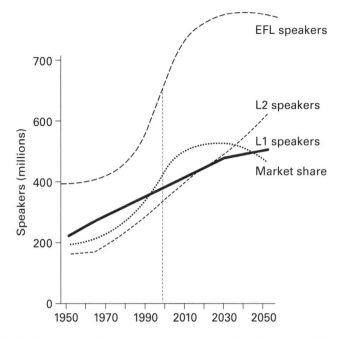

David
Graddol

Figure D8.1.1 Estimates of first-language speakers of English from 1950 to 2050 as calculated by the engco model, together with speculations regarding L2 and EFL communities

Will satellite TV channels bring English into every home, creating a global audiovisual culture?

Satellite TV has been regarded as a major driver of global English. Star TV in Asia, for example, used English and Mandarin in their start-up phases, because these are the 'big' languages which reach the largest audiences. MTV is frequently credited with bringing US English to the world through music and popular culture. Thus English language programmes reach the middle classes in South and South-east Asia in whom the companies who pay for advertising are most interested. But the extensive use of English language material also reflects the easy availability of English language product on the world market. However, as satellite operators develop, they need to expand their audiences by increasing their reach in individual countries – this means going beyond English-speaking audiences. As their income streams develop and as technological innovation (such as digital transmission) makes additional channels available, operators will be able to finance and operate channels more suited to local and niche audiences. Such economic and technological logic explains why English programming has been so prominent in the 1990s. Evident now is the same logic driving an increase in the number of languages and community interests serviced by satellite and cable TV. English language programmes will remain, particularly in certain content areas (such as sport and news), but they will become one of many offerings, rather than the dominant programming.

National networks in English-speaking countries will continue to establish operations in other parts of the world, but their programming policies will emphasise local languages. CBS, for example, intends to establish a news and entertainment channel in

David
Graddol

Brazil, broadcasting in Portuguese, not English; CNN International is launching Spanish and Hindi services; Star TV and MTV are rapidly localising – introducing programming in an increasing number of languages [. . .].

National networks based in other languages will also establish a greater presence in the global audio-visual market. Ray and Jacka (1996), for example, note that Doordarshan, the Indian state-television company, will lease transponders on a new satellite with a footprint stretching from South-east Asia to Europe. They comment, 'this signals two major changes: the loosening grip of Murdoch on global satellite broadcasting and the entry of Doordarshan into global broadcasting to Indian diasporic audiences. [. . .] there can be no doubt that India will become an even stronger force in world television in the very near future' (Ray and Jacka, 1996: 99). Spanish television networks in Mexico are similarly establishing a global presence, producing programming for Europe as well as for Spanish speakers elsewhere in the Americas.

It is thus clear that two trends will dominate the second wave of satellite broadcasting: other major world languages will increase their global reach and the larger providers will localise their services. Both trends indicate a more crowded and linguistically plural audio-visual landscape in the twenty-first century.

Will English continue to be associated with leading-edge technology?

Leading-edge technology, particularly computers and information technology, has been largely English based in several respects. First, its research and development is focused in the US, though often in close collaboration with Japanese transnational companies (TNCs). Second, the literature and conferences in which research findings are reported and through which researchers keep up to date with developments elsewhere, are English based. Third, communications technology and document-handling software have developed around the English language. Indeed, the notorious history of the ASCII coding set which has plagued the use of computer systems for non-English languages for many years, is one example. Fourth, the installed user base of new technology is primarily located in the US, resulting in support manuals, help lines, on-screen menu systems and so on, appearing first in English.

The close association between English and information technology may prove a temporary phenomenon. As software and technology become more sophisticated, they support other languages much better. Desktop publishing and laser printing are now capable of handling hundreds of lesser used languages and a wide range of scripts and writing systems. Computer operating systems and software are now routinely versioned for many languages. In many cases the user can further customise the product, allowing even very small languages, unknown to the manufacturers, to be accommodated. So whereas English speakers used to enjoy the best and latest technology, this is no longer so true.

Will economic modernisation continue to require English for technology and skills transfer?

Currently, English is to be found at the leading edge of economic modernisation and industrial development (p. 32). The typical pattern of economic modernisation involves technology and skills transfer from the Big Three regions (North America, Europe and Japan) as a result of investment by TNCs, often via joint-venture companies: a process associated closely with English.

David
Graddol

But as countries benefit from such transfer and 'come up to speed', there develop local networks of small companies supplying the large TNC enterprises. Since many such suppliers use local employment, this secondary economic activity does not stimulate English to the same degree as the primary activity around TNCs.

There is yet a third wave to be expected in economic development. Just as the Big Three TNGs transfer technology, not simply to produce goods more cheaply but also to create new markets, so countries like Thailand and Malaysia are looking towards their neighbours, including Vietnam, Laos and Cambodia, as future trading partners. The development of such regional trade, in which no Big Three country is directly involved, may diminish the primacy of English as the language of technology transfer: the necessary level of expertise can be obtained closer to home and more cheaply. Sources of management and technology transfer in Asia now include Singapore, Hong Kong, Taiwan, Korea, Malaysia and Thailand. This third-wave technology transfer – often associated with less than leading-edge technology – may be less reliant on English. But it is equally possible that English provides the means for such countries to extend into regional markets.

There is no doubt that it would be extremely helpful to have a better understanding of how the next phases of globalisation will affect the use of English.

What impact will the Internet have on the global use of English?

The Internet epitomises the information society, allowing the transfer of services, expertise and intellectual capital across the world cheaply, rapidly and apparently without pollution or environmental damage. At present 90% of Internet hosts are based in English-speaking countries. It is not surprising, therefore, that the majority of traffic and the majority of Web sites are based in English and that those users based in other countries and who normally work in other languages, find they have to communicate with others in the cyberspace community through the medium of English.

Many studies, however, have shown how well the Internet supports minority and diasporic affinity groups. Although early studies of 'nationally oriented' Internet newsgroups (containing discussions of national or regional culture and language) seemed to indicate a preference for using English (for example, soc.culture.punjabi), others which have become more recently active (such as soc.culture.vietnamese) extensively use the national language. It is not yet clear why some groups use English less than others, but an overall trend away from the hegemony of English in such groups is visible and often surfaces as an explicit topic of discussion.

One reason may be that the Internet user base is developing rapidly in Asia and non-English-speaking countries. And software technology, such as browser and HTML standards (which govern the HyperText Markup Language in which Web pages are written), now also supports multilingual browsing [. . .].

The quantity of Internet materials in languages other than English is set to expand dramatically in the next decade. English will remain pre-eminent for some time, but it will eventually become one language among many. It is therefore misleading to suggest English is somehow the native language of the Internet. It will be used in cyberspace in the same way as it is deployed elsewhere: in international forums, for the dissemination of scientific and technical knowledge, in advertising, for the promotion of consumer goods and for after-sales services.

David
Graddol

In the meantime, local communication on the Internet is expected to grow significantly. This, and the increasing use of email for social and family communication, will encourage the use of a wider variety of languages. English is said to have accounted for 80% of computer-based communication in the 1990s. That proportion is expected to fall to around 40% in the next decade.

Note

1   The engco forecasting model has been designed by The English Company (UK) Ltd as a means of examining the relative status of world languages and making forecasts of the numbers of speakers of different languages based on demographic, human development and economic data. The figures reported in this document are based on demographic projections from *World Population Prospects 1950–2050 (1996 Revision)* and *Sex and Age Quinquennial 1950–2050 (1996 Revision)* in machine readable data sets made available from the United Nations in 1997, on economic data for 1994 from the World Bank, and from estimates of proportions of national populations speaking different languages taken from national census data and a variety of reference sources.

The main purpose of the model is to explore the potential impact of urbanisation and economic development on the global linguistic landscape of the twenty-first century. A more detailed explanation of the assumptions made by the engco model can be found on The English Company (UK) Ltd's Internet site (http://www.english.co.uk) along with details of any other reports and revised projections which may become available from time to time.

D8.2 Issues to consider

❑   Graddol seems confident that English will remain the language of technology and industry. How might advances in technology affect the development of English in the future? One way into considering this is to think about the effect of technological innovations on English in the past (for example, the widespread use of the printing press, the Industrial Revolution, etc.). Consider the potential impact on both written and spoken English.

❑   In terms of social attitudes towards English, what is the likely effect of a steadily increasing number of people speaking English as a second or foreign language?

❑   What might be the impact of the globalisation of English on local dialect varieties?

❑   To what extent do you think the scenarios suggested by Graddol will result in the development of a World Standard English? And what would any World Standard be like? For instance, would you expect it to be essentially a variety of British Standard English?

GLOSSARY OF LINGUISTIC TERMS

accent   A speaker's accent is the way that he/she pronounces their particular variety of the language that they speak. For example, the Birmingham accent differs phonologically from the Newcastle accent. A speaker's accent can indicate where he/she is from, what social class they belong to, how educated they are, etc. It is not uncommon to hear people speaking Standard English with a regional accent, though it would be unusual to hear someone speaking a regional dialect using Received Pronunciation. (See also *dialect*).

adjective   Adjectives can either function as the head of an adjective phrase ('I am *very hungry*') or as modifiers in a noun phrase (The *large brown* cow). Most adjectives are gradable and have a base form, a comparative form and a superlative form. It is often possible to tell whether a word is an adjective by seeing if you can make a comparative or superlative form, as in *tall* (base form), *taller* (comparative) and *tallest* (superlative). Usually, adjectives specify the properties of a noun and can be descriptive (The *large brown* cow) or evaluative (The *most beautiful* cow).

adverb   Adverbs function as the head of an adverb phrase. Sometimes the head is preceded by modifiers, which are often adverbs of degree. Here are some examples (the adverb phrases are underlined and the head is in italics): The professor gesticulated <u>*wildly*</u>; He shouted <u>exceptionally *loudly*</u>; The students applauded <u>very *enthusiastically* indeed</u>. Adverbs can also function as modifiers in adjective phrases (the adjective phrases are underlined and the modifying adverbs are italicised): I am <u>*extremely* hungry</u>; The professor was <u>*very* pleased</u>; It was <u>*too* hot</u>. Adverbs often end in –*ly*, but be careful – sometimes what looks like an adverb is actually an adjective – e.g. *friendly*. Some adverbs also have comparative and superlative forms (e.g. She danced *well/better/best*; He danced *gracefully/more gracefully/most gracefully*). Adverbs give more information about the action, process, state, etc. described in the verb phrase. Adverbs can express manner (*quickly, well*), place (*here, there, somewhere*), time (*now, then, last night, six weeks ago*), duration (*constantly, briefly, always*), frequency (*daily, weekly*) and degree (*hardly, rather, quite*).

conjunction   Conjunctions link phrases and clauses and can be either co-ordinating (e.g. *and, but, or, either, nor, neither*) or subordinating (e.g. *although, when, after, because, since, whereby, while, unless, as, but*). There are more subordinating than co-ordinating conjunctions. Subordinating conjunctions introduce a clause within a sentence that is linked to the main clause but which cannot stand on its own.

consonant   A consonant is a speech sound that is produced when the outflow of air from the lungs is restricted in some way by the articulators (e.g. teeth, lips, tongue).

determiner   Determiners introduce noun phrases (e.g. <u>*A* tiger</u> ate <u>*the* hunters</u>). The definite and indefinite articles (*the* and *a* respectively) are determiners, as are demonstratives like *this, that, those, these, my, your, all, any, some, most.*

dialect A dialect is a sub-variety of a particular language. Dialects differ in terms of words, grammatical structures and pronunciations. For example, speakers of Yorkshire dialect may use words or grammatical structures that are not used in other dialects of English. Similarly, their pronunciation will vary from that of speakers of other dialects. The term *dialect* is considered by some linguists to have negative connotations. For example, non-linguists often think of dialects as corruptions of a standard form. To avoid these problems, linguists sometimes use the term *variety* as a neutral alternative. Note that the term *dialect* incorporates differences in pronunciation, while the term *accent* refers solely to phonological characteristics. (See also *accent.*)

digraph A digraph is a two-letter combination that represents one phoneme. For example, the digraph *<sh>* represents the phoneme /ʃ/, as in the English word *ship*. A digraph is a type of grapheme. (See also *grapheme* and *graph.*)

diphthong A diphthong is a long vowel that is composed of two distinct vowel sounds with a glide between them, e.g. /au/, as in *south.*

discourse If we think of the elements that make up language as being hierarchically structured, then morphemes combine to form words, words combine to form phrases, phrases combine to form clauses, and clauses combine to form sentences (see the introduction to section C for more details). In each case, the unit of language that we are dealing with is larger than the last. The term *discourse* refers to the next level up in the hierarchy; i.e. language above the level of the sentence. *Discourse* is language that is meaningful and unified – that is, coherent (either syntactically or pragmatically). *Discourse* can refer to both written and spoken language. Additionally, *discourse* is used to refer to dynamic, communicative interaction between speakers and hearers, and writers and readers.

grammar Grammar refers to the structures that govern the formation of meaningful words and sentences in a language. Grammar can be sub-divided into morphology ('word grammar') and syntax ('sentence grammar'). (See also *morphology* and *syntax.*)

graph A graph is a single letter that represents a particular phoneme. So the graph *<k>* represents the phoneme /k/. A graph is a type of grapheme. (See also *grapheme* and *digraph.*)

grapheme A *grapheme* is a symbol used to represent a particular phoneme. Graphemes are indicated by angle brackets. For example, in English the grapheme *<sh>* represents the phoneme /ʃ/ and the grapheme *<p>* represents the phoneme /p/. (See also *graph* and *digraph.*)

graphology Graphology is the study of the appearance of language in its written form. It may be useful to think of graphology as the written equivalent of phonology. That is, while the phonological level of language comprises the speech sounds of that language, the graphological level comprises its visual characteristics. (See also *phonology.*)

inflection An inflection is a morphological ending on a word or change in the form of a word that affects its grammatical function. For example, *<-er>* is an inflection that can be appended to the base form of adjectives to form a comparative.

lexis   The term *lexis* is a technical term to refer to the vocabulary of a language. The related term *lexical item* (or *lexeme*) is a more precise way of describing what non-linguists might call a word. For example, linguists would say that *jumping*, *jumped* and *jumps* are all different forms of the same lexical item, *jump*.

monophthong   A monophthong is a pure vowel, e.g. /æ/, as in *cat* (compare this with a *diphthong*).

morpheme   A morpheme is the smallest meaningful unit of language. Note that phonemes combine to form morphemes. Morphemes can be free (e.g. 'chair', 'hunt') or bound ('chair-s', 'hunting'). (See also *morphology*.)

morphology   Morphology is the study of word-structure and how morphemes can combine to form meaningful words. (See also *grammar* and *syntax*.)

noun   Nouns can function as the head of a noun phrase, as in *The bright blue racing car*. 'Car' is the head of this phrase; without the word *car* this phrase is incomplete. However, the head of a noun phrase is not always the final word in the phrase. Sometimes the head word can be post-modified (as opposed to the pre-modification in the above example) – consider *The bright blue racing car that won the race*. Also, some noun phrases (NPs) can be just one word long, as in *Cows* (NP) *eat* (VP) *grass* (NP). A good test for a noun is to see whether you can put the definite article (*the*) before it. If you can, it is likely to be a noun. You can sometimes recognise a noun by its suffix. Typical suffixes include: *leader*, *racism*, *station*, *happiness*, *prosperity*. Some nouns can also be pluralised by adding either <*-s*>, <*-es*> or <*-ies*>. Nouns often refer to physical things – e.g. people, places, objects, substances. These are concrete nouns. However, nouns can also refer to abstract concepts. Abstract nouns include *happiness*, *love*, *anniversary*, *pain*, *thought*.

orthography   Orthography refers to the spelling system of a language. The study of a language's orthography is therefore the study of spelling in that language.

phoneme   A phoneme is the smallest unit of sound. This can be indicated by considering minimal pairs – that is, words that differ in just one phoneme. For example, the words *tip* and *tap* are distinguishable only because of their different vowel sounds. This means that the /I/ and /æ/ must be distinct phonemes, because replacing the phoneme /I/ in *tip* with /æ/ changes the meaning of the word. Compare, on the other hand, the phonemes /t/ and /ʔ/. Replacing the /t/ in *bottle* with the glottal stop does not change the meaning of the word (compare /bɒtəl/ and /bɒʔəl/), therefore /t/ and /ʔ/ must be considered variants of the same phoneme, rather than distinct phonemes. (See also *phonology*.)

phonology   Phonology is the study of speech sounds in language. It is sometimes convenient to imagine language to be composed of a number of different structural levels. In such a model of language, the phonological level comprises the speech sounds of the language in question. (See also *graphology*.)

pragmatics   Pragmatics is the study of meaning and how context affects this. If a librarian in the university library asks me if I have my library card and I say 'Damn! I've forgotten my wallet!', it is likely that the librarian would infer my answer to mean 'no', on the basis of being able to infer that my wallet is where I usually keep it. But if, on entering the pub, I say 'Damn! I've forgotten my wallet!', whoever I happen to be with might understand me to mean 'Can you pay for the drinks?' (and I can guess what their answer would be!). Pragmatics tries to explain how meanings can be inferred that are different from the surface-level meaning of the utterance.

preposition   Prepositions usually express relations of position in space and time. They are always followed by a noun phrase, e.g. Dorothy travelled _over the rainbow,_ I parked the car _outside_ the house.

pronoun   Pronouns can be used in place of a noun phrase. For example, in the sentence 'The exceptionally scatty lecturer smiled warmly', we can replace the noun phrase (_The exceptionally scatty lecturer_) with a pronoun, e.g. 'He smiled warmly'. Pronouns cannot be modified with determiners or adjectives.

semantics   Semantics is the study of meaning, incorporating word-meaning and sentence-meaning. While pragmatics considers the effects of context on meaning, semantics does not. (See also _pragmatics._)

syntax   Syntax is the study of sentence structure and the rules governing the formation of meaningful sentences in a language. Note that in this case, 'rules' means descriptive as opposed to prescriptive rules; see C4 for more details on this distinction. (See also _morphology_ and _grammar._)

text   We are used to thinking of _text_ as referring to written language but linguists often use the term in a technical sense. _Text_, in this case, is the product of discourse, either written or spoken. So, a transcript of an interview is a text, even though the original discourse was spoken language.

utterance   An utterance is a unit of spoken language that may or may not have the formal characteristics of a sentence.

variety   The term _variety_ can be used as a neutral alternative to _dialect_ to avoid any negative connotations that the latter term may have. Since non-linguists tend to think of dialects as being specifically regional forms of language (e.g. Scouse, Lancashire), _variety_ can be particularly useful to refer to non-geographical aspects of language variation (e.g. linguistic differences based on social class). _Variety_ is also used to refer to international variants of a language (e.g. Australian English, Indian English, etc.).

verb   Main verbs function as the head of a verb phrase (VP). Sometimes the verb phrase will consist of just the main verb, and other times there may be auxiliary verbs before it. Here are some examples of VPs (underlined), with the main verb in italics: Cows _eat_ grass, I was _avoiding_ work, The mice must have _eaten_ all the cheese! Verbs have five different forms (see the table below). For regular verbs, the past and past participle form are the same. For irregular verbs, these are different. Verbs can refer to physical actions (_run, jump_), states of being (_is_), mental processes (_think, believe, understand_), etc.

	Infinitive	Present	Past	Present participle	Past participle
Regular	walk	walk/s	walked	walking	walked
Irregular	drink	drink/s	drank	drinking	drunk
	give	give/s	gave	giving	given
	fly	fly/ies	flew	flying	flown

vowel A vowel is a speech sound that is produced when the airflow from the lungs is not impeded as it is in the production of consonants. Different vowel sounds are achieved by varying the shape of the mouth cavity.

FURTHER READING

This book is a starting point. It provides a broad overview of some of the major aspects of the history of English and my hope is that it will leave you wanting to explore this topic further. Below are some suggestions as to books and articles that you will find useful for investigating particular topic areas in more detail.

GENERAL HISTORIES OF ENGLISH

❏ Baugh and Cable (2002) has long been a standard introduction to the history of English and is particularly good on the external history of the language. Blake (1996) is a history of Standard English that dispenses with the traditional division of the language into Old, Middle, Early Modern and Modern varieties and as such provides an interesting alternative perspective on the way that the history of English is often packaged, as does Crystal (2005). Watts and Trudgill (2002) contains articles examining alternative histories of English, and Wales (2006) looks specifically at the development of Northern English. For a focus on the social and cultural aspects of the history of English, as well as some of the debates surrounding these, try Knowles (1997).

❏ For more information on the internal history of the language, Pyles and Algeo (1993) provides considerable detail. Freeborn (2006) is a comprehensive and chronologically ordered survey that is especially good on the development of written English, and has a strong emphasis on the examination of primary sources. Fennell (2001) is an excellent and highly accessible textbook that combines both an internal and external history of the language, and is an ideal next step once you have read an entry-level textbook such as this one.

❏ For a solid description of English at its various stages, see Smith (2005). Volume 5 of *The Cambridge History of the English Language* focuses on the development and history of English in Britain and overseas. Barber (1993) is also a good overview, and the *Oxford History of English* (Mugglestone 2006) is another highly accessible source.

OLD ENGLISH

❏ Three very accessible introductions to Old English language are McCully and Hilles (2005), Hogg (1992) and Hough and Corbett (2007). When you feel ready to tackle something at a higher level, Mitchell (1995) is an excellent and very readable account of Old English and also provides a good deal of contextual information about the Anglo-Saxon world. Mitchell and Robinson (2007) is an extremely thorough guide to Old English grammar.

❏ Volume 1 of *The Cambridge History of the English Language* (Hogg 1992) provides in-depth coverage of English from its earliest origins up until 1066.

❏ An understanding of phonetics and grammar is undoubtedly of help when it comes to deciphering Old English. If you feel you need to brush up on the basics, Jeffries (2006) is an ideal introductory textbook focusing on the description of English at all linguistic levels. For a specialist text on phonetics and phonology try Collins and Mees (2004), and for grammar and vocabulary, Jackson (2002).

MIDDLE ENGLISH

❏ A standard textbook on Middle English, which also contains considerable discussion of Middle English literature, is Burrow and Turville-Petre (1996). Smith and Horobin (2005) is a good, general introduction to Middle English and Horobin (2007) is a very accessible account of Chaucer's variety. Machan (2003) provides a fascinating account of the status and use of Middle English during the Middle English period.

❏ Volume 2 of *The Cambridge History of the English Language* (Blake 1992) provides comprehensive coverage of English from the Norman Conquest to the advent of printing.

EARLY MODERN ENGLISH

❏ A good descriptive account of Early Modern English is Barber (1997). Görlach (1991) is a detailed and comprehensive study, with a greater focus on the mechanisms for change and development in the language, as is Nevalainen (2006).

❏ For a discussion of some of the pragmatic aspects of spoken Early Modern English see Culpeper and Kytö (2000). Culpeper and Kytö (1999) is a corpus-based study of non-standard varieties in Early Modern English dialogues, and also includes some consideration of the methodological issues associated with studying EModE speech.

❏ On the issue of standardisation see especially Wright (2000) and Nevalainen and Tieken-Boon van Ostade (2006).

❏ For comprehensive coverage of the period see volume 3 of *The Cambridge History of the English Language* (Lass 1999).

EIGHTEENTH-CENTURY ENGLISH TO THE PRESENT DAY

❏ Volume 4 of the *Cambridge History of the English Language* (Romaine 1998) provides detailed coverage of many aspects of the language of this period.

❏ Bailey (1996) and Görlach (1999) are comprehensive overviews of nineteenth-century English.

❏   Biber et al. (1999) is a comprehensive, corpus-based grammar of spoken and writ-
     ten Present Day English, while Leech (2003) and Mair and Leech (2006) examine
     recent grammatical developments in English.

WORLD ENGLISHES

❏   For an introduction to the notion of World Englishes see Jenkins (2003).
❏   Crystal (2003) is a good introduction to some of the important themes concern-
     ing English as a global language, while Bailey and Görlach (1984) provides in-
     depth surveys of the development and spread of English around the world.
❏   Volume 6 of *The Cambridge History of the English Language* focuses particu-
     larly on the development of English in North America, and Tottie (2002) is an
     accessible introduction to the linguistic and sociolinguistic aspects of American
     English.

REFERENCES

Aitchison, J. (2001) *Language Change: Progress or Decay?* 3rd edition. Cambridge: Cambridge University Press.

Algeo, J. (ed.) (2001) *The Cambridge History of the English Language, Vol. 6: English in North America*. Cambridge: Cambridge University Press.

Altendorf, U. (2003) *Estuary English: Levelling at the Interface of RP and South-Eastern British English*. Tübingen: Narr.

Arnold, T. (1871) *Select English Works of John Wyclif*. Oxford: Clarendon Press.

Arnould, E.-J. (1958) 'Deux siècles de contacts culturels franco-anglais (871–1066)', *Annales de Normandie* 8: 71–85.

Bailey, R. (1996) *Nineteenth-Century English*. Ann Arbor: University of Michigan Press.

Bailey, R. W. and Görlach, M. (1984) *English as a World Language*. Cambridge: Cambridge University Press.

Barber, C. (1976) *Early Modern English*. London: André Deutsch.

Barber, C. (1993) *The English Language: A Historical Introduction*. Cambridge: Cambridge University Press.

Barber, C. (1997) *Early Modern English*. 2nd edition. Edinburgh: Edinburgh University Press.

Baugh, A. C. and Cable, T. (2002) *A History of the English Language*. 5th edition. London: Prentice Hall.

Benskin, M. (2004) 'Chancery Standard', in Kay, C., Hough, C. and Wotherspoon, I. (eds) *New Perspectives on English Historical Linguistics: Volume II: Lexis and Transmission*, pp. 1–40. Amsterdam: John Benjamins.

Berndt, R. (1965) 'The linguistic situation in England from the Norman Conquest to the loss of Normandy (1066–1204)', *Philologica Pragensia* 8: 145–63.

Biber, D. and Clark, V. (2002) 'Historical shifts in modification patterns with complex noun phrase structures: how long can you go without a verb?', in Fanego, T., Pérez-Guerra, J. and José López-Couso, M. (eds) *English Historical Syntax and Morphology: Selected Papers from 11ICEHL*, pp. 43–66. Amsterdam: John Benjamins.

Biber, D., Johansson, S., Leech, G., Conrad, S. and Finegan, E. (1999) *Longman Grammar of Spoken and Written English*. London: Longman.

Bishop, C. J. E. (1962) 'Mercian "second-fronting"', *Archivum Linguisticum* 14: 130–45.

Bishop, T. A. M. (1971) *English Caroline Minuscule*. Oxford: Clarendon.

Björkman, E. (1969) *Scandinavian Loan-words in Middle English*. New York: Greenwood Press.

Blake, N. (ed.) (1992) *The Cambridge History of the English Language, Vol. 2: 1066–1476*. Cambridge: Cambridge University Press.

Blake, N. (1996) *A History of the English Language*. Basingstoke: Palgrave.

Blank, A. (1999) 'Why do new meanings occur? A cognitive typology of the motivations for lexical semantic change', in Blank, A. and Koch, P. (eds) *Historical Semantics and Cognition*, pp. 61–89. Berlin: Mouton de Gruyter.

Bugaj, J. (2004) *Middle Scots Inflectional System in the South-West of Scotland*. Frankfurt: Peter Lang.

Burchfield, R. (ed.) (1994) *The Cambridge History of the English Language, Vol. 5: English in Britain and Overseas: Origins and Development*. Cambridge: Cambridge University Press.

Burchfield, R. (1994) 'Introduction', in Burchfield, R. (ed.) *The Cambridge History of the English Language, Vol. 5: English in Britain and Overseas: Origins and Development*. Cambridge: Cambridge University Press.

Burridge, K. and Mulder, J. (1998) *English in Australia and New Zealand*. Oxford: Oxford University Press.

Burrow, J. A. and Turville-Petre, T. (1996) *A Book of Middle English*. 2nd edition. Oxford. Blackwell.

Cameron, A. (1982) 'Review: *Spezifisch anglisches Wortgut in den nordhumbrischen Interlinearglossierungen des Lukasevangeliums* by Franz Wenisch', *Speculum* 57(4): 956–7.

Campbell, A. (1959) *Old English Grammar*. Oxford: Clarendon.

Carney, E. (1994) *A Survey of English Spelling*. London: Routledge.

Cassidy, F. G. (1984) 'Geographical variation of English in the United States', in Bailey, R. W. and Görlach, M. (eds) *English as a World Language*, pp. 177–209. Cambridge: Cambridge University Press.

Cawdrey, R. C. (1604) *A Table Alphabeticall*. London.

Clover, B. (1888) *The Mastery of the French Language in England from the XIth to the XIVth Century, Including the Phonetics and Morphology of the Norman French Language, With Special Reference to the Law Reports Contained in the Year Books*. New York: Corning and Co.

Collins, B. and Mees, I. (2004) *Practical Phonetics and Phonology: A Resource Book for Students*. London: Routledge.

Collins, P. and Peters, P. (1988) 'The Australian corpus project', in Kytö, M., Ihalainen, O. and Rissanen, M. (eds) *Corpus Linguistics, Hard and Soft*, pp. 103–20. Amsterdam: Rodopi.

Cooke, D. (1988) 'Ties that constrict: English as a Trojan horse', in Cumming, A., Gagne, A. and Dawson, J. (eds) *Awareness: Proceedings of the 1987 TESL Ontario Conference*, pp. 56–62. Toronto: TESL Ontario.

Corbett, J., McClure, J. D. and Stuart-Smith, J. (2003) 'A brief history of Scots', in Corbett, J., McClure, J. D. and Stuart-Smith, J. (eds) *The Edinburgh Companion to Scots*, pp. 1–17. Edinburgh: Edinburgh University Press.

Crowley, J. P. (1981) 'The Study of Old English Dialects'. Unpublished PhD thesis: University of North Carolina at Chapel Hill.

Crowley, J. P. (1986) 'The study of Old English dialects', *English Studies* 67: 97–104.

Crystal, D. (1994) *Rediscover Grammar*. London: Longman.

Crystal, D. (1995) *The Cambridge Encyclopedia of the English Language*. Cambridge: Cambridge University Press.

Crystal, D. (2000) *Language Death*. Cambridge: Cambridge University Press.

Crystal, D. (2001) 'The future of Englishes', in Burns, A. and Coffin, C. (eds) *Analysing English in a Global Context*, pp. 53–64. London: Routledge.

Crystal, D. (2003) *English as a Global Language*. 2nd edition. Cambridge: Cambridge University Press.

Crystal, D. (2005) *The Stories of English*. London: Penguin.

Culpeper, J. and Kytö, M. (1999) 'Investigating non-standard language in a corpus of Early Modern English dialogues: methodological considerations and problems', in Taavitsainen, I., Melchers, G. and Pahta, P. (eds) *Writing in Non-Standard English*, pp. 171–87. Amsterdam: John Benjamins.

Culpeper, J. and Kytö, M. (2000) 'Data in historical pragmatics: spoken interaction (re)cast as writing', *Journal of Historical Pragmatics* 1(2): 175–99.

Davies, N. (2000) *The Isles: A History*. Basingstoke: Papermac.

Dillard, J. L. (1985) *Toward a Social History of American English*. Berlin: Walter de Gruyter.

Dillard, J. L. (1992) *A History of American English*. London: Pearson Education.

Dunning, T. (1993) 'Accurate methods for the statistics of surprise and coincidence', *Computational Linguistics* 19(1): 61–74.

Eagleson, R. (1984) 'English in Australia and New Zealand', in Bailey, R. W. and Görlach, M. (eds) *English as a World Language*, pp. 415–38. Cambridge: Cambridge University Press.

Ekwall, E. (1960) *The Concise Oxford Dictionary of English Place-Names*. Oxford: Oxford University Press.

Emerson, O. F. (1921) *John Dryden and a British Academy*. London: Oxford University Press.

Fennell, B. (2001) *A History of English: A Sociolinguistic Approach*. Oxford: Blackwell.

Fisiak, J. (1968) *A Short Grammar of Middle English*. London: Oxford University Press.

Flasdieck, H. M. (1928) *Der Gedanke einer Englischen Sprachakademie*. Jena: Germany.

Förster, M. (1902) 'Ein Englisch-Französisches rechtsglossar', *Beitrage zur Romanischen und Englischen Philologie. Festgäbe für Wendelin Förster*, pp. 205–12. Halle: Niemeyer.

Foxe, J. (1563) *Actes and Monuments*. London.

Freeborn, D. (2006) *From Old English to Standard English*. 3rd edition. Basingstoke: Palgrave.

Freeman, E. (1924) 'A proposal for an English Academy in 1660', *Modern Language Review* 19: 291–300.

Gneuss, H. (1972) 'The origin of standard Old English and Æthelwold's school at Winchester', *Anglo-Saxon England* 1: 63–83.

Görlach, M. (1991) *Introduction to Early Modern English*. Cambridge: Cambridge University Press.

Görlach, M. (1999) *English in Nineteenth-century England: An Introduction*. Cambridge: Cambridge University Press.

Graddol, D. (1997) *The Future of English?* London: British Council.

Green, J. (1982) 'The Sheriffs of William the Conqueror', *Anglo-Norman Studies* 5: 129–45.

Green, L. J. (2002) *African American English*. Cambridge: Cambridge University Press.

Haugen, E. (1966) 'Dialect, language, nation', in Pride, J. B. and Holmes, J. (eds) (1972) *Sociolinguistics*, pp. 97–111. Harmondsworth: Penguin.

Held, D., McGrew, A., Goldblatt, D. and Perraton, J. (1999) *Global Transformations: Politics, Economics and Culture.* Cambridge: Polity Press.

Hogg, R. (ed.) (1992) *The Cambridge History of the English Language. Volume 1: The Beginnings to 1066*, pp. 409–51. Cambridge: Cambridge University Press.

Hogg, R. (2002) *An Introduction to Old English.* Edinburgh: Edinburgh University Press.

Horobin, S. (2007) *Chaucer's Language.* Basingstoke: Palgrave.

Hough, C. and Corbett, J. (2007) *Beginning Old English.* Basingstoke: Palgrave.

Hunter Blair, P. (1962) [1956] *An Introduction to Anglo-Saxon England.* Cambridge: Cambridge University Press.

Iglesias-Rábade, L. (1987) 'Norman England: a historical sociolinguistic approach', *Revista Canária de Estudios Ingleses* 15: 101–12.

Jackson, H. (2002) *Grammar and Vocabulary: A Resource Book for Students.* London: Routledge.

James, E. (2001) *Britain in the First Millennium.* London: Arnold.

Jeffries, L. (2006) *Discovering Language: The Structure of Modern English.* Basingstoke: Palgrave Macmillan.

Jenkins, J. (2003) *World Englishes: A Resource Book for Students.* London: Routledge.

Johnson, F. R. (1944) 'Latin versus English: the sixteenth century debate over scientific vocabulary', *Studies in Philology* 41(2): 109–35.

Johnson, S. (1983) [1755] *A Dictionary of the English Language.* London: Times Books.

Jones, M. A. (1995) *The Limits of Liberty: American History 1607–1992.* Oxford: Oxford University Press.

Judd, E. L. (1983) 'TESOL as a political act: a moral question', in Handscombe, J., Orem, R. A. and Taylor, B. P. (eds) *On TESOL '83*, pp. 265–73. Washington DC: TESOL.

Kachru, B. (1984) 'South Asian English', in Bailey, R. W. and Görlach, M. (eds) *English as a World Language*, pp. 353–83. Cambridge: Cambridge University Press.

Ker, N. R. (1957) *Catalogue of Manuscripts Containing Anglo-Saxon.* Oxford: Clarendon.

Kibbee, D. (1991) *For to Speke Frenche Trewely. The French Language in England 1000–1600: Its Status, Description and Instruction.* Amsterdam: John Benjamins.

Knowles, G. (1997) *A Cultural History of the English Language.* London: Arnold.

König, E. (1980) 'On the context-dependence of the progressive form in English', in Rohrer, C. (ed.) *Time, Tense and Quantifiers: Proceedings of the Stuttgart Conference on the Logic of Tense and Quantification.* Tübingen: Max Niemeyer.

König, E. (1995) 'He is being obscure: non-verbal predication and the progressive', in Bertinetto, P. M., Bianchi, V., Higginbotham, J. and Squartini, M. (eds) *Temporal Reference, Aspect and Actionality*, 2 vols, pp. 155–68. Turin: Rosenberg and Sellier.

Krapp, G. P. (1910) *Modern English.* New York.

Krapp, G. P. (1925) *The English Language in America.* New York: The Century Company.

Kufner, H. (1972) 'The grouping and separation of the Germanic languages', in Van Coetsem, F. and Kufner, H. (eds) *Toward a Grammar of Proto-Germanic*, pp. 71–97. Tübingen: Niemeyer.

Labov, W. (1966) *The Social Stratification of English in New York City*. Washington DC: Center for Applied Linguistics.

Labov, W. (1972) *Language in the Inner City*. Philadelphia: University of Pennsylvania Press.

Labov, W. (1978) 'On the use of the present to explain the past', in Baldi, P. and Werth, R. N. (eds) *Readings in Historical Phonology*, pp. 275–312. Pennsylvania: Pennsylvania State University Press.

Lass, R. (ed.) (1999) *The Cambridge History of the English Language, 1476–1776*. Cambridge: Cambridge University Press.

Leech, G. (2003), 'Modality on the move: the English modal auxiliaries 1961–1992', in Facchinetti, R., Krug, M. and Palmer, F. R. (eds) *Modality in Contemporary English*, pp. 223–40. Berlin: Mouton de Gruyter.

Leech, G. (2004), 'Recent grammatical change in English: data, description, theory', in Altenberg, B. and Aijmer, K. (eds) *Advances in Corpus Linguistics. Proceedings of the 23rd ICAME Conference, Gothenburg, 2002*. Amsterdam: Rodopi.

Leech, G. and Smith, N. (2006) 'Recent grammatical change in written English 1961–1992: some preliminary findings of a comparison of American with British English', in Renouf, A. and Kehoe, A. (eds) *The Changing Face of Corpus Linguistics*, pp. 185–204. Amsterdam: Rodopi.

Legge, M. D. (1979) 'Anglo-Norman as a Spoken Language', *Anglo-Norman Studies* 2: 108–17.

Leith, D. (1983) *A Social History of English*. London: Routledge.

Leith, D. (1997) *A Social History of English*. 2nd edition. London: Routledge.

Ljung, M. (1980) *Reflections on the English Progressive*. Gothenburg Studies in English 46. Gothenburg: Acta Universitatis Gothoburgensis.

Leonard, R. (1968) 'The Types and Currency of Noun and Noun Sequences in Prose Usage 1750–1950'. Unpublished MPhil thesis: University of London.

Leonard, R. (1984) *The Interpretation of English Noun Sequences on the Computer*. Amsterdam: North Holland.

Loyn, H. R. (1962) *Anglo-Saxon England and the Norman Conquest*. London: Longman.

Machan, T. (2003) *English in the Middle Ages*. Oxford: Oxford University Press.

McCully, C. and Hilles, S. (2005) *The Earliest English: An Introduction to Old English Language*. London: Longman.

Mackenzie, F. (1939) *Les relations de l'Angleterre et de la France d'après le vocabulaire*. Paris: Droz.

Mair, C. (1997) 'The spread of the going-to-future in written English: a corpus-based investigation into language change in progress', in Hickey, R. and Puppel, S. (eds) *Language History and Language Modelling: A Festschrift for Jacek Fisiak on His 60th Birthday*, pp. 1537–43. Berlin: Mouton de Gruyter.

Mair, C. and Hundt, M. (1995) 'Why is the progressive becoming more frequent in English? A corpus-based investigation of language change in progress', *Zeitschrift für Anglistik und Amerikanistik* 43: 111–22.

Mair, C. and Leech, G. (2006) 'Current change in English syntax', in Aarts, B. and MacMahon, A. (eds) *The Handbook of English Linguistics*, pp. 318–42. Oxford: Blackwell.

Marckwardt, A. H. (revised by J. L. Dillard) (1980) *American English*. Oxford: Oxford University Press.

Marckwardt, A. H. and Rosier, J. L. (1972) *Old English Language and Literature*. New York: W. C. Norton and Co.

Mencken, H. L. (1967) [1936] *The American Language: An Inquiry into the Development of English in the United States*. One volume abridged edition. New York: Alfred A. Knopf.

Mills, A. D. (1998) *A Dictionary of English Place Names*. 2nd edition. Oxford: Oxford University Press.

Mitchell, B. (1995) *An Invitation to Old English and Anglo-Saxon England*. Oxford: Blackwell.

Mitchell, B. and Robinson, F. C. (2007) *A Guide to Old English*. 7th edition. Oxford: Blackwell.

Moore, S., Meech, S. B. and Whitehall, H. (1935) 'Middle English dialect characteristics and dialect boundaries', *Essays and Studies in English and Comparative Literature*, pp. 1–60. Ann Arbor: University of Michigan Publications.

Mugglestone, L. (ed.) (2006) *The Oxford History of English*. Oxford: Oxford University Press.

Myres, J. N. L. (1970) 'The Angles, the Saxons and the Jutes', *Proceedings of the British Academy* 56: 145–74.

Nevalainen, T. (2006). *An Introduction to Early Modern English*. Edinburgh: Edinburgh University Press.

Nevalainen, T. and Tieken-Boon van Ostade, I. (2006) 'Standardisation', in Hogg, R. and Denison, D. (eds) *A History of the English Language*, pp. 271–311. Cambridge: Cambridge University Press.

Nielson, H. F. (1981) 'Old Frisian and the Old English dialects', *Us Wurk* 30: 49–66.

O'Grady, W. and de Guzman, V. P. (1996) 'Morphology: the analysis of word structure', in O'Grady, W., Dobrovolsky, M. and Katamba, F. (eds) *Contemporary Linguistics: An Introduction*. 3rd edition, pp. 132–80. London: Longman.

Orton, H., Sanderson, S. and Widdowson, J. (eds) (1978) *The Linguistic Atlas of England*. London: Croom Helm.

Övergaard, G. (1995) *The Mandative Subjunctive in American and British English in the 20th Century*. Stockholm: Almqvist and Wiksell International.

Pennycook, A. (2001) 'English in the world/the world in English', in Burns, A. and Coffin, C. (eds) *Analysing English in a Global Context*, pp. 78–89. London: Routledge.

Phillipson, R. (1992) *Linguistic Imperialism*. Oxford: Oxford University Press.

Price, O. (1668) *English Orthographie*. Oxford: Henry Hall.

Pyles, T. and Algeo, J. (1993) *The Origins and Development of the English Language*. 4th edition. Fort Worth: Harcourt Brace Jovanovich.

Quirk, R., Adams, V. and Davy, D. (1975) *Old English Literature: A Practical Introduction*. London: Edward Arnold.

Ray, M. and Jacka, E. (1996) 'Indian television: an emerging regional force', in Sinclair, J., Jacka, E. and Cunningham, S. (eds) *New Patterns in Global Television: Peripheral Vision*. Oxford: Oxford University Press.

Read, A. W. (1938) 'Suggestions for an Academy in England in the latter half of the eighteenth century', *Modern Philology* 36(2): 145–56.

Reaney, P. H. (1960) *The Origin of English Place Names*. London: Routledge.

Reed, C. E. (1967) *Dialects of American English*. Amherst: University of Massachusetts Press.

Romaine, S. (1988) *Pidgin and Creole Languages*. London: Longman.

Romaine, S. (ed.) (1998) *The Cambridge History of the English Language, Vol. 4: 1776–1997*. Cambridge: Cambridge University Press.

Rothwell, W. (1983) 'Language and government in medieval England', *Zeitschrift für Französischen Sprache und Literatur* 93: 258–70.

Salzman, L. F. (1967) *Building in England down to 1540*. Oxford: Clarendon.

Samuels, M. L. (1963) 'Some applications of Middle English dialectology', *English Studies* 44: 81–94.

Samuels, M. L. (1972) *Linguistic Evolution*. Cambridge: Cambridge University Press.

Scragg, D. G. (1974) *A History of English Spelling*. Manchester: Manchester University Press.

Sebba, M. (1997) *Contact Languages: Pidgins and Creoles*. Basingstoke: Palgrave.

Serjeantson, M. S. (1935) *A History of Foreign Words in English*. London: Routledge and Kegan Paul.

Serpollet, N. (2003) 'Should and the subjunctive: a corpus-based approach to mandative constructions in English and French'. Unpublished PhD thesis: Lancaster University.

Shastri, S. V. (1988), 'The Kolhapur Corpus of Indian English and work done on its basis so far', *ICAME Journal* 12: 15–26.

Shelly, P. Van Dyke (1921) *English and French in England*. Philadelphia: University of Pennsylvania Press.

Sheridan, T. (1756) *British Education*. London.

Simpson, D. (1986) *The Politics of American English, 1776–1850*. Oxford: Oxford University Press.

Smith, A. H. (1933) *Three Northumbrian Poems*. London: Methuen.

Smith, J. (2005) *Essentials of Early English*. 2nd edition. London: Routledge.

Smith, J. and Horobin, S. (2005) *An Introduction to Middle English*. Edinburgh: Edinburgh University Press.

Smith, N. (2003a), 'A quirky progressive? A corpus-based exploration of the will + be + -ing construction in recent and present day British English', in Archer, D., Rayson, P., Wilson, A. and McEnery, T. (eds) *Proceedings of the Corpus Linguistics 2003 Conference*. Lancaster University: UCREL Technical Papers 16: 714–23.

Smith, N. (2003b), 'Changes in modals and semi-modals of strong obligation and epistemic necessity in recent British English', in Facchinetti, R., Krug, M. and Palmer, F. R. (eds) *Modality in Contemporary English*, pp. 241–66. Berlin: Mouton de Gruyter.

Smyser, H. M. (1948) 'The list of Norman names in the Auchinleck Ms. (Battle Abbey Roll)', in Holmes, Jr., U. T. and Denomy, A. J. (eds) *Mediaeval Studies in Honor of Jeremiah Denis Matthias Ford*, pp. 257–87. Cambridge, MA: Harvard University Press.

Stenton, F. M. (1955) *The Latin Charters of the Anglo-Saxon Period*. Oxford: Clarendon Press.

Stockwell, P. (2002) *Sociolinguistics: A Resource Book for Students*. London: Routledge.

Stockwell, P. (2007) *Sociolinguistics: A Resource Book for Students*. 2nd edition. London: Routledge.

Todd, L. (1974) *Pidgins and Creoles*. London: Routledge and Kegan Paul.

Todd, L. (1984) 'The English language in West Africa', in Bailey, R. W. and Görlach, M. (eds) *English as a World Language*, pp. 281–305. Cambridge: Cambridge University Press.

Toon, T. E. (1984) 'Contemporary American English', in Bailey, R. W. and Görlach, M. (eds) *English as a World Language*, pp. 210–50. Cambridge: Cambridge University Press.

Toon, T. E. (1992) 'Old English dialects', in Hogg, R. (ed.) *The Cambridge History of the English Language. Volume 1: The Beginnings to 1066*, pp. 409–51. Cambridge: Cambridge University Press.

Tottie, G. (2002) *An Introduction to American English*. Oxford: Blackwell.

Trapp, J. B., Gray, D. and Boffey, J. (2002) *Medieval English Literature*. 2nd edition. Oxford: Oxford University Press.

Trudgill, P. (1974) *The Social Differentiation of English in Norwich*. Cambridge: Cambridge University Press.

Trudgill, P. and Hannah, J. (2002) *International English*. 4th edition. London: Arnold.

Vising, J. (1923) *Anglo-Norman Language and Literature*. London: Oxford University Press.

Vleeskruyer, R. (ed.) (1953) *The Life of St Chad*. Amsterdam: North Holland.

Wales, K. (2006) *Northern English: A Cultural and Social History*. Cambridge: Cambridge University Press.

Walpole, H. (1758) *Catalogue of the Royal and Noble Authors of England*. Middlesex: Strawberry Hill.

Watts, R. and Trudgill, P. (eds) (2002) *Alternative Histories of English*. London: Routledge.

Williams, J. M. (1975) *Origins of the English Language*. New York: The Free Press.

Wilson, R. M. (1939) *Early Middle English Literature*. London: Methuen.

Wolfram, W. and Thomas, E. R. (2002) *The Development of African American English*. Oxford: Blackwell.

Wright, L. (ed.) (2000) *The Development of Standard English, 1300–1800: Theories, Descriptions, Conflicts*. Cambridge: Cambridge University Press.

INDEX

accents 30, 183, 184
  see also dialects and regional differences
acceptance 60
accusative case 41–3
acronyms 115–16
adjectives 93, 183
  comparatives/superlatives 104–6
adverbs 93, 183
Ælfric 129
African-American English
  early representation of 112–13
  origins 69–70
Aitchison, Jean
  Language Change 147
  shifting sounds 147–54
Alfred the Great 7–8, 10–11, 136
Algeo, J. 82
American English 66–8
  African-American English and 69–70
  archaisms in 68–9, 163–4
  changed meanings 160–3
  colloquialisation 176–7
  colonies and independence 25–6
  loan words 67, 108–9
  Mencken on 160–6
  qualitative study of nouns 174–5
  qualitative study of verbs 166–73
  Webster's spelling reforms 110–11
*An Invitation to Old English and Anglo-
  Saxon England* (Mitchell) 128
analytic/synthetic language 40, 52–3
Angles 4
Anglo-Saxon Chronicle 140
Anglo-Saxon heptarchy 5
Anglo-Saxon language 4–6, 132
  peasantry and 140–1
  place names 88, 89
  settlement of people 135

Apollonius of Tyre 85
articulators 54
Asthana, Anushka 101–2
Augustine of Canterbury 6–7
Australian English 27
  colloquialisms 114–15
  development of 70–2

back-formation 116
Bacon, Francis 105
Barber, C. 61, 65
  comparatives/superlatives 106
  Quakers and pronouns 103
The Battle of Maldon 7–8
Baugh, Albert C. 5, 30, 69
  on an English Academy 154–60
  French borrowings 47
  A History of the English Language
    (with Cable) 154
BBC *see* British Broadcasting
    Corporation
St Bede 135
  *Ecclesiastical History of the English
    People* 4–5, 46
Benskin, Michael 21
Berndt, R. 140, 141
Biber, D. 174
The Bible
  King James version 19–20
  the Lord's Prayer 86–7, 95
  Tyndale's translation 19, 23
  Wycliffe's translation 18–19
Black Death 14
Blank, A. 120
blending 116–17
Bolton, Edmund 155
Boudica 3
brand names 117

Britain
    Anglo-Saxons 4–6
    industrial revolution 28
    Norman invasion 11–14, 48, 53
    political use of English 14
    Roman period 3–4
    trade and empire 25–7
    Viking invasions 7–8, 11
British Broadcasting Corporation
    prescriptivism and 101–2
    RP and 29–30
British Empire 25–7
British Philological Society 29
Britons 3
Bruton-Simmonds, Ian 101–2
bubonic plague 14
Bunyan, John 105
Burchfield, R. 70
Burridge, K. 70–1, 78
Burrow, J. A. 15

Cable, Thomas 5, 30, 69
    on an English Academy 154–60
    French borrowings 47
    A History of the English Language
        (with Baugh) 154
Cædmon's Hymn 46–7
calquing 76
Cameron, A. 87
Cameroon pidgin 75–6
Campbell, Alistair 133
Canada 25–6
The Canterbury Tales (Chaucer) 20–1,
    93–4
Carney, E.
    American spelling 110–12
cases 41, 84–5, 174
Cassidy, F. G. 67
Cawdrey, Richard
    A Table Alphabeticall 23, 96–7
Caxton, William 18–19, 22–3, 60
Celtic languages
    family tree 81, 82, 83
    Old English and 133, 137
    place names 88
    Scots and 3, 45

chain shifts
    push and drag 58, 148–52
Chancery English 18, 21–2, 24, 60–1
Chaucer, Geoffrey 50
    The Canterbury Tales 20–1, 93–4
Cheke, Sir John 66
Christianity
    translations of the Bible 19–20
    West Saxon dialect 9–10
    written language of monasteries 136
    see also Latin language
Churchill, Winston 33
Clark, V. 174
Claudius, Emperor 3
clipping 117, 118
Cnut, King 133
Cochrane, James 102
Cockney dialect
    Australian English and 71
code-switching 13
codification 60–1
coinage 117
Collins, B.
    Practical Phonetics (with Mees) 37
colonisation 25
colloquialisation 176–7
communication technology
    development of 31
    global use of English 33, 179–80
compounding 40
compounds 115
    Old English 40
conjunctions 93, 183
consonants 54–5, 183
contact languages 74–6
    see also loanwords
contractions 175
conversion 117
Cooke, D. 77
Cooke, Thomas 158
creoles *see* pidgins and creoles
Crowley, Joseph P.
    Old English dialects 134–9
Crystal, David
    on Bede 4–5
    examining language 2

global use of English 31–2, 77
  on King James Bible 19–20
culture
  identity and global English 77

Danes 7
Danish language *see* Scandinavian
    languages
dative case
  Old English 42–3, 84–5
Davies, Norman 11
Defoe, Daniel
  Essay upon Projects 156–7
derivation 116
determiners 93, 183–4
diacritics 49
dialects and regional differences 184
  boundaries 10–11
  convergence 68
  development of 60
  dialect-levelling 68
  Early Modern 65
  Estuary English 30, 152–4
  the Great Vowel Shift 144–7
  historical evidence 137–8
  isoglosses 15–16
  Middle English 15–16, 57
  mix in Australia 71
  Old English 8–11, 86–7, 134–9
  variety and 186
  see also accents
dictionaries and grammars
  Early Modern 23–4, 95–100
  Johnson's 24, 96, 129–30, 159
  OED 29
  Webster and American spelling 110–11
digraphs 37, 110–11, 184
  Middle English 49
  Old English 37
Dillard, J. L. 68, 112
diphthongs 184
  diphthongisation 57
  Estuary English 152–3
  Great Vowel Shift 144–5
  Old English 37, 47
  producing sounds 56–7

discourse 184
  globalisation 33
'The Dream of the Rood' 134
Dryden, John 155–6, 158
Dutch language
  American English and 67, 108

Eagleson, R. 27
Early Modern English 16
  American archaisms from 163–4
  Chancery standard 18, 21–2, 60–1
  development of 16–25
  gradable adjectives 104–6
  orthography 97–100
  prescription and description 95–7
  pronouns 103
  spelling and orthography 61–2
  the verb 'do' 106–8
  vocabulary expansion 66
  written form 60–1
Ecclesiastical History of the English People
    (Bede) 46
Education Act of 1870 29
Edward the Confessor 11–12, 13, 139
Ekwall, E. 88
elaboration 60
Ellis, A. J. 163
Elyot, Sir Thomas 66
Emerson, O. F. 156
English as a foreign language 31
  Middle English and the French
    52–3
  rise in 178–9
  see also global use of English
English language (Present Day)
  accents and 183
  colloquialisation 176–7
  development 28–31
  future development of 124–5
  global use of 31–4
  qualitative study of nouns 174–6
  qualitative study of verbs 166–73
  'Scottish Standard English' 45
  Standard English 11, 18, 20, 22, 29–30,
    33, 60–1, 64, 69, 72, 76–8, 100–1,
    105, 116–18, 122–4

understanding change 80–1
see also Early Modern English; Middle
   English; Old English; World
   Englishes
Estuary English 30, 152–4
Ethelbert of Kent 6
etymology 24, 29, 87–8, 91
Evelyn, John 155–6
external history 2
extralinguistic change 2

Franklin, Benjamin 164
Franks Casket inscriptions 138
French language 147
   Académie français 154
   American English and 67, 108
   French speakers of English 52–3
   Middle English 47, 53, 91, 92, 93
   Norman invasion 11–12, 139–43
   place names 89

gender
   Old English 42
   pronoun use 174–5, 177
genitive (possessive) case 174
   Early Modern pronouns 62–4
   Old English 42–3, 84–5
German language
   American English and 67, 108
   shifting sounds 149–50
Germanic languages
   Anglo-Saxon settlement 4–6
   family tree 81, 82
   Old English vocabulary 128–9
   Vikings 7–8
global use of English 31–4
   attitudes towards 76–7
   conformity or diversity 78
   cultural aspects of dominance 122
   future development of 124–5
   rate of rising use 178–9
   satellite broadcasting 179–80
   standards and registers 122–4
   see also World Englishes
globalisation 32
Görlach, M. 62

Graddol, David
   The Future of English? 178–82
grammar 184
   codification 95
   morphology 185
   quantitative study of change 166–77
   syntax 186
   see also prescriptivism
graphemes 37, 184
   Middle English 51
   Old English 47
graphology 184
graphs 37, 184
Great Vowel Shift 16–17, 24, 34, 152
   Chinese language 151–2
   diagram of 148
   Estuary English 152–4
   German language and 149–50
   Leith on 144–7
   Middle English 51, 54, 57–60
   Uniformitarian Principle 58–9
Green, L. J. 69–70
Guthrie, Lord Charles 101
Guzman, V. P. de 117

Hannah, J.
   Australian English 70–1, 114–15
   Indian English 72–3
Haugen, E. 60–1
Held, David 32
Henry V 14, 18
Hilles, S. 4
Horobin, S. 50
Hundred Years War 14
Hunter Blair, Peter 5

iambic pentameter 105
Indian English 72–4
   British colonisation 26–7
industrial revolution 28
inflection 40, 184
   case endings 41–2
   gender 42
   Middle English changes 51–3
   number 43
   Old English 129

Scandinavian languages 52
  verbs 43–4
Inkhorn Controversy 66
inkhorn terms 66
internal history 2
International Phonetic Alphabet 37
internet 31, 181–2
intralinguistic change 2

Jacka, E. 180
Jacot de Boinod, Adam 102
Johnson, Dr Samuel 129–30
  dictionary of 24, 96, 159
Jonson, Ben 104
Judd, E. L. 77
Jutes 4, 135

Kachru, B. 27
Kentish dialect 8, 135
  Great Vowel Shift 146–7
  textual evidence 137–8
Kersey, John 24
Kibbee, Douglas
  on French in England 139–43
  For to Speke Frenche Trewely 139
Knowles, G. 19
koinés 134
Krapp, G. P. 112, 160–1, 163–4

Labov, William 17, 69
  the Uniformitarian Principle 58–9
Lancashire 8
language and languages 2
  acceptance 61
  creole 69–70, 74–6, 112, 120
  development of 2, 60
  family tree 81–4
  hierarchy of 80
  koinés 134
  pidgins 27, 69, 74–6, 112–13, 120–1
  struggle for survival 77, 122
Lass, Roger 58–9
Latimer, Hugh 104
Latin language
  Christianity and 6–7, 9–10
  family tree 82, 83

Middle English and 48, 92, 93
  as official language 141–2
  Old English and 132
  place names 88–9
  Roman Britain 3–4
Leacock, John
  The Fall of British Tyranny 112–13
Leech, Geoffrey 166–77
Leith, Dick 103
  the Great Vowel Shift 144–7
lexicon 24
lexis 185
lingua franca 33
linguistics 80–1
loanwords
  open and closed class 93
  see also individual languages
London dialects
  Cockney 71
  Early Modern 20, 21–3
  Estuary 152–4
the Lord's Prayer 86–7, 95
Lyons, Sir Michael 101

MacAlpin, Kenneth 45
McCully, C. 4
Machan, T. 58–9
macrons 37
Marckwardt, A. H. 45
  American archaisms 68–9
  Native American loanwords 109
Martinet, André 148
Meech, S. B. 135
Mees, I.
  Practical Phonetics (with Collins) 37
Mencken, H. L.
  The American Language 160–6
Mercian dialect 8–9, 10, 135, 136
  textual evidence 137–8
Middle English 14, 16
  The Canterbury Tales 93–4
  dialect areas 15–16
  emergence of 47–8
  French and 47–8
  Great Vowel Shift 57–60, 144–7
  historical period of 14

inflection 51–3
loanwords 91–4
Scandinavian languages 91–2, 93
spelling and pronunciation 48–51,
    53–60
vocabulary 53
Midlands dialect
    Middle English 20
Mitchell, Bruce 40
    *An Invitation to Old English and
        Anglo-Saxon England* 128
    Old English vocabulary 128–34
monophthongs 45, 185
    Old English 47
Moore, W. 135
morphemes 116, 185
morphology 185
Mulder, J. 70–1, 78
Murray, James 29

Native American languages
    American English and 67, 109
Nevalainen, T. 20
New Guinea English
    Tok Pisin 120–1
New Zealand 27
Nicoll, James D. 133
nominative case 41
Normandy 139
Norse languages *see* Scandinavian
    languages
Northumbrian dialect 8–9, 10, 135
    Cædmon's Hymn 46–7
    Great Vowel Shift 144–5
    the Lord's Prayer 86–7
    Old English 45
    textual evidence 137–8
Nottingham, University of
    Key to English Place Names 90
nouns 41–3, 53, 72–5, 93, 174, 185
number
    Indian plurals 72
    inflection 43

objects
    synthetic/analytic language 40–1

O'Grady, W. 117
Old English
    Anglo-Saxons 4–6, 37
    borrowings 132–3
    case 84–5
    compared to Middle 94
    dialects of 8–11, 86–7, 134–9
    earliest origins 3
    family tree of 82, 83
    i-mutation 131, 133–4
    Latin and 3–4
    monastic texts 136
    Norman French and 13
    Old Norse 8
    oral culture 9
    place names 87–91
    pronunciation 84
    spelling and sound 36–9
    varieties of 44–7
    verbs 43–4
    Vikings and 45
    vocabulary 39–40, 128–34
Oldmixon, John 158
onomatopoeia 117
oral culture 9
orthography 185
    Early Modern English 61–2, 97–100
Orton, H. et al.
    The Linguistic Atlas of England 145
Oswald of Northumbria 9–10
Övergaard, G. 173
Oxford English Dictionary 29

Pennycook, A. 76–7
phonemes 185
    digraphs and 184
    Middle English 49–50
phonology 185
Picts 3, 4
pidgins and creoles 27
    African-American English and 69–70
    decreolisation 75
    early representation of 112–13
    mixing 74
    process of 75–6
    reduction 74

simplification 74
Tok Pisin 120–1
place names
    habitative and topographical 87
    Old English 87–91, 138
possessives *see* genitive (possessive) case
Practical Phonetics (Collins and Mees) 37
pragmatic information
    Early Modern verbs 66
pragmatics 185–6
prefixes 116
    i-mutation and 131
prepositions 186
prescriptivism
    attitudes of 100–2
    Early Modern English 95–7
    an English Academy 154–60
    prescription and description 95–7,
        100–2
    registers 122–4
    Swift's proposal 157–9
Price, Owen
    English Orthographie 97–100
pronouns 93, 186
    Early Modern 62–4
    polite forms 64, 103
    quantitative study of 174–5
pronunciation
    American English 69
    Great Vowel Shift 16–17, 144–7, 148
    Middle English 50–2, 53–60
    Old English 37–9
    push/drag chains 148–52
    Received Pronunciation 29–30, 146
    see also World Englishes
Pyles, T. 82

Quakers
    you and thou 103
Quirk, R. 85

Ray, E. 180
Reaney, P. H. 88
Received Pronunciation (RP) 29–30
    accent and 183
    American English and 69

Reed, C. E. 67
regional differences *see* dialects and
        regional differences; World
        Englishes
registers 123
rhythm
    iambic pentameter 105
Robinson, F. C. 135
Romaine, S. 120–1
Rosier, J. L. 45
Rothwell, W. 141
Ruthwell Cross 134, 139

Samuels, M. L. 2, 20
Saxons 4
    see also Anglo-Saxon language
Scandinavian languages
    family tree 81, 82, 83
    inflections 52
    Middle English borrowing 53, 91–2,
        93
    Northumbria 45
    Old English 132–3, 137
    place names 88, 89
Scots (language)
    Old English and 45, 47
Scots (people) 3, 4
Scragg, D. G. 61
selection 60
semantic change
    broadening and narrowing 118–19
    close relations 120
    cultural sources 118–19
    emotional sources 120
semantic field 109
semantics 186
Shakespeare, William 104, 105
Shelly, P. Van Dyke 140–1
Sheridan, Thomas Brinsley 159
simplification 120–1
Skinner, Stephen
    A New English Dictionary 23
Smith, A. H. 46
Smith, Nick
    quantitative grammatical change
        166–77

Sociolinguistics (Stockwell) 37
Spanish language
  American English 108
speech sounds
  consonants 54–5
  labial articulation 54
  phonology 185
  plosives 54
  voiced and unvoiced 54
  vowels 55–7
  see also pronunciation
spelling
  Early Modern English 61–2
  Middle English 48–50
  standardisation 59–60
  Webster's American English 110–11
  Standard English *see* English language
    (Present Day)
Stockwell, Peter
  Sociolinguistics 37
subjects
  synthetic/analytic language 40–1
suffixes 116
Swift, Jonathan 110
  A Modest Proposal 23
  proposal to reform language 157–9
syntax 186
synthetic language 40

television, global 179–80
text-messaging 123–4
texts 186
Thorpe, Vanessa 101–2
Tieken-Boon van Ostade, I. 20
Todd, L. 74–6
Tok Pisin 120–1
Toon, T. E. 67
transatlantic telegraph cable 31
Trudgill, Peter 17
  Australian English 70–1, 114–15
  Indian English 72–3
Turville-Petre, T. 15
Tyndale, William 19, 23

Uniformitarian Principle 58–9
utterances 186

variety 186
verbs 186
  'do' 106–8
  Early Modern 65–6
  Indian English 72–3
  modal 167–71
  passive voice 172–3
  phrases 186
  progressive aspect 171–2
  regularisation 64
  strong and weak 65
  subjunctive mood 173
  weak and strong 43–4
vernacular languages 3
Vikings 7
vocabulary
  enlargement of 115–20
  lexis 185
  open and closed class 93
vocal folds 54
voiced and unvoiced sounds 54
Vortigern 4
vowels 187
  chain shift 58
  front and back 55
  Great Shift 57–60
  open and close 55
  producing sounds 55–7
  rounded and unrounded 55

Wales 5
Walpole, Horace 156
Webster, Noah 26
  *American Dictionary of the English
    Language* 110–11
  *Compendious Dictionary of the English
    Language* 110
West African English
  pidgins and creoles 74–6
West Saxon dialect 8–10, 135–6
  Cædmon's Hymn 46–7
  the Lord's Prayer 86–7
  textual evidence 137–8
Widdecombe, Ann 101
William of Malmesbury 140
William the Conqueror 12–14, 139